W9-BWV-409

THE INSTANT CURRICULUM

Over 750 Developmentally Appropriate
Learning Activities for
Busy Teachers of Young Children

Dedication

To our friend, colleague, and teacher, Jan Smith. You are an inspiration always. The field of early childhood bears your footsteps.

And to our children and grandchildren:

Richele Bartkowiak and Tiffany Markle
Austin Markle, Gabrielle and Madison Britt, and Evan Bartkowiak

Kate Wright, Doug Townsend, and David Townsend
Lee, Blair, and Georgia Wright
Austin, Blake, and Cara Townsend
Adam and Matthew Rossano

May your lives be filled with the wonder of wonder!
—P.S. and J.R.

**NEW!
Revised
Edition**

THE
Instant
CURRICULUM

Over 750
Developmentally
Appropriate
Learning Activities
for Busy Teachers of
Young Children

Pam Schiller
and Joan Rossano

Illustrated by Deborah C. Wright
and Kathleen Kerr

gryphon house, inc.
Beltsville, Maryland

Copyright

© 2005 Pam Schiller and Joan Rossano
Printed in the United States of America.

Published by Gryphon House, Inc.
P.O. Box 207, Beltsville, MD 20704
301.595.9500; 301.595.0051 (fax); 800.638.0928 (toll-free)

Visit us on the web at www.gryphonhouse.com

Library of Congress Cataloging-in-Publication Data

Schiller, Pamela Byrne.
The instant curriculum revised : over 700 developmentally appropriate learning activities for busy teachers of young children / Pam Schiller andJoan Rossano ; illustrations by Deborah Wright.
    p. cm.
    Includes index.
    Summary: "Resource book for teachers in early childhood education, providing over 750 activities to use in the classroom"-- Provided by publisher.
    ISBN 978-0-87659-002-7
1. Early childhood education--Activity programs. 2. Curriculum planning. 3. Child development. I. Rossano, Joan. II. Title.
LB1139.35.A37S36 2005
372.19--dc22

2005001905

Bulk Purchase

Gryphon House books are available for special premiums and sales promotions as well as for fundraising use. Special editions or book excerpts also can be created to specification. For details, contact the Director of Marketing at Gryphon House.

Disclaimer

Gryphon House, Inc. and the authors cannot be held responsible for damage, mishap, or injury incurred during the use of or because of activities in this book. Appropriate and reasonable caution and adult supervision of children involved in activities and corresponding to the age and capability of each child involved, is recommended at all times. Do not leave children unattended at any time. Observe safety and caution at all times.

Every effort has been made to locate copyright and permission information.

Gryphon House is a member of the Green Press Initiative, a nonprofit program dedicated to supporting publishers in their efforts to reduce their use of fiber-sourced forests. This book is made of 30% post-consumer waste. For further information visit www.greenpressinitiative.org.

Table of Contents

Introduction **17**

**Chapter 1: Bringing the Inside Out—
Self-Expression Through Art** **21**
Drawing **22**
   Drawing Tools 22
   Drawing Surfaces 22
   Crayon Melt 22
   Doodli-Do 22
   Good Graffiti 23
   Meat Tray Art 23
   Buttermilk Drawings 23
   Sugar Water Drawings 23
   Scented Markers 23
   Seurat Dots 24
   Wet Sand Drawings 24
   Magnifying Glass Assistance 24

Painting **25**
   Scratch-and-Sniff Paint 25
   Fingerpaint and Fingerpaint Relief 25
   Splatter Painting 25
   Cotton Swab Painting 26
   Textured Painting .26
   Bubble Painting 26
   Deodorant Bottle Painting 26
   Spray Painting 26
   Roller Painting 27
   Squirt Bottle Painting 27
   Gadget Painting 27
   Sponge Painting 27
   Feather Painting 28
   Epsom Salt Paint 28
   Icing Paint 28
   Puff Paint 28
   Salt Paint 28

Designs **29**
   Fingerpaint Baggies 29
   Marble Prints 29
   Car Tracks 29
   Straw Blowing 30
   Glue Drop Designs 30
   Shaker Art 30
   Absorption Designs 30
   Mobiles 31
   Rubbings 31
   Sand Designs I 31
   Sand Designs II 32
   Mondrian Masterpieces 32
   Template Designs .33
   Stained Glass Windows 33
   More Stained Glass Windows 33
   Rock Salt Designs .33

Prints **34**
   Cookie Cutter Prints 34
   Gadget Printing 34
   Bubble Prints I 34
   Bubble Prints II 34
   Sponge Prints 35
   Blotto Prints I 35
   Blotto Prints II 35
   Hand Mural 36
   Hand Wreaths 36
   Fingerprint Creations 36
   Footprints 36

Collages **37**
   Torn Paper Collages 37
   Torn Paper Silhouettes 37
   Tissue Paper Collages 37
   Nature Collages 38
   Confetti Art 38
   Humpty Dumpty Reconstruction 38

Happy Face Montage 38
Monochromatic Masterpieces 39
Shapes on Shapes 39
Textured Collages .39

Sculpting and Molding **40**
Papier-Mâché 40
Goop and Gak 40
Cloud Dough 40
Playdough Sculpting 41
Wood Sculpting 41
Box Sculpting 41
Stabiles 42
Sandcastles 42
Mud Pies 42
Soap Suds Clay 42
Foil Sculptures 42

Art and Crafts Recipes **43**
Bubble Soap 43
Cloud Dough 43
Colored Glue 43
Colored Rock Salt .43
Epsom Salt Solution 43
Face Paint/ Body Paint 44
Fingerpaint Recipe #1 44
Fingerpaint Recipe #2 44
Fingerpaint Recipe #3 44
Body Paints 44
Gak 45
Goop 45
Icing Paint 45
Paints 46
Papier-Mâché Paste 46
Paste 46
Playdough Recipe #1 46
Playdough Recipe #2 46
Playdough Recipe #3 47
Puff Paint 47
Salt Paint 47
Scented Playdough 47

Scratch-and-Sniff Paint 47
Soap Paint 47
Soapsuds Clay 47

Chapter 2: A Pot, a Pan, and a Wooden Spoon—Cooking 49
No-Cook Recipes **51**
Milkanilla 51
Purple Cow Shakes 51
Baggie Ice Cream 52
Can Ice Cream 52
Butter 52
Sun Salad 52
Peanut Butter 53
Peanut Butter Balls 53
Friendship Mix 54
Banana Pudding 54
Shake-a-Puddin' 54
Banana Wheels 54
Candy Mints 55
Glittery Sugar Mallows 55
Tooty Fruity 56
Apple and Carrot Salad 56
Fruit Sticks 56
Sandwich Animals .56
Sandwich Fillings .57

Toaster Oven/Oven Recipes **57**
Toast Tidbits 57
Pizza Faces 58
Bear Claws 58
Pigs in a Blanket 58

Refrigerator/Freezer Recipes **59**
Marzipan 59
Gelatin Jigglers 59
One-Cup Salad 59
Party Pops 59

Hot Plate/Electric Skillet/ Popper Recipes 60

    Shooting Stars 60

    Chili Popcorn 60

    Skillet Cookies 60

    Donuts 61

    Grilled Cheese Delights 62

Chapter 3: The Magic of Make Believe—Dramatic Play 63

Imaginative Play **66**

    Prop Boxes 66

    Car Wash 68

    Gas Station 68

    Tent Town 68

    Drive-Throughs 69

    Dinner Is Served 69

    Baby Bathtime 70

    The Nursery 70

    Box House 71

    Box Hideaway 71

    Pantry Match 71

    What's in the Trunk? 72

Creative Play **72**

    Floral Arrangements 72

    My Hat 72

    Mad Hatters 73

    Bakery Goods 73

    Little Designers 73

    Baubles, Beads, Bangles, and Belts 74

    What Is It? 74

    Stocking Snakes 74

    Soft Blocks 75

    Let's Pretend 75

Chapter 4: Expanding Horizons— Language and Literacy 77

Listening **80**

    "Go-fers" 80

    Listening Walk 80

    Sound Canisters 80

    Where's the Sound? 81

    Follow the Sound 81

    Mystery Sounds 81

    Musical Hot and Cold 81

    Gossip 82

    Ears Up 82

    Which Instrument Do You Hear? 82

    Do You Hear What I Hear? 82

    The Sound of Silence 83

    I've Got Rhythm 83

    Sound Makers 83

    Taped Directions 84

    I Spy 84

    Listening Stories 84

    Simon Says 84

    Twin Tunes 85

    Listening Tunes 85

    Clapping Names 85

    The Long and the Short of It 86

Oral Language **86**

    Reading Vocabulary 86

    Singing Vocabulary 86

    Word of the Day 87

    A Picture's Worth a Thousand Words 87

    Baggie Book Photo Album 87

    Vocabulary Fun 88

    Shopping Fun 88

    Sequencing Concrete Objects 88

    In the Bag 89

    Positional Words 89

    Opposites 89

    Opposites Hunt 90

    Sign Language Vocabulary 90

    Show-and-Tell 90

Ticklers 90

Deluxe Show-and-Tell 91

String a Story 91

Nursery Rhyme Pantomimes 91

Magic Mirror 91

Magic Pebble 92

Magic Wand 92

Sally Sad and Harry Happy 92

Puppet Party 92

What Do You Know About This? 93

Posing Questions .93

Recipe Dictation .93

Flannel Board Stories 93

Expanding Story Concepts 93

Word Police 94

Phonological Awareness **94**

Hicky Picky Bumblebee 94

Clapping Words 94

Silly Sentences 95

Tongue Twisters 95

Alliteration Fun 95

Alliterative Songs .95

The Sounds of Rain 96

Onomatopoeia Songs 96

Name Game 96

Pick-a-Pair 96

Rime Time 97

Rhyme or Reason .97

Rhyming Game 97

Fill-In Nursery Rhymes 98

Rhythmic Nursery Rhymes 1 98

Rhythmic Nursery Rhymes II 98

Whispered Rhymes 98

Rhyme in a Can 98

Say and Touch 99

Letter Knowledge and Recognition **99**

What's Missing? 99

Whoops! 100

What's the Order? 100

Can You Remember? 100

Wallpaper Lotto .101

Alphabetical Order 101

Which Letter Is Missing? 102

Gel Bags 102

Playdough Letters 102

Pretzel Letters 102

Thumbprint Letters 103

Freckle Names 103

Letter Tracing 103

Letter Matching .103

Pair, Think, and Share 104

Circle the Letter 104

Letter Tic Tac Toe 104

Sand Writing 104

Sand Letters 104

Finger Writing 104

Tactile Letters 105

Tablecloth Lotto 105

Lucky Letters 105

Bingo 106

Scrabble Letters .106

E-I-E-I-O 106

Mail Call 106

Manual ABC's 107

Print Awareness **107**

Top, Middle, and Bottom 107

More Top, Middle, and Bottom 107

Left to Right 108

Cozy Comics 108

"Reader Wiggle" 109

Name Puzzles 110

Letter Puzzles 110

String a Letter 110

Cereal Box Puzzles 110

Labels 111

Nametags 111

Grocery Put Away 111

Funny Funny Papers 112

Story Dictation .112

Experience Charts 112
Classroom Pen Pals 113
Rebus Charts .113
Rebus Treasure Hunt 113
Rebus Recipes 114
Nursery Rhyme Fill-Ins 114
Writing Rhymes 114
Story Starters .114
Wordless Books 114
Baggie Books .115
Lists 115
Journal Writing 116
Pen Pal Buddies 116
News Events 116

Comprehension 117
Story Detectives 117
True/Not True 117
Questioning Strategies 117
Story Map 118
Word Webs 119
Story Re-Enactments 119
Story Pantomime 120
Action Stories .120

**Chapter 5 : First Things First—
Making Math Meaningful** 121
Free Exploration 123
Junk Boxes 123
Naming Attributes 124
I Spy 124
Can You Find It? 124
Tree Tag 1 124
Tree Tag 2 125
Hand Match-Up 125
Descriptive Vocabulary 125
More Vocabulary 125

Spatial Relationships 126
Top, Middle, and Bottom 126
Little Box Surprises 126
Inside Outside 126
Over and Under 127
Where's the Button? 127
"Going on a Bear Hunt" 127
Circle Commands 129
Twister 129

Classification .130
Classmate Classifications 130
Classification Books 130
Button Match .130
Shoes, Shoes, Shoes 131
Eyes Open, Eyes Shut 131
Classifying Snacks 131
Classifying by Color 132
Classifying by Shape 132
Classifying by Size 133
Classifying Using Senses Other Than Sight .135
Open-Ended Classification 136
Classification Applications 137

Patterning 138
People Patterns 138
Object Patterns 138
Paper Patterns 138
Crayon Patterns 138
Paper Chains .139
Set Patterns 139
Block Patterns 139
Fruit Kabobs .139
Vertical Patterns 140
Circular Patterns 141
Wrap-Around Patterns 141
Movement Patterns 142
Musical and Sound Patterns 142
Cultural Patterns 143
Environmental Patterns 144

One-to-One Correspondence 145

    Equal Sets 145

    Unequal Sets 147

Ordering 149

    Ordering by Height 149

    Ordering by Length 150

    Ordering by Weight 151

    Ordering by Liquid Measurement 151

    Ordering by Position and Size 152

    Ordering by Comparing Sets 153

Numeration 154

    Math Number Bags 154

    Beanbag Throw 155

    Number Cards .155

    The Shape of Things 156

    Number Clips .156

    Counting Patterns 156

    Pasting Sets 157

    Plates and Clips 157

    Mix It Myself Snack 157

    Piggy Banks 158

    Card Match 158

    Musical Numbers 158

    Circle 'Round the Zero 159

    Number Bingo 159

    My Number Book 159

    Golf Tee Combinations 160

    Living Sets 160

    Washer Drop .160

    Candy Sets 161

    Crunchy Sets .161

    Mud Cakes 161

    And One More 161

    Egg Carton Shake 162

    Target Practice 162

    Subtraction Action 162

    In the Bag 162

Shapes 163

    Cookie Cutter Shapes 163

    Shape Construction 163

    Playdough Shapes 163

    Shape Hunt 163

    Musical Shapes 164

    Squares and Rectangles 164

    Triangles and Rectangles 164

Measurement 165

    Linear Measurement 165

    Weight Measurement 166

    Capacity Measurement 167

    Temperature Measurement 167

    Time Measurement 168

Graphs 169

    Brothers and Sisters 169

    My Favorite Juice 169

    Color of the Day 169

    Popular Pets 170

    More Popular Pets 170

    From Pictorial to Symbolic 170

    How Do I Get to School? 171

    My Favorite Fruit 171

    Let's Vote 171

Fractions 172

    The Same Amount for Everyone 172

    What Is a Half? 172

Chapter 6: The Universal Language—Music and Movement . . .173

Songs 174

    Happy Birthday 174

    Variations of Old-Time Favorites 174

    Different Voices 174

    Sing and Listen 175

    Crescendo 175

    Do As I Do 175

Circle Songs .175

Roofs and Windows 176

Hummin' 177

"If You're Happy and You Know It"
    Variations 177

"Itsy Bitsy Spider" Variations 177

"Twinkle, Twinkle, Little Star" Variations . .177

Singing Discussions 178

Chants **178**

Who Took the Cookie? 178

Giant Stomp .179

"The Flight of the Fairies" 179

"Oni Woni" 180

Creative Movement **180**

Giants and Elves 180

Olympic Streamers 180

Preschool Fitness 181

Around the Chairs 181

Butterfly Wings 181

Cool Music 181

Circles to Music 182

Friendship Circles 182

Pompoms 182

Freckles and Stripes 182

Hi-Low 183

Ball Roll 183

"Hey! My Name Is Joe" 183

"Tooty-Ta" 184

"Metamorphosis" 184

Moving Freely **185**

Deejay for the Day 185

On Stage 185

Music Makers **185**

Tabletop Band 185

Leader of the Band 186

Bottle Maracas 186

Drum and Sticks 186

Body Rhythms 186

Bottle Band 186

Homemade Music Makers 187

Dances **187**

Scarf Dancing 187

Paper Plate Flying 187

Shadow Dancing 188

Preschool Limbo 188

Swish and Sway 188

Pick Your Partner 189

Dance, Thumbkin, Dance 189

Games **190**

Musical Beanbags 190

Pass the Beanbag 190

Freeze 190

Who's That Traipsing on My Bridge? 191

Cooperative Musical Chairs 191

Snack Pass 191

Hopscotch 192

Paper Chase 192

Inchworm Race 192

Chapter 7: Building Muscle Mastery—
Physical Development 193

Gross Motor **195**

Obstacle Course 195

Big Steps, Giant Steps 195

Hula Hoop Toss 195

Musical Cues .196

Mirror Reflections 196

Amazing Mazes 196

Blanket Toss .197

Homemade Balls 197

Basket Balance 198

Walk a Crooked Line 198

Duck Waddles 198

Spider Walk 198

Back-to-Back Lifts 199

Tunnels 199

Broad Jumps .199

Ring That Bell 200

Shovel Pickup 200

Indoor Croquet 200

Log Rollers 200

"The Little Ants" 201

Fine Motor **202**

Bubbles in My Hand 202

Balls and Cups 202

Catch Me If You Can 202

Liquid Movers 202

Wire Creations 202

Easy Cutouts .203

Nut Sorting 203

Seed Sorting .203

Colorful Confetti 203

Clay Letters 204

Shaving Cream Designs 204

Tracing Fun 204

Tracing Lids 204

Cookie Cutter Tracing 205

Cups of Color 205

Little Ships 205

Greeting Card Puzzles 205

Water Transfer 206

Button Transfer 206

Torn Paper Creations 206

Paper Folding 206

Grass Tug of War 206

Weaving Variations 207

Shadow Puppets 207

Finger Puppets 207

Me Puzzles 207

Napkin Folding 208

Paper Cutting 208

Button Sweeping 208

Playdough Fun 208

Chapter 8: The Wonder of Wonder—Science **209**

Air **211**

Sacks of Air 211

Air Pushers 211

Air Pusher Experiment 212

Air Movers 212

Circle Kites 212

Bubbles Up 213

Bubble Machines 213

Floaters and Droppers 213

When the Wind Blows 213

Air Conditioning Hoops 214

Helicopters 214

Raisin Elevators 214

Sound: What We Hear When Air Moves . . .215

Water **217**

Liquid 217

Solid 218

Evaporation (Gas) 219

Diffusion 219

Insoluble Substances 220

Force and Motion **221**

Force 221

Friction: Resistance to Motion 222

Gravitation: Force That Attracts 225

Magnetism: Another Kind of Force 227

Simple Tools **229**

Pulleys 229

Water Transfer 229

Filter Catch 230

Kitchen Tools 230

Easy Movers .230

Light and Color **231**

Color Shadows 231

Playdough Color Mixing 231

Color Tubes 231

Rose-Colored Glasses 232

Color Mixer 232

Shadow Puppets 232

Guess Who? 233

Sun Art 233

Rainbows 233

Strobe Light 234

Me and My Shadow 234

Sundial 234

Scattered Light 235

Mirror Magic 235

Mirror Drawing 235

Periscopes 235

Lemon Juice Magic 236

Weather and Seasons 236

"The Weather Song" 236

Cloud Watch 236

Wind Walk 237

Rain Gauge 237

Shadow Tracing 237

Season Walks 237

Seasonal Trees 238

Spotlight on Seasons 238

Seasonal Observation Bottles 239

Senses 239

The Eyes Have It 239

What's for Snack? 239

Sound Makers 240

Taste Test 240

Tactile Temperatures 240

Hot and Cold 240

Sounds Abound 240

Puffs of Smell 241

The Nose Knows 241

A World of Scents 241

Scented Bubbles 241

Sensory Alert 241

Change of State 242

Stone Soup 242

Ice Meltdown 242

Soda Fizz 242

Gelatin Jigglers 243

Plants 243

Nature Bracelets 243

Tire Garden 244

Vegetable Garden 244

Hairy Larry 244

Grocery Bag Leaves 245

Leaves—All Sizes, All Shapes 245

Leaf Rubbings 245

Treasure Hunt 246

Window Garden 246

Egg Carton Planters 246

Mini-Terrariums 247

Little Sprouts 247

Sweet Potato Vines 248

What's a Nut? 248

Natural Dyes 248

Animals 249

Feed the Birds 249

Bird Bath 249

Pinecone Bird Feeders 249

Looking Loops 250

Ant Watch 250

Ant Helpers 250

Bug Bottles 251

Animal Habitats 251

Who Lives Where? 252

Feathers, Fur, Scales, and Shells 252

Animal Homes 252

Mothers and Babies 252

Insect Body Parts 253

Chapter 9: Everyone's a Piece of the Puzzle—Social Studies 255

Feeling Good About Me .256
 I Am Special 256
 My Name Means a Lot 256
 Accentuate the Positive 257
 V.I.P. Treasure Chest 257
 Artist of the Week 258
 Responsibility Roster 258
 Responsibility Straws 259

Understanding and Controlling Emotions 259
 My Feelings 259
 Happy and Sad .260
 Feeling 260
 Face to Face 260

My Family 261
 Family Portrait 261
 Family Tree 261
 Names for Relatives 261
 Classroom "Concerts" 262

Sharing and Cooperating 262
 Tips for Taking Turns 262
 Pass It Along 262
 Tips for Sharing .262

Participating and Contributing 263
 Classroom Quilt .263
 Trash Truck 263
 Litter Brigade 263
 Sidewalk Art Sale 264

Likenesses and Differences 264
 International Feast 264
 Home, Sweet Home 264
 There Is More Than One Way 265
 See, Touch, and Hear 265
 Goodbye, Adios, and Sayonara 266

Community Workers and Friends 266
 Career Prop Boxes 266
 Job Fair 267
 Small Mall 267
 Senior Citizens' Day 267

Concepts of Time 268
 Yesterday, Today, and Tomorrow 268
 Tomorrow Box 268
 Growing Up 268
 Bygones 268
 Morning, Noon, and Night 269

Environmental Awareness 269
 Use and Reuse 269
 Recycled Products 269
 Clothes Corner .270
 Pen Pals 270
 Crayon Conservation 270
 Sandbox Tools 270
 Re-Bow 270
 Recycled Soap 271
 Bits and Pieces .271
 Rainwater Recycle 271
 Rainbow Bottles 271
 A Tree From Me .272

Health and Safety 272
 Safety Rituals 272
 A Healthy Song .273
 Cross-Lateral Brain Energizers 273
 Breathe Deeply .274
 Thirsty Brains Can't Think 274
 Homemade Toothpaste 274
 Squeaky Clean .275
 Food Group Pyramid 275
 Paper Plate Food Collage 276
 Heartbeats 276
 Traffic Lights 277
 Stop Signs 277
 Stop, Look, and Listen 277
 Stop, Drop, and Roll 278

Chapter 10: Preparing for the Future—Critical Thinking and Problem Solving 279

Critical Thinking ....
and Problem Solving 281

Arm Stretchers 281
Two Parts, Three People! 281
How Many People in Your Family? 282
What Can You Do With This? 282
What Will Go in This? 282
Water Brigade 283
Follow the Arrows 283
Ping-Pong Races 283
Where's the Birdie? 284
Wacky Wednesday 284
Is This Cup Full? 285
Separating Solids 285
Spill Cleanup 286
From Many to One 286
Puzzle Challenge 286
Funnel Race 286
Greeting Card Cut-Ups 287
Pass the Purse 287
Bubbles Aloft 287
Rollers and Clunkers 287
Back Together Again 287
Go-Togethers 288

Chapter 11: Adapting to Change—Transitions 289

Transitions 290

Pretend Places 290
Who Am I? 290
Musical Cues 290
Cues From Classics 291
Groovy Moves 291
Weather Walks 291
Butterfly Flutter 292

Wacky Walks 292
Roll Call 293
Rhyming Roll Call 293

Chapter 12: Keeping Connected—Families as Partners 295

Families as Partners 296

Printed Labels 296
What We Did This Week 296
Second Time Around 296
Special Guest Day 296
Family Networking 297
Calendars 297
Communication Notes 297
Newsletters 297

Appendix 299

Theme Connections Charts 300
Songs, Chants, and Fingerplays 319
Games 338

Indexes 345

Theme Index 346
General Index 348

Introduction

This book was written to serve as a resource for teachers of comprehensive early childhood programs. The title, ***The Instant Curriculum, Revised,*** denotes activities and a commitment to reducing both the amount of time teachers spend preparing and the amount of money they spend purchasing special supplies.

Each chapter represents a primary domain included in a comprehensive early childhood curriculum. The chapters begin with an overview, which provides the basic philosophy behind that particular curriculum area. The activities are designed to encourage the development of skills and to provide practice with specific concepts. Underlying the structure of this book is the basic belief that children should be actively involved in the learning process and that learning experiences are connected to each other.

The most crucial role of the early childhood teacher is to help children develop the skills they need to become lifelong learners. Themes provide a springboard for creativity when planning curriculum. They also provide a format for children to connect information. But a child's success in school is predicted not by his knowledge of specific facts or by her precocious ability to read so much as by the skills he or she has mastered, such as being able to wait, to listen, and to follow directions; to communicate both feelings and ideas; to think critically; to move with agility, and many others. As accountability in early childhood classrooms continues to increase, the curriculum focus will shift away from themes and toward a focus on the scope and sequence of developmental skills.

This book's focus on concepts and skills provides a flexible format that allows you to select activities that strengthen a specific skill area for one child or the entire group. It also allows you to add your own unique spin by customizing the selected activity to match curriculum themes. For example, you could change the Pasting Sets activity (page 157) in the Math chapter from pasting circles and squares to pasting sets of cats and dogs for an animal theme. In the same fashion, the E-I-E-I-O activity (page 106) in Language and Literacy can be used with a farm theme and the Megaphones activity (page 215) in the Science chapter can be used with a music or sound and movement theme.

If you use a thematic approach you will find a chart in the appendix (pages 300-319) that provides suggestions for connecting themes to the skills and concepts developed by the activities in The Instant Curriculum, Revised. Many activities will fit within a variety of themes. Most activities can be modified to fit a theme by simply changing the materials to ones that represent the theme. For example, stuffed animals for an animal themes can be changed to vehicles for a transportation theme.

Although each activity is assigned to a specific area, its potential is not limited to that area. In the early childhood classroom, learning is integrated. For example, to develop the concept of four (Math curriculum area), a teacher using an integrated approach will provide opportunities to clap-count the number four (Music and Movement), collect four leaves on a nature walk (Science), or use four colors on a collage (Art).

In the early childhood classroom, we have the opportunity to integrate our curriculum in a way that is both meaningful and realistic to children. We are not only able to address the needs of the whole child (cognitive, physical, and social emotional development) in a way that supports the equal value of each area, we are also able to provide activities that honor and respect the many talents and abilities of children. In the early childhood classroom, Science is Art and Art is Science. Music is Math and Math is Music. We are able to teach many disciplines in an interconnected and natural way. Our classrooms are realistic reflections of the world.

Two chapters (Literacy and Language, and Math) are sub-divided into skill areas. In both chapters, activities move in a developmental continuum that, if used in order, allows children to develop an easier skill into a more complex skill. By using the activities in these chapters as they are presented, you will optimize the learning opportunities for children. In today's climate, early childhood teachers are being held to a new level of accountability, especially in the areas of Literacy and Language and Math. Learning to be purposeful in developing lessons and practice opportunities (learning center support) will help you in meeting these new expectations. The organization of the Literacy and Language and Math chapters will also help you learn to articulate your goals and objectives in a way that will match accountability standards.

Teachable Moments are interspersed throughout the book and explained on the next page.

A special feature of this book is the Critical Thinking and Problem Solving chapter. Although problem solving and critical thinking activities have been included within each curriculum area, this chapter focuses on the potential application of these skills to all areas of learning because these skills are significant for children's success in an ever-changing world.

The Instant Curriculum also features special chapters on Transitions and Family Connections. Both are integral aspects of the early childhood classroom. Transitions help keep the classroom running smoothly. Family Connections provide continuity for children and help us maintain partnerships with families.

Throughout the book, we emphasize allowing children to learn at their own level of development and progress accordingly. We also emphasize providing choices for children and encouraging children to experiment and discover. In this way, young children will develop skills to learn how to learn and will feel confident in their ability. Learning will become an interesting process, one that continues for a lifetime.

Using Teachable Moments

Alert teachers can take advantage of opportunities that arise during the day to help children increase their understanding of specific skills and concepts. The following are a few examples:

Child: "Is it cold outside?"
Teacher: "Why don't you feel the window and find out."

Child: "This is too heavy to move over to the sandbox."
Teacher: "Do we have anything out here on the playground that will help you move it?"

Child: "What do you want us to use to clean up all this water on the table?"
Teacher: "Try this paper towel and a piece of paper and find out which one works best."

Child: "My hands are cold!"
Teacher: "Try rubbing them together. How do they feel now?"

Child: "Oh, I've dropped the paper clip on the carpet and I can't find it!"
Teacher: "Do we have anything on the Science Table that could help you find it?" (magnet)

Child: "I can't get the Styrofoam out from under the shelf."
Teacher: "Do you think you could use the rhythm stick? Will blowing on it make it move?"

Child: "The ball is in the mud puddle."
Teacher: "What do you see that would help get it out without getting your feet wet?" (stick, broom, another ball)

A Final Thought

When interacting with children, use open-ended questions rather than ones that require only a "yes" or "no" answer. "What do we have that will reach the top shelf?" "Why do you think that happened?" Open-ended questions (which are written in italics throughout the book) are included for many activities. Use these or create your own questions.

Although this book is a compilation of over 750 activities, it is only a starting place. We hope you will add your own ideas and creativity. No one knows the children in your classroom better than you. Here's to a classroom full of fun and learning!

Bringing the Inside Out— Self-Expression Through Art

Overview

The purpose of art in the early childhood curriculum is to encourage children to explore artistic media and provide a vehicle for the creative expression of each individual child. Art is not imitating the work of others (a teacher's model), nor is it coloring inside the lines of a drawing. It is a process, not a product. It is often messy and incomplete by adult standards, but it is a representation of the child's world as he sees it and can express it.

Your role is to establish an environment conducive to creativity, by providing appropriate materials and maintaining the right attitude. A variety of materials appropriate for each child's developmental level brings out the creative abilities that ALL children possess. Respect the work of each child; avoid comparisons and judgments. Every child's effort is valuable enough to be displayed, but it is not necessary to display every child's work at one time. Less is more in the early childhood classroom. Select three or four children each week and display their art. Everyone will likely stop to take a look at the work of the "featured artists."

Ask the children to talk about their work. *"Tell me about your picture"* indicates interest in a child's work; *"What is it?"* might leave a child feeling inadequate with her artistic expression. A rich atmosphere and a caring and knowledgeable teacher are key components to the developing artist.

Using materials in a manner in which the limits are set only by the artistic media provided and the children's imagination will let them express their own unique perception of the world.

This chapter offers open-ended activities in which each child can feel successful and where the process is valued more than the product. Experiences with a variety of art media and in a variety of art forms are provided with suggestions for extended applications.

Brain Fast Facts

☆ The skill of handling a brush or crayon is wired in the left hemisphere of the brain. The emotion and communication aspects of art are wired in the right hemisphere.

☆ Creativity is at its peak in the early childhood years.

Drawing

Drawing Tools

☆ Give the children a variety of drawing tools to explore. Provide pencils of different widths and lead numbers, pens, colored markers, chalk, colored pencils, and crayons.

☆ Encourage them to try some unusual drawing utensils such as a cotton swab, bird feather, twig, or plastic fork. Provide paint so the children can dip a utensil in paint and then draw on paper with these unusual utensils.

☆ Ask the children to pick their favorite drawing tool and describe why they like using it. *Which tool is easiest to use? Which one is most difficult?*

Drawing Surfaces

☆ Provide sheets of sandpaper, textured wallpaper, wax paper, foil, and cardboard for the children to use as drawing surfaces.

☆ Encourage the children to describe the effect each surface has on their work. *Which surface was the most fun to use?*

Crayon Melt

☆ Place a warming tray on low setting. Cover it with several sheets of newspaper to protect the children from the hot edges of the tray.
Safety Note: This activity must be closely supervised and an adult should be present at all times.

☆ Place a sheet of art paper on top of the newspaper and let the children take turns coloring with wax crayons. The children will discover a change in the "feel" of the way the crayon moves and a change in how the drawing looks.

Doodli-Do

☆ Make a variety of doodle marks on sheets of drawing paper and give one sheet to each child.

☆ Encourage the children to create drawings from the doodle marks.

☆ Ask the children to describe their drawings to each other.

Good Graffiti

☆ On days when the ground is soggy and children can't play on the grass, give them chalk to draw on the sidewalk or patio. This activity is fun even on sunny days when the playground is dry.

Meat Tray Art

☆ Provide each child with a Styrofoam meat tray and crayons.
☆ Let the children draw directly on the trays.
☆ Punch two holes on top and insert a strip of yarn to make a hanger.

Holiday Adaptations: This makes a nice Mother's Day, Father's Day, or holiday gift.

Buttermilk Drawings

☆ Sponge over art paper with a thin layer of buttermilk.
☆ Encourage the children to draw on the paper with colored chalk in the design of their choosing, creating a thick, smooth, chalky drawing.

Sugar Water Drawings

☆ Give each child a small baby food jar.
☆ Put three tablespoons of sugar in each jar and add enough lukewarm water to fill the jar.
☆ Shake the jar until the sugar is dissolved. When the water becomes clear, ask the children how the sugar disappeared.
☆ Pour the sugar water into bowls. Provide each child with colored chalk. The children draw pictures by dipping the chalk into sugar water.
☆ When dry, the pictures will sparkle with crystallized sugar.

Scented Markers

☆ Give the children scented markers and invite them to create drawings that reflect the scent of the marker they are using.

Seurat Dots

☆ If available, show the children some of the artwork created by Seurat. He was an artist who used dots to create his drawings. This art technique is called *pointillism*. It is the light between the dots that gives life to his drawings and paintings.

☆ Encourage the children to draw a picture and then use a crayon or marker to fill in the drawing with dots.

☆ Invite the children to experiment making designs with a Lite-Brite. This may help them better understand how Seurat used light space to create a picture.

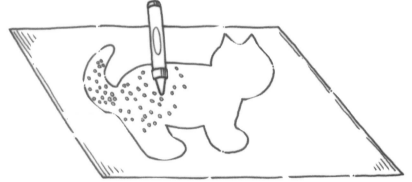

Wet Sand Drawings

☆ Before outdoor play time, add water to the sand in the sandbox.

☆ Invite the children to gather around the perimeter of the sandbox, leaning into the sandbox and making designs in the sand with sticks, combs, and potato mashers.

☆ Provide a watering can for children to re-moisten the sand when needed.

Magnifying Glass Assistance

☆ Ask the children to draw a picture while looking through a magnifying glass.

☆ Talk with them as they draw. How does the different view affect your drawing?

☆ If available, show the children some of Picasso's artwork. Particularly interesting for this activity would be some of his work that distorts normal proportions of images.

Painting

Scratch-and-Sniff Paint

☆ Mix Scratch-and-Sniff Paint as directed on page 47.

☆ Invite the children to use the mixture as paint. When it dries, scratching it will release an aroma.

☆ Challenge the children to identify the aroma released by each paint. *Which aroma do you like best? Have you smelled this aroma before? Where?*

Fingerpaint and Fingerpaint Relief

☆ Provide fingerpaint (see page 44 for several recipes) for the children.

☆ Place fingerpaint directly on a tray or tabletop. Encourage the children to explore it, making designs in the paint with their fingers.

☆ Add texture to the paint by adding a small amount of sand or birdseed.

☆ When the children have created a design that they wish to keep, with or without texture, show them how to make a print of their design by placing a piece of drawing paper on top of it and pressing it gently with their hands.

Splatter Painting

☆ Give each child an old toothbrush, a large strainer, and a sheet of drawing paper.

☆ Encourage the children to place buttons, small blocks, and other objects on their paper to create a design. If desired, let the children cut their own templates from heavyweight paper.

☆ Have the children dip their toothbrush into paint and rub it across the strainer to splatter the paint around their templates.

☆ When the paint dries, the children remove the templates to reveal the design.

Cotton Swab Painting

☆ Give each child a cotton swab and a small container of tempera paint.

☆ Encourage the children to create a drawing using the cotton swab as a drawing tool.

Textured Painting

☆ Mix ½ cup of paint with different ingredients to create texture using the chart provided on page 46 of this chapter.

☆ Give the children brushes and paper and invite them to explore the various textures of the paints.

☆ When the paint dries, have them run their hands over the paint and describe what they feel.

Bubble Painting

☆ Mix bubble soap (see page 43 for recipe). Add 2 tablespoons of tempera paint to the mixture.

☆ Cover the floor with butcher paper and invite the children to blow bubbles with a regular bubble blower.

☆ Have the children describe what happens when the bubbles land on the paper and pop. *What shapes did you make? What happens when two bubbles land near each other?*

Deodorant Bottle Painting

☆ Mix tempera paint to a creamy consistency by adding 2 tablespoons of liquid starch to each cup of paint.

☆ Remove the tops of empty roll-on deodorant bottles, pour paint into bottles, and replace the roll-on tops.

☆ Invite the children to roll the paint on art paper to create their own designs.

Spray Painting

☆ Protect the floor with newspaper or a plastic liner.

☆ Provide templates of circles, squares, leaves, and other objects for the children to use to create a design on their paper or encourage them to cut their own templates.

☆ Fill a spray bottle (with adjustable spray settings) with a watery solution of tempera paint. Invite the children to lightly spray their paper and templates.

☆ When the paint dries, the children can lift the templates to see the resulting design.

Roller Painting

☆ Obtain several used, small wall painting roller brushes (the edger type).

☆ Children can paint at the easel or on a wall protected by plastic and covered with art paper.

Squirt Bottle Painting

☆ Prepare several bottles of thick tempera paint (consistency of mustard) in plastic squirt bottles. Each bottle of paint should contain a different color.

☆ Encourage the children to squirt colors on art paper to create designs.

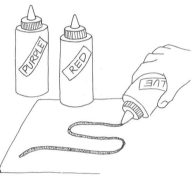

Gadget Painting

☆ Provide several interesting items for the children to use as tools for painting (such as a feather duster, bottle brush, wisp broom, and other common objects) and a shallow tray of paint.

☆ Invite the children to explore the various items as tools for painting.

☆ Discuss the tools the children choose to use. *How does the tool work as a brush? Is it easy to paint with? How is it different from a paintbrush?*

Sponge Painting

☆ Attach sponges to clothespins. Encourage the children to dip the sponges into a shallow tray of paint and use them as paintbrushes.

☆ Talk with the children as they paint. *What designs are you making? How is using a sponge for a brush different than using a regular paintbrush? Is it easier to paint or is it more difficult?*

Feather Painting

☆ Provide children with a tray of tempera paint and feathers that have a long and sturdy shaft.

☆ Encourage the children to use the feathers as a painting and drawing tool. They can paint with the top of the feather (the vane) and draw with the shaft of the feather.

☆ Discuss the use of the feather as a brush and as a pen as the children are working. *Does the feather make a good writing tool?*

Epsom Salt Paint

☆ Mix Epsom Salt Paint as directed on page 43. Provide paintbrushes and paper.

☆ Encourage the children to paint a picture. When the paint dries it will have a glazed appearance. It is more fun to use Epsom Salt Paint on colored paper or as a glaze over a crayon drawing.

☆ Have the children talk about the way the paint changes the look of their pictures.

☆ Ask questions. *Do you like the glazed look? What are some good things to paint with this type of paint?*

Icing Paint

☆ Mix Icing Paint as directed on page 45. Provide brushes or Popsicle sticks and stiff paper or cardboard.

☆ Invite the children to use the Icing Paint to create a swirling textured picture.

☆ This paint has the consistency of icing and is great for creating pictures of oceans and skies.

☆ Talk with the children as they paint. *What things can you make with this paint? How is this paint different? Is it thinner or thicker than the usual paint?*

Puff Paint

☆ Mix Puff Paint as directed on page 47. Provide fingerpaint paper or other appropriate surface for fingerpainting.

☆ Encourage the children to fingerpaint with the Puff Paint.

☆ Talk with them as they paint. Discuss the feel of the paint.

Salt Paint

☆ Mix one teaspoon of salt into fingerpaint.

☆ Encourage the children to enjoy the gravel-like texture of the paint.

☆ Ask them to describe the texture of the paint. *Is it grainy? Is it rough? How is this fingerpaint different from the usual fingerpaint you use? Which type of paint do you prefer?*

The Instant Curriculum

Designs

Fingerpaint Baggies

☆ Fill large, plastic zipper-closure bags with four tablespoons of fingerpaint (see page 44 for recipe).

☆ Place a sealed bag on the table in front of each child.

☆ Encourage the children to create and re-create designs as they move their fingers over the top of the bag of paint.

Marble Prints

☆ Place a sheet of paper on a cookie sheet or inside a shallow cardboard box.

☆ Dip marbles into tempera paint. Use a plastic spoon or fork to remove the marbles from the paint.

☆ Place marbles on the cookie sheet or in the box and let children rotate the box to move the marbles around, creating a design.

☆ Use golf balls for a slightly different effect.

Car Tracks

☆ Pour tempera paint over a sponge (or paper towel). Prepare a different color for each sponge.

☆ Place small toy cars next to each color of prepared tempera.

☆ Encourage the children to roll cars across the tempera-soaked sponges and then roll the cars on art paper to create a colored, overlapping track design.

Straw Blowing

☆ Use a spoon to place a small amount of tempera paint on each child's paper.

☆ Give each child a straw (straws that are cut in half are easier to handle).

☆ Encourage the children to blow through a straw to move paint across the paper and create a design.

Glue Drop Designs

☆ Use food coloring or tempera paint to tint two or three small containers of glue.

☆ Provide art paper and toothpicks for each color of glue.

☆ Encourage the children to dot the glue on their paper.

☆ Or add food coloring or tempera paint to small bottles of glue and let the children squeeze the drops onto their paper to create designs.

Seasonal Adaptation: Use blue food coloring to tint a small container of glue. Encourage the children to draw a picture with markers or crayons, and then turn it into a rainy day scene by dabbing blue glue dots over the picture.

Shaker Art

☆ Fill salt shakers with powdered tempera paint.

☆ Invite the children to dip a paintbrush into glue and paint a design on a piece of paper.

☆ Let the children shake the tempera paint onto their glue design.

Absorption Designs

☆ Mix three or four colors of food coloring with water. Place each color in a separate jar.

☆ Place an eyedropper in each jar.

☆ Place a paper towel or coffee filter on a layer of thick newspaper in a shallow pan.

☆ Encourage the children to use eyedroppers to drop color onto the paper towels.

☆ As the color spots overlap, children will discover different colors.

☆ Talk with the children about *absorption*. Point out how the more porous and thick the paper, the better it absorbs the paint.

☆ Discuss the colors that occur when the different colors overlap.

Mobiles

☆ Take the children on a nature walk to locate small branches to use as the base of a mobile. If wooded areas are unavailable, use a coat hanger instead of a branch as the base.

☆ Ask the children to draw pictures of things that are of interest to them or things they like.

☆ Challenge the children to draw a circle around each item and cut it out.

☆ Punch holes in the top of each of their pictures and tie on pieces of yarn ranging in length from 8" to 12".

☆ Help the children tie their artwork onto the branch or coat hanger to create a mobile.

Rubbings

☆ Provide a limited number of large cardboard cutout shapes, such as a diamond, a square, a circle, and a rectangle.

☆ Encourage the children to place the cutouts under a piece of paper and rub a crayon over the paper to create a rubbing.

☆ Challenge the children to turn the shapes into other designs by adding details with crayons. For example:
   ★ a diamond becomes a kite by adding string
   ★ a square becomes a table by adding legs
   ★ a circle becomes a face by adding eyes, mouth, and a nose
   ★ a rectangle becomes a window by adding lines to create windowpanes

Sand Designs I

☆ Color sand by mixing it with powdered tempera paint or by placing a small amount of sand on a paper plate and rubbing colored chalk over it. The chalk will erode and mix with the sand to create colored sand.

☆ Place the sand in salt shakers.

☆ Encourage the children to make a design with glue and then sprinkle the colored sand on top. Children can shake off the excess sand to see the design.

Sand Designs II

☆ Color sand by mixing it with powdered tempera paint or by placing a small amount of sand on a paper plate and rubbing colored chalk over it. The chalk will erode and mix with the sand to create colored sand.

☆ Give each child a small jar. (Plastic baby food jars work well.)

☆ Show the children how to fold a paper plate in half and use it as a funnel to pour a small amount of colored sand into the jar.

☆ Encourage them to layer the colors of sand in the jar until it is completely full and then glue on the lid.
Note: Keep layers of sand relatively thin, ¼" to ½" deep. Sand designs will be more attractive if each layer is uneven.

Mondrian Masterpieces

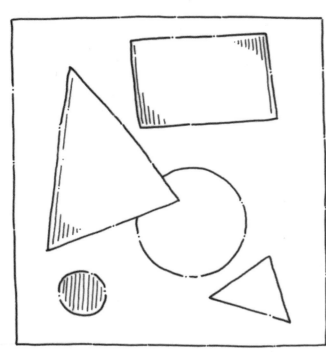

☆ Mondrian was a 19th/20th century Dutch painter. His work covers a wide range from landscapes to portraits, but he is best known for his bold, abstract, geometric pieces of art. He frequently used yellows, reds, grays, blacks, and whites in his designs.

☆ Show some of Mondrian's work, if possible.

☆ Give the children geometric shapes cut from yellow, gray, white, red, and blue construction paper and encourage them to create a geometric collage.

☆ Or offer the children easel paper, brushes, and tempera paint (red, yellow, blue, black, gray, and white). Encourage the children to create Mondrian masterpieces.

☆ Encourage the children to discuss their designs. *Which color did you like using best? Which shape did you use most often?*

Template Designs

☆ Give the children geometric templates, such as plastic lids, coasters, meat trays, bottle lids, and other uniquely shaped objects, to trace around to create a design.

☆ Encourage them to color in their designs using crayons.

Stained Glass Windows

☆ Add liquid detergent to tempera paint to create a thicker consistency.

☆ Cover the wall and floor area with newspaper for protection.

☆ Define a space for each child on a window using masking tape. Let the children take turns painting directly on the window inside the area defined by tape.

☆ Remove tape when all the painting is done and fill in the tape lines with dark paint.

More Stained Glass Windows

☆ Give the children small containers of hair gel in as many pastel colors as available.

☆ Use masking tape to designate an area of the window for each child.

☆ Invite the children to paint a colorful design on the windows using a brush and hair gel. Designs will wash off easily when you are ready to have clean windows again.

Rock Salt Designs

☆ Dye rock salt using the recipe for colored rock salt on page 43.

☆ Give the children glue and stiff paper or cardboard.

☆ Invite them to create designs using glue, and then sprinkle with colored rock salt.

Prints

Cookie Cutter Prints

☆ Give the children several cookie cutters, a shallow tray of tempera paint, and a piece of paper.

☆ Encourage them to dip the cookie cutter in the paint and make prints on their paper.

Gadget Printing

☆ Prepare tempera paint and pour it on a paper towel "sponge."

☆ Provide children with several objects, such as a kitchen whisk, fork, potato masher, and any other suitable gadget, to press on the color-soaked towel and make prints on art paper.

Bubble Prints I

☆ Mix 1 tablespoon of liquid detergent, 1 teaspoon of glycerin, and a small amount of tempera paint in a small bowl of water.

☆ Use a hand mixer to create bubbles.

☆ Give the children a piece of drawing paper and invite them to lay it on top of the bowl of bubbles to make a circular or bubble design.

Bubble Prints II

☆ Give each child a 3" x 5" piece of bubble wrap with large "bubbles," drawing paper, and a shallow tray of tempera paint.

☆ Encourage them to dip the bubble wrap into the tray of paint and then press it onto their drawing paper.

Sponge Prints

☆ Cut sponges into a variety of shapes or buy commercially made shaped sponges.

☆ Prepare tempera paint and pour a thin layer into a flat dish or meat tray.

☆ Encourage the children to dip sponges into the paint and print designs on butcher paper or drawing paper.

Holiday Adaptation: Use printed paper to wrap special-occasion gifts.

Blotto Prints I

☆ Give each child a piece of folded construction paper.

☆ Have them dab paint on one side only.

☆ While the paint is still wet, fold the other side over the design. Show them how to rub their hands on the outside of the paper, and then open to reveal a duplicated picture.

Variation: Place paint on the folded paper with a small dollop at the top and a larger dollop underneath. When the children open their paper it will look like a butterfly. Encourage them to add details (antennae) with markers or crayons.

Blotto Prints II

☆ Give children a cutout butterfly shape that has been folded.

☆ Prepare paint in a thick consistency. (You can thicken the paint by adding liquid starch to the mixture.)

☆ Encourage the children to dot color on one wing, or paint the wing entirely with a variety of colors.

☆ Fold the other wing over and rub. Colors will blend as they are reproduced on the top wing.

☆ Display butterflies on a dry tree limb anchored in a bucket of sand.

1.

2.

3.

Fold line

Hand Mural

☆ Prepare tempera paints in different colors and pour on folded paper towels in pie pans or meat trays.

☆ Ask the children to press their hands on the paint-soaked towels and print on a large sheet of butcher paper hanging on the wall. Hands can overlap in a design of their choice.

☆ Have a rinse bucket and towel available for painted hands.

☆ Encourage the children to find a hand that is larger than their hand and one that is smaller than their hand.

Hand Wreaths

☆ Give each child a piece of green construction paper and a pencil.

☆ Invite the children to trace around their hands and then cut out the resulting handprint.

☆ Shape the handprints into a wreath or a tree on the bulletin board.

Fingerprint Creations

☆ Place a stack of paper towels on a plate and pour tempera paint on it.

☆ Encourage the children to press their index finger on the paint pad and create a design on butcher paper or individual sheets of art paper.

☆ Depending on the colors available, children can print oranges or lemons on a tree, scales on a fish, feathers on an owl, or decorative balls on a tree.

☆ Children may also create mice by using a black marker to add eyes and a tail. They can create a worm by connecting fingerprints and using a marker to add eyes and legs.

☆ Encourage the children to name the animals they create.

Footprints

☆ Provide a shallow tray of tempera paint, an 8' strip of butcher paper, a tub of soapy water, and a towel.

☆ Invite the children to take off their shoes, step into the tempera paint, and then walk the length of the butcher paper.

☆ Have someone waiting at the other end of the paper with soapy water and a towel.

☆ Identify one of each child's footprints by writing the child's name beside the print.

☆ Talk with the children about their footprints. *Whose print is the largest? Smallest? Name the toes on the foot. Which prints are right feet? Which prints are left feet?*

Collages

Torn Paper Collages

☆ Give the children scraps of colorful paper and invite them to tear the paper into any type of shapes they desire.

☆ Ask the children to glue the torn pieces of paper on a piece of drawing paper to form a collage.

Torn Paper Silhouettes

☆ Provide each child with a large shape that has been randomly torn from light-colored paper.

☆ Ask the children to paste the shape on darker background art paper.

☆ Encourage the children to use crayons to turn the shape into a picture.

Tissue Paper Collages

☆ Provide children with cut pieces of tissue paper, liquid starch, brushes, and art paper.

☆ Encourage them to paint starch over the paper and place tissue paper on it in a design of their choice.

Nature Collages

☆ Give each child a sack and go on a nature walk.
☆ Let the children collect leaves, twigs, flower, bark, moss, and other small items of interest.
☆ Upon return to the classroom have the children glue their nature treasure on a piece of paper or cardboard to create a collage.

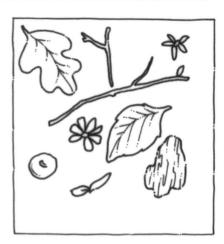

Confetti Art

☆ Save used hole punches from other projects. Separate by color and store in clear plastic jars.
☆ Encourage the children to draw designs with glue using an old paintbrush, a dry marker, or cotton swab.
☆ Let them sprinkle colored hole punches over their glue designs.

Humpty Dumpty Reconstruction

☆ Save shells from boiled eggs.
☆ Break the shells into small pieces.
☆ Cut out egg shapes from drawing paper.
☆ Have the children paint glue on egg-shaped paper and sprinkle crushed eggshells on the glued area.

Happy Face Montage

☆ Have the children look through magazines for happy faces and cut them out.
☆ Encourage them to glue the pictures onto a piece of paper to create a collage of happy faces.

Mono- chromatic Masterpieces

☆ Give each child a piece of red paper. Provide many small bits of other red materials, such as red wrapping paper, red cloth, red feathers, red tissue paper, red ribbon, and other red art materials.

☆ Challenge the children to create a monochromatic collage.

☆ Repeat on other days with other colors.

Shapes on Shapes

☆ Cut out one large circle (or square or triangle) from a grocery bag, wallpaper, construction paper, or butcher paper for each child.

☆ Cut a number of similar small shapes for each child.

☆ Invite the children to glue the small circles on the large circle (or small triangles on large triangle) in a design of their choosing.

☆ They can add color with crayons or markers.

Textured Collages

☆ Collect a variety of different textured, colored fabric pieces and cut them into usable sizes.

☆ Pre-sort the fabrics according to prints (such as stripes, floral prints, and dots) or leave them in independent categories.

☆ Have the children cover their papers with glue and then arrange the fabrics, creating their own design.

Sculpting and Molding

Papier-Mâché

☆ Prepare papier-mâché paste (see page 46 for recipe).

☆ Give each child a form to work with, such as a milk carton, box, old ball, or any other suitable object.

☆ Ask the children to tear strips of newspaper to use with the paste.

☆ Show them how to dip the newspaper strips into the paste, remove the excess paste, and then lay the strip over their form.

☆ Make sure the children smooth out the wrinkles in the paper as they continue to layer the paper on their form.

☆ When the paper is completely dry, usually after a couple of days, provide poster paint or acrylic paint and encourage the children to paint a design on their form.

Ball

News

Paste

Cover form

Goop and Gak

☆ Mix a batch of Goop or Gak, or both, and let the children have fun molding and sculpting with it. (See recipes on page 45.)

☆ Talk with them as they work about the feel of the mixture. *Is it rough? Is it smooth? Is it cool to the touch?*

☆ If the children are playing with both Goop and Gak, ask them how the mixtures are different and alike.

Cloud Dough

☆ Make Cloud Dough (see recipe on page 43) for the children to explore.

☆ Ask the children why they think the dough is called "cloud dough."

Playdough Sculpting

☆ Mix playdough prior to class, using one of the recipes on pages 46-47.

☆ When cool, place in covered containers or plastic bags.

☆ Children can use and re-use the playdough, molding it into shapes of their choice.

Wood Sculpting

☆ Obtain small pieces of lumber from a lumber store or from parents.

☆ Provide glue and let the children arrange and glue the pieces together, creating their own designs.

Box Sculpting

☆ Provide boxes in a variety of sizes, from small jewelry boxes to shoeboxes.

☆ Encourage the children to glue boxes together and on top of each other, creating their own unique configurations.

☆ If desired, provide small bits of cloth and ribbon to add design interest.

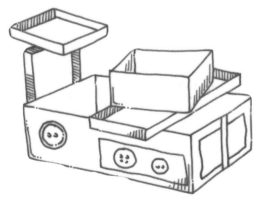

Stabiles

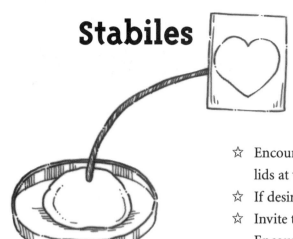

☆ Provide each child with a drinking cup lid, pipe cleaners, playdough (or modeling clay), and objects cut out from greeting cards (or small magazine pictures).

☆ Ask the children to glue cutouts on one end of the pipe cleaner, put playdough into the cup lid, and insert the other end of the pipe cleaner into the playdough,

☆ Encourage the children to arrange several pipe cleaners on cup lids at various heights and twisted in different shapes.

☆ If desired, place the stabile lids in a small box to display them.

☆ Invite the children to share their work with their friends. Encourage them to describe what they have created. *Are the pipe cleaners easy to shape?*

Sandcastles

☆ On a warm, sunny day, moisten the sand in the sandbox to the consistency of beach sand.

☆ Let children put on bathing suits and make sandcastles.

☆ Provide leaves and twigs for "landscaping," if desired.

☆ Have a water hose ready to rinse off the sandcastle builders when they are finished!

Mud Pies

☆ For summer water play (when children are in bathing suits), place pans of water in the sandbox so children can mix sand and water to make mud pies.

☆ Place a tire or other smooth surface in the sandbox to use as a display table for "cookies," "pies," and other sculpted creations.

☆ Ask the children to describe and name the pies they make. Talk with them about why the pies are called "mud pies."

Soap Suds Clay

☆ Mix Soap Suds Clay (see page 47 for recipe) for the children to explore.

☆ Talk with the children as they work with the clay. *How does it feel different from playdough? How is it like playdough? Which do you prefer to work with and why?*

Foil Sculptures

☆ Give each child a 1' square sheet of aluminum foil.

☆ Encourage them to shape the foil into creations of their own choosing.

☆ Talk with them as they work. *Is the foil easy to work with? What sounds does it make? How does it feel? Is it heavy? Light?*

The Instant Curriculum

Art and Crafts Recipes

Any recipe using a potentially dangerous material or piece of equipment, such as alcohol, talcum powder, or anelectric mixer, or one that requires heating or hot water should be completed by adults only. Other recipes can be made with the children with constant and careful supervision.

Bubble Soap

☆ Gently mix 1 teaspoon of glycerin, ½ cup of liquid detergent, and ½ cup of water. For best results, let the mixture sit overnight before blowing bubbles.

Cloud Dough

☆ Mix 1 cup of vegetable oil, 6 cups of flour, and ½ cup of water. Continue adding water, 1 tablespoon at a time, until the mixture forms the consistency of dough. The oil makes this mixture greasy, providing a tactile experience different from playdough.

Colored Glue

☆ Add tempera paint to glue to make various colors. Let the children "squeeze" their pictures (using squeeze bottles) instead of painting.

Colored Rock Salt

☆ Dye rock salt by placing food coloring in alcohol and letting the salt sit in the mixture for about 10 minutes. Drain on a paper towel.

Epsom Salt Solution

☆ Mix 1 cup of hot water with 4 tablespoons of Epsom salt. Allow mixture to cool. Use as a paint. When this mixture dries, it creates a glazed appearance.

Face Paint/ Body Paint

☆ Mix 2 tablespoons of cold cream, ½ teaspoon of glycerin, 1 teaspoon of cornstarch, 1 teaspoon of dry tempera, and 1 teaspoon of detergent. Make sure the detergent is one that is gentle to the skin.

Fingerpaint Recipe #1

☆ Pour a tablespoon of liquid starch onto paper or directly onto tabletop. Sprinkle on a little powdered tempera. Let the children mix.

Fingerpaint Recipe #2

☆ Dissolve ⅓ cup of cornstarch in ¾ cup of cold water in a saucepan. Add 2 cups of hot water and cook on a stove or hot plate until the mixture is clear. Add 1 envelope of Knox gelatin dissolved in ¼ cup of cold water. Blend well. Add ½ cup of Ivory Flakes (or Ivory Snow) and blend well. Allow mixture to cool. Divide into containers. Add desired color of powdered tempera to each container.
Safety Note: If children are helping to make the fingerpaint, closely supervise the use of a stove or hot plate.

Fingerpaint Recipe #3

☆ Mix 1 ½ cups of laundry starch with ½ cup of cold water and stir into a creamy paste. Add 1 quart of boiling water until the mixture becomes transparent or glossy-looking. Stir continually. Add ½ cup of talcum and allow the mixture to cool. Add 1 ½ cups of soap flakes and stir until they are evenly distributed. Pour into containers and add powdered tempera to color. Allow mixture to cool before using.

Body Paints

☆ Mix 2 tablespoons of cold cream, ½ teaspoon of glycerin, 1 teaspoon of cornstarch, 1 teaspoon of liquid detergent, and 1 teaspoon of dry tempera. Mix the ingredients together to create Body Paints. Make several different colors.
☆ Provide small brushes.
☆ Demonstrate how to use the paint to paint flowers, suns, moons, and other simple images on the back of your hand or on your forearm.
☆ Encourage the children to explore painting a design on their own hands or arms or on the hands or arms of a friend.

☆ Talk with the children as they paint. Ask questions. *How does the brush feel on your skin? Does it tickle? How is this painting like a tattoo? How is it different?*

Gak

☆ Combine 2 cups of glue, 1 ½ cups of water, and food coloring (if colored Gak is desired). In a larger bowl mix 2 teaspoons of Borax and 1 cup of hot water. Stir until smooth. Slowly add glue mixture to Borax. It will thicken quickly and be difficult to mix. Mix well and drain off excess water. Let stand for a few minutes, and then pour into a shallow tray. Let dry for 10 minutes. Store Gak in a plastic, zipper-closure bag (it will keep for two to three weeks).

Goop

☆ Cook 2 cups of salt and ½ cup of water for 4 to 5 minutes on low heat. Remove from heat. Add 1 cup of cornstarch and ½ cup of water. Return to heat. Stir until mixture thickens. Allow mixture to cool before using. Store in a plastic, zipper-closure bag or in a covered container.

Icing Paint

☆ Mix 1 cup of powdered tempera paint, 2 tablespoons of wallpaper paste, and ¼ to ½ cup of liquid starch. Mix until thick enough to spread like frosting. Use Popsicle sticks to spread on cardboard or other stiff surface.

Paints

☆ Add the following ingredients to one pint of tempera paint to change paint consistency:

- ★ Slimy Paint: add 2 tablespoons of corn syrup
- ★ Gritty Paint: add ½ teaspoon of sand
- ★ Slippery Paint: add 1 teaspoon of glycerin
- ★ Lumpy Paint: add 1 tablespoon of flour
- ★ Rough Paint: add 1 tablespoon of sawdust
- ★ Shiny Paint: add ½ cup of sugar
- ★ Sparkly Paint: add ½ cup of salt (use immediately)
- ★ Creamy Paint: add ¼ cup of liquid starch
- ★ Thick Paint: mix 3 parts tempera powder to 1 part water

Helpful Hints:

☆ Add liquid soap to all paints to make it easier to wash out of clothes.

☆ Add 1 teaspoon of alcohol to paint to keep it from souring.

Papier-Mâché Paste

☆ Mix 2 cups of wheat paste and 2 ½ cups of water.

Paste

☆ Mix 2 tablespoons of flour with a small amount of water to form a paste. Pour 2 cups of boiling water into the paste mixture. Boil for 3 minutes in a double boiler. Add ½ teaspoon of alum and ½ teaspoon of oil of wintergreen. Add food coloring, if desired. Allow mixture to cool before using. This paste will keep for about two weeks (more in cooler climates).

Playdough Recipe #1

☆ Combine 3 cups of flour, 1 ½ cups of salt, 3 tablespoons of vegetable oil, 2 tablespoons of cream of tartar, and 3 cups of water. Cook over very low heat until mixture is no longer sticky to the touch. When cool, store in a plastic container or plastic, zipper-closure bag for use and re-use.

Playdough Recipe #2

☆ Dissolve 1 tablespoon of alum in 1 tablespoon of oil and 1 cup of boiling water. Add 1 cup of flour and ½ cup of salt. Knead when cool. Store in plastic containers or in plastic, zipper-closure bags for use and re-use.

Playdough Recipe #3

☆ Combine 1 cup of flour, ½ cup of salt, 1 cup of water, 1 tablespoon of vegetable oil, and 2 teaspoons of cream of tartar. Heat mixture over low heat until it forms a ball. Knead after the mixture cools. Store in a covered container for use and re-use.

Puff Paint

☆ Mix 2 tablespoons of tempera paint, ⅓ cup of white glue, and 2 cups of shaving cream. Use like fingerpaint.

Salt Paint

☆ Mix 1 teaspoon of salt into fingerpaint for children to enjoy a tactile fingerpainting experience.

Scented Playdough

☆ Add 1 teaspoon of scented extract (peppermint, vanilla, lemon) to a basic playdough recipe. If desired, use scented massage oils in place of extract.

Scratch-and-Sniff Paint

☆ Mix flavored gelatin as directed but use only half the amount of water called for. Use the mixture for paint. When it dries, children can scratch and sniff it.

Soap Paint

☆ Mix 1 cup of soap flakes and enough water to form a consistency of whipping cream. Beat with a mixer until it looks like shaving cream. Add food coloring, if desired. Use like fingerpaint.

Soapsuds Clay

☆ Mix ¾ cup of soap powder (laundry detergent) and 1 tablespoon of warm water in a bowl. Beat with an electric mixer until it has the consistency of clay.

A Pot, a Pan, and a Wooden Spoon— Cooking

Overview

When cooking with young children, it is important to remember that the process is equally as important as the product. Much will be learned as children slice fruits and vegetables, mix and measure ingredients, count items, and witness changes of state as dry ingredients become liquid and liquids become solids. Cooking is probably one of the best examples of a single learning experience that incorporates and integrates a number of cognitive, physical, and emotional skills. The following are a few of the things children will experience as they cook.

Cooking is an excellent **sensory** experience. Children will learn about different textures, including *gooey, cold, hot, wet, hard, rough, bumpy, smooth*, and dozens of others. They will hear a variety of sounds: *sizzling, crunching, popping, squirting, gurgling*, and many more. They will see food change from brittle to soft and liquid to solid. They will witness evaporation, the impact of friction, changes in color as foods cook, and changes in the way textures affect the way food looks. Aromas that occur during cooking will help children sharpen their discrimination among different scents. Last, but not least, children will experience a variety of tastes.

Cognitively, children will learn about colors, shapes, and sizes. They will learn about fractions and scientific principles. They will learn how to follow directions, how to use proper tools, and about the concept of time.

Language is introduced and practiced during cooking activities. Terms such as *more/less, bigger/smaller, in/out, pour, stir, shake, spread, peel, crack, grind, grate*, and *boil* are experienced concretely.

Children also develop appropriate **social** behaviors when they cook. They learn the importance of cooperation when working in a group, sharing, taking turns, planning ahead, delayed gratification, and the proper use of utensils.

Cooking is an active experience and, therefore, allows children to practice both **fine** and **gross motor skills.** They will stir, knead, press, pinch, cut, spread, roll, pour, and pound.

Cooking also offers the opportunity for children to learn about **proper nutrition.** Through cooking experiences, they can be introduced to healthy, balanced meals. They can learn to make choices that are nutritionally sound.

Finally, children are **learning to cook,** and they are having fun. Children love to cook. Because cooking is generally reserved for adults, and children might not participate in food preparation at home, they will jump at the chance to try cooking activities at school. Both boys and girls can be helpful "junior chefs."

Because there are so many positive outcomes of cooking together, you may want to make it the subject of one of your school or class newsletters, or letters you send home to families about what the children are learning. Use the information above to help families become aware of the many things that their children can learn from sharing in meal preparation or just cooking for fun.

Important points to remember when cooking with young children:
☆ Always consider safety issues. When using certain pieces of equipment, particular substances, or heat, an adult should do these steps.
☆ Provide several measuring experiences before using a recipe that requires extensive measuring. Some of the best opportunities for measuring experiences occur during play in the sand and water table.
☆ Demonstrate the correct way to use both dry and liquid measuring utensils. Let the children practice using them.
☆ Provide a child-sized workspace.
☆ Review safety rules.
☆ Introduce new vocabulary.
☆ Clean up as you go along. Set up three dishpans—one for washing, one for rinsing, and one for drying.
☆ Talk with the children as they sample the product. *How does it taste? Is it sweet? Is it tart? Is it creamy or crumbly?*
☆ Evaluate the process. Ask questions related to the total experience. *What went well today? What problems did we encounter? Did everyone share the work?*

Brain Fast Facts
☆ Cooking activities integrate all five senses. The more senses involved in the learning experience the greater the likelihood the information will receive a high priority for processing.

- ☆ Select recipes that allow for the participation of several children or recipes that prepare individual portions.
- ☆ Set out all materials prior to beginning.
- ☆ Always wash hands prior to starting.
- ☆ Check for allergies each time you select a recipe.
- ☆ Be aware of cultural and religious food limitations when planning cooking activities.

No-Cook Recipes

Milkanilla

- ☆ Invite each child to mix ½ teaspoon of sugar, ⅛ teaspoon of vanilla, and a drop of food color with 6 ounces of milk. Stir and drink.
- ☆ Ask the children why they think this drink is called "Milkanilla."
- ☆ Encourage them to think of a new name for this drink.

Purple Cow Shakes

- ☆ Encourage each child to place a small scoop of vanilla ice cream, 2 tablespoons of grape juice, and 2 tablespoons of milk in a plastic baby food jar. Let them shake, shake, shake!
- ☆ Recite "The Purple Cow" by Gelett Burgess with the children as they enjoy their shakes. Can anyone tell you which word in the poem rhymes with "cow?"

I never saw a purple cow,
I never hope to see one.
But I can tell you, anyhow,
I'd rather see than be one.

Baggie Ice Cream

☆ Help each child place ½ cup of milk, 1 tablespoon of sugar, and ¼ teaspoon of vanilla in a small plastic, zipper-closure bag and seal it.

☆ Place each bag in a large zipper-closure bag. Add 3 tablespoons of rock salt and ice cubes and seal. Shake. This makes one serving of ice cream.

☆ Teach the children the chant: "You scream. I scream. We all scream for ice cream."

☆ This activity is great for demonstrating change of state. Encourage the children to talk about what makes a liquid turn into a solid.

Can Ice Cream

☆ Place 2 cups of milk, 2 tablespoons of sugar, and 1 teaspoon of vanilla in a small coffee can and close the lid.

☆ Place the small can inside a larger can and add ice cubes and a little rock salt.

☆ Invite the children to roll the can back and forth across the floor to keep the mixture inside moving. In about 15 minutes, you will have ice cream.

☆ Talk with the children about the role the rock salt plays in the freezing process. (The salt keeps the ice from melting.)

Butter

☆ Put out a carton of whipping cream to bring it to room temperature.

☆ Let each child place 2 tablespoons of whipping cream (at room temperature) in a small baby food jar.

☆ Encourage the children to shake their jars until the cream becomes solid. Pour off the excess water and add salt to taste.

☆ Talk with the children about where cream comes from. Encourage them to think of other dairy products that are made from milk.

☆ Spread the resulting butter on crackers and enjoy.

Sun Salad

☆ Give each child a peach half and some grated cheddar cheese.

☆ Show them how to turn the peach half pit side down on their plate and add grated cheese around the edges to create sunrays.

☆ Have the children brainstorm ideas about how they might make a "moon salad."

Peanut Butter

☆ Invite the children to shell peanuts. Have the children count the peanuts inside each shell. *What is the most common number of peanuts inside each shell? Does anyone see only one peanut in a shell?*

☆ Place 1 cup of peanuts, 1 ½ tablespoons of vegetable oil, and ¼ teaspoon salt in a blender. Blend to desired smoothness.

☆ Serve on crackers or on apple slices.
   Safety Note: Before serving children any food, check for allergies.

☆ Teach the children "The Peanut Butter Song." Discuss the sticky consistency of peanut butter. *What makes it so sticky?*

The Peanut Butter Song by Pam Schiller (Tune: "Three Blind Mice")
Peanut butter,
Peanut butter,
See how it spreads,
See how it spreads,
It sticks to my knife, and it sticks to my bread.
It sticks to my tongue and the top of my mouth.
Have you ever tried to talk with a mouth full of
Peanut butter,
Peanut butter?

Peanut Butter Balls

☆ Mix ½ cup of peanut butter, ½ cup of honey, and 1 cup of nonfat powdered milk together.

☆ Invite the children to roll the dough into small balls. Encourage them to brainstorm ways to make their peanut butter balls a uniform size.

☆ The balls are less sticky and easier to eat if they have been refrigerated for a couple of hours.

☆ Discuss the ingredients in this snack with the children. *Are they healthy items? If so, why?*
   Safety Note: Before serving children any food, check for allergies.

Friendship Mix

☆ Have the children bring in small snack items such as bite-size cereal, pretzels, dried fruit, and other ingredients to share with their classmates.

☆ Place each of the items in separate small bowls and give each child a small cup.

☆ Encourage the children to mix their own snack mix by placing a spoonful of selected items into their cup.

☆ Encourage the children to think of why this snack might be called "Friendship Mix."

Banana Pudding

☆ Help children mix a package of instant banana pudding with milk (according to directions on the box).

☆ Encourage the children to slice bananas using a plastic knife.

☆ Give each child a small cup. Encourage them to place a vanilla wafer in the bottom of their cup, and then add a few slices of bananas and a couple of spoonfuls of pudding.

☆ Discuss the layers in their cups. *Which item is on the bottom? Which item is on the top? What is in the middle?*

Shake-a-Puddin'

☆ Invite each child to place 1 tablespoon of instant pudding and ¼ cup of milk into a small plastic jar and shake until thick.

☆ As the children enjoy their pudding, ask them to describe the texture.

Banana Wheels

☆ Let the children slice bananas using plastic knives.

☆ Place 1 teaspoon of dry flavored gelatin in a plastic, zipper-closure bag.

☆ Encourage the children to put three or four banana slices in the bag and shake. They can remove the Banana Wheels with toothpicks and eat.

☆ Ask them why they think these snacks are called "Banana Wheels."

Candy Mints

☆ Blend together 2 tablespoons of margarine, 2 tablespoons of shortening, 3 tablespoons of warm water, a few drops of red food coloring, and 1 teaspoon of peppermint flavoring. Add 5 cups of powdered sugar.

☆ Encourage the children to knead the ingredients together until thoroughly mixed.

☆ Invite the children to roll the dough into small balls and then pat them into mints.

☆ Say the following rhyme with the children as they roll:

Pat-a-Mint by Pam Schiller (Tune: "Pat-a-Cake")
Pat-a-mint,
Pat-a-mint,
Baker's man.
Pat me a mint as fast as you can.
Roll 'em up, pat 'em down,
Nice and round.
Roll 'em up, pat 'em down
Round and round.

☆ Because this snack is mostly sugar, limit children's intake to just one or two small mints. Ask them if they think the snack is healthy or if it is a treat.

Glittery Sugar Mallows

☆ Place ¼ cup of sugar in a plastic, zipper-closure bag or inside a small plastic jar.

☆ Add one or two drops of food coloring and shake to mix.

☆ Pour one small can of canned (evaporated) milk in a small bowl.

☆ Give each child a large marshmallow. Encourage them to dip their marshmallows into the milk and then into the colored sugar mixture to create "Glittery Sugar Mallows."

☆ Ask the children about the nutrient value of this snack. *Is this a healthy choice or is it just a good-tasting snack?*

Tooty Fruity

☆ Invite the children to use a rolling pin to crumble six zwieback biscuits.

☆ Mix the crumbs with ¼ cup of melted butter and ¼ cup of white corn syrup. Stir until well mixed. Set it aside.

☆ Help the children grate the rind of one orange. Mix the grated rind and ½ cup raisins into the biscuit mixture.

☆ Grease an 8" square pan and press the mixture into the pan. Chill overnight in the fridge.

☆ The next day, cut the "Tooty Fruity" into squares and serve. Talk about the name of this snack. *What is interesting about the name Tooty Fruity?* (rhyming name)

☆ Ask the children to think of another name for this snack that would rhyme, such as "Rooty Fruity" or "Looty Fruity."

orange

white corn syrup

Zwieback toast ↓

butter ↓

raisins

Apple and Carrot Salad

☆ Let the children help peel, slice, and grate one carrot and two apples.

☆ Mix the grated carrot and apples with ½ cup of raisins, ⅓ cup of mayonnaise, and one teaspoon of lemon juice.

☆ As the children sample the salad, ask them to describe the texture and the taste

Fruit Sticks

☆ Give the children strawberries, grapes, and pineapple chunks and a wooden skewer.

☆ Encourage the children to put the fruit pieces on the stick as they would a shish kabob.

☆ Challenge the children to use the fruits to create a pattern on their sticks.

Safety Note: Wooden skewers have sharp points. Supervise closely.

Sandwich Animals

☆ Give each child two slices of bread and a slice of cheese or turkey. Have them lightly butter their bread and then add the cheese or turkey.

☆ Encourage the children to select an animal cookie cutter and press it hard to cut their sandwich into an animal shape.

☆ As the children eat their sandwiches, have them brainstorm other fillings they could put in their sandwich. *What other foods can you cut with a cookie cutter?*

Sandwich Fillings

☆ Make sandwiches using some of the suggestions below for the filling. Suggestions for fillings:
   ★ Peanut Butter and Jelly—equal parts peanut butter and jelly.
   ★ Nananutter—equal parts peanut butter and mashed bananas.
   ★ Cream Cheese and Fruit—mix softened cream cheese with raisins or fruit cocktail.
   ★ Peanut Butter Surprise—mix peanut butter and crushed pineapple or bacon bits.
   ★ Honey Butter—mix equal parts peanut butter and honey.
☆ Invite the children to sample the sandwiches. *Which filling do you like the best?*

Toaster Oven/Oven Recipes

With proper supervision, children can help with all the steps except toasting and cooking.

Toast Tidbits

☆ Invite the children to spread margarine on a slice of bread to make their own toast. For cinnamon toast, let them sprinkle their buttered bread with a mixture of sugar and cinnamon.
☆ Put the cinnamon/sugar mixture in a salt shaker so the children are better able to control the amount of topping.
☆ Toast in a toaster oven until brown (adult only).
☆ While the children are eating their toast, informally stimulate their imaginations by commenting on the shape of the toast after biting into it. *My toast looks like a tree. Leroy, what does yours look like? Lisa Marie, try turning your toast the other way.*
☆ Children can continue biting their toast in different places to create imaginary shapes.

Pizza Faces

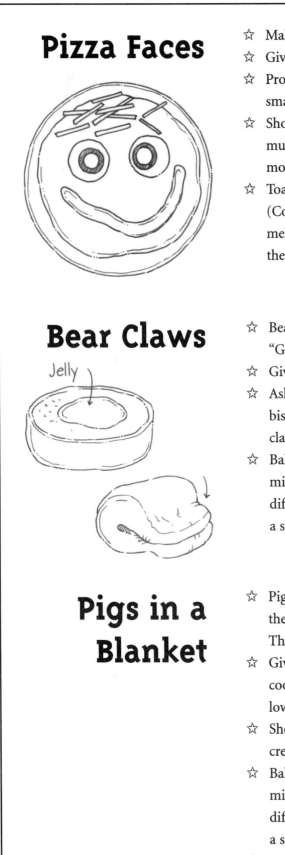

Jelly

☆ Making Pizza Faces can help reinforce facial feature concepts.

☆ Give each child ½ of an English muffin.

☆ Provide pepperoni, red peppers, sliced olives, grated cheese, and a small bowl of pizza sauce.

☆ Show the children how to brush a little sauce on top of their muffin and then use the other items to create eyes, noses, mouths, and hair.

☆ Toast in a toaster over for 3 minutes at 350° (adult only). (Cooking times vary with different ovens. When the cheese melts, it is generally a sign the muffins are ready to take out of the oven.)

Bear Claws

☆ Bear Claws are great to make as an extension activity following "Going on a Bear Hunt" (see pages 127-128).

☆ Give each child an uncooked refrigerated biscuit.

☆ Ask the children to spread a small amount of jelly on top of their biscuit, fold it over, and pinch the edges together to create a "bear claw."

☆ Bake in a toaster oven at 350° for 4 minutes on one side and 2 minutes on the other side (adult only). (Cooking times vary with different ovens. When biscuits turn golden brown, it is generally a sign they are ready to turn or take out of the oven.)

Pigs in a Blanket

☆ Pigs in a Blanket are great to make when doing a Farm Animal theme or as an extension activity following the story of "The Three Little Pigs."

☆ Give each child an uncooked refrigerated biscuit and a small pre-cooked sausage link (consider using a healthy sausage link that is low fat and/or low sodium).

☆ Show the children how to fold their biscuit around the sausage to create a "blanket."

☆ Bake in a toaster oven at 350° for 4 minutes on one side and 2 minutes on the other side (adult only). (Cooking times vary with different ovens. When biscuits turn golden brown, it is generally a sign they are ready to turn or take out of the oven.)

☆ Ask the children why this snack is called "pigs in a blanket." Ask them how they think dough is made.

Refrigerator/Freezer Recipes

Marzipan

☆ Invite the children to mix 7 ounces of coconut, 3 ounces of any flavored gelatin, ⅔ cup of sweetened condensed milk, 1 ½ teaspoons of sugar, and 1 teaspoon of almond extract.

☆ Encourage the children to create shapes of their choice and place the candy on a tray. Chill until dry.
Note: Serve occasionally as a treat.

Gelatin Jigglers

☆ Mix flavored gelatin with half the amount of water suggested on the box. Let congeal. Cut into squares or use a cookie cutter to cut out shapes.

☆ Be sure to point out the change of state that occurs as the gelatin liquid turns to a solid.

One-Cup Salad

☆ Let the children mix together 1 cup of each item: bananas, fruit cocktail, miniature marshmallows, crushed pineapple, and sour cream.

☆ Ask the children why this salad is called "One-Cup Salad."

☆ This is a good recipe for reinforcing the concept of both the number one and the measurement cup.

☆ Point out how this is different than a typical garden salad.

Party Pops

☆ Invite the children to help fill an ice tray with orange juice.

☆ Have them place a chunk of pineapple in each section of the ice tray.

☆ Place in the freezer for 30 minutes.

☆ Remove and place a Popsicle stick into each pineapple chunk. Freeze.

☆ This makes a great snack for a warm summer day.

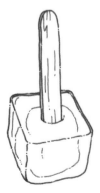

Hot Plate/Electric Skillet/ Popper Recipes

With proper supervision, children can help with all the steps except those using a hot plate, electric skillet, or popcorn popper.

Shooting Stars

☆ Cover the floor with butcher paper or a shower curtain liner. Draw circles, squares, and other shapes on the paper or liner.

☆ Place a popcorn popper in the middle of the paper and pop popcorn in the popper without the lid.
Safety Note: Make sure that children are sitting at least 5' away from the popper. This activity requires adult supervision at all times.

☆ Challenge the children to describe where the popcorn lands, such as next to the circle, inside the circle, or beside the square.

Chili Popcorn

☆ Make popcorn in a hot air popper or in the microwave.

☆ Pour 1 tablespoon of melted margarine over the popped corn.

☆ Invite the children to mix ¼ teaspoon of ground cumin, 1 ¼ teaspoon of chili powder, and a dash of salt.

☆ Pour the seasoning mixture over the popcorn and mix thoroughly.

☆ Encourage the children to describe the taste of the popcorn. *Is it more or less salty than regular popcorn? Is it spicy? Do you like it better than regular popcorn?*

Skillet Cookies

☆ Invite the children to help measure and mix together 2 cups of uncooked oats, ¾ cup of whole wheat flour, 1 teaspoon of cinnamon, and ½ teaspoon of salt. Set dry mixture aside.

☆ Next let the children help mix 1 cup of softened butter, 1 cup of sugar, 2 eggs, 2 tablespoons of water, and 1 teaspoon of vanilla.

☆ Mix the two sets of ingredients together and add 1 cup of raisins.

☆ Preheat an electric frying pan to 350 degrees. Help the children drop cookie dough by rounded teaspoons onto the surface of the electric frying pan. Cook for 4 minutes on each side.
Safety Note: This activity requires adult supervision at all times. Do not leave children alone while the electric frying pan is on.

Donuts

☆ Give each child an uncooked refrigerated biscuit. Show them how to punch a hole in the biscuit using a plastic bottle cap.

☆ Place the biscuits in a fryer for approximately two to three minutes (adult only).

☆ Turn the biscuits about halfway through the frying time. Do not allow children to place the biscuit in the oil or take it out of the oil.
Safety Note: This activity must be supervised by an adult at all times.

☆ Remove the donuts from the oil and allow them to cool. Encourage the children to dust the cooled donuts with powdered sugar. This works best if powdered sugar is placed in a salt shaker.

☆ Teach the children "The Donut Song." Encourage them to sing as they eat.

The Donut Song (Tune: "Turkey in the Straw")
Oh, I ran around the corner,
And I ran around the block,
I ran right in to the baker shop.
I grabbed me a donut
Right out of the grease,
And I handed the lady
A five-cent piece.
She looked at the nickel,
And she looked at me,
She said, "This nickel
Ain't no good to me.
There's a hole in the nickel
And it goes right through."
Said I, "There's a hole in your donut, too!
"Thanks for the donut. Good-bye!" (more said than sung)

The Bagel Song (Tune: "Turkey in the Straw")

Oh, I ran around the corner,

And I ran around the block,

I ran right in to the baker shop.

I grabbed me a bagel

Right off of the tray,

And I handed the lady

A nickel to pay.

She looked at the nickel,

And she looked at me,

She said, "This nickel

Ain't no good to me.

There's a hole in the nickel

And it goes right through."

Said I, "There's a hole in your bagel, too!

"Thanks for the bagel. Good-bye!" (more said than sung)

Grilled Cheese Delights

☆ Give each child two slices of bread and a slice of cheese. Ask them to butter their bread and place the slice of cheese between the two slices of bread (buttered side facing out).

☆ Place the sandwich in a skillet and let it cook on low heat, 3 minutes on one side and 2 minutes on the other (adult only). (Since heat settings vary with different skillets, you may just wish to leave the sandwich in the skillet until it browns on each side.) Let sandwiches cool before serving them to the children.

Safety Note: This activity requires adult supervision at all times.

The Magic of Make Believe— Dramatic Play

Overview

Dramatic play is essential for developing creativity and imagination. Young children need no written lines to memorize or rules to follow. Through imitation and fantasy, the world is theirs; and through dramatic play they take charge. It allows them to express their inner feelings within a context that is both meaningful and non-threatening.

Through dramatic play, children learn to get along with others. They learn to negotiate, compromise, and take turns. One of the primary goals of early education is to help children develop and practice the nuances of socializing with others.

Dramatic play allows children to practice problem solving in practical and meaningful ways. It encourages children to anticipate consequences, arrange situations, adapt to unplanned events, and learn to work within situational limits.

One of the most important outcomes of dramatic play is the development of children's language capabilities. Dramatic play allows children to experience language in a natural context and in a way that no other part of the preschool environment can offer. Children learn new vocabulary as they explore the props they are using in play. They learn how to be more precise and descriptive in their expressions as their peers indicate a need for more information, and their syntax becomes more refined as they model the language of others.

It is important to provide a variety of props to stimulate children's play. Providing prop boxes is an easy way to have stimulating materials right at children's fingertips. A prop box is a collection of real items related to the development or enrichment of dramatic play activities around a central theme. These items can be stored in a sturdy box, which can be easily labeled and stacked for storage.

The possibilities for prop materials are endless. They can be gathered with the help of families and can come from local vendors, garage sales, surplus stores, secondhand stores, and attics. The following is a list of several prop boxes that will add to the adventure in the Dramatic Play Center. More complete descriptions and suggestions for other prop boxes can be found on pages 66-67.

Prop Box Theme	Materials
Artist	variety of paper, easel, paints, chalks, pallet (made from cardboard), variety of brushes, smocks (old shirt)
Auto Repair Garage	supply catalog, funnels, wiring, filters, small or play hammer, tire pump, jumper cables, spark plugs, keys, pliers, gears, screwdriver, flashlight, old shirts, work gloves
Bakery	rolling pins, measuring cups and spoons, playdough, cookie cutters, mixing bowls, mixing spoons, cake pans, cookie sheets, baker hat, apron, telephone
Camping	tent, sleeping bag, lantern, backpack, sticks for a fire, pots and pans, outdoor chair, boots, fishing pole
Dancer	leotards, tights, tutu, ballet shoes, tap shoes, mirror, CD player and CDs
Eye Doctor	glasses, eye chart, small flashlight (with no batteries)
Flower/Gift Shop	vases, silk or plastic flowers, ribbons, sign, pliers, floral wire, cards, scissors, tape, order forms, cash register, foil, boxes, wrapping paper, telephone
Grocery Store	empty food containers, shopping baskets, cash register, play money, coupons, price tags, large paper bags
Mail Carrier/ Post Office	mail sack, letters (envelopes), stamps, mail sorter (divided box with name labels), magazines, rubber bands, pencils, pens, hole punch, ink pad
Pizza Place	pizza trays, menus, empty packaging for pizza ingredients, playdough, pizza boxes, dishes, napkins, tablecloths, water pitchers, cash register, play money

The Instant Curriculum

Restaurant	menus, napkins, tablecloth, plastic dishes, silverware, order forms, cash register, play money, aprons
Salon/Spa	mirrors, empty bottles (shampoo, conditioner, hair spray, and so on), blow dryer with cord removed, rollers, combs, brushes, play manicure supplies, appointment book, telephone, cash register, play money, smocks
Scientist	microscope, lab coat (long shirt), magnifying glass, slides
Scuba Diver	fins, diving mask, air tanks (empty 2-liter soda bottles), seashells, plastic fish
Teacher/School	books, paper, chalk board, pencils, pens, chalk, lesson plan/grade book, workbooks, flash cards, alphabet wall cards, charts

Brain Fast Facts

☆ Social-emotional well-being is wired between birth and age four.

☆ Children between the ages of two and five use imaginative play to organize more complex mental and emotional patterns.

☆ Interactive communication accelerates the development of creativity.

The opportunity for dramatic play is not limited to the Dramatic Play Center. It occurs naturally all over the classroom as well as on the playground. Pretending to refuel a motorcycle on the playground, re-enacting stories during story circle, building a city in the Block Center, pretending to be an artist when painting at the easel, and walking to "giant" music during Music and Movement time are all examples of dramatic play activities that may occur within the classroom and throughout the day. In this book, there are story re-enactment ideas in the Literacy and Language chapter and ideas for walking like giants or elves in the Music and Movement chapter, but they still hold within their context the opportunity for children to extend and enrich their imaginations, language, and problem-solving skills.

Transitions provide a further opportunity for dramatic play. Moving from one room to another like bunnies, butterflies, or clowns provides an interesting way to achieve an objective and have fun doing it.

Your role is one of unobtrusive observer. The direct flow of dramatic developments should be uninterrupted unless problems are rising or the direction of the activity is moving to unacceptable behaviors. It takes practice to know how to intercede without controlling the situation.

In order to stimulate new plots and ideas, rotate materials in the Dramatic Play Center on a regular basis. Materials also need to be appealing to both boys and girls.

During the early years, children are just beginning to form concepts and understanding of the skills necessary for social interactions. Dramatic play greatly enhances the formation of these skills, but is dependent upon a teacher who understands the value of dramatic play to the social, emotional, and cognitive development of young children.

Imaginative Play

Prop Boxes

Prepare the following prop boxes and bring them out throughout the year.

Office Prop Box

☆ To prepare an office prop box, include items such as an old typewriter or computer keyboard and monitor (with cords cut), pads of paper, tape dispensers, old telephone, boxes, briefcases, and other office-related objects.

☆ Involve families in preparing this prop box so that the children might have possible substitutions or identifiable items from a family member's workplace.

☆ Bring the box into an area with small tables and chairs that the children can arrange as they choose.

  ☆ Talk with the children as they play and provide vocabulary as needed. For example, children are probably not familiar with typewriters. Explain the keyboard and its features. Compare it to a computer.

  ☆ Ask the children if they know anything about the places where their family members work.

  ☆ Take them on a quick trip down to the administrator's office and let them look at all the items necessary for the administrator to do his or her work. Take a clipboard with you and make a list of work tools.

Circus Prop Box

☆ Prepare a circus prop box by including such items as clown costumes, ballet shoes and tutus, wigs, a small umbrella, a round plastic tub, a straw with yarn on the end for an animal tamer, and balls for juggling.

☆ Ask the children to bring in stuffed animals for the week that this prop box is in use.

☆ Set up the prop box in an area where children can arrange chairs for an audience and put a masking tape line on the floor for a tightrope.

☆ Talk with the children about their experiences with a circus. *Have you ever seen the circus? Which animal is your favorite circus animal? Why? What makes clowns funny?*

Beauty Salon Prop Box

☆ Make a beauty salon prop box by including items such as hairdryers (with cord cut), plastic rollers, combs (sterilized), empty hair spray bottles, empty shampoo and conditioner bottles, towels, telephone, calendar, pencils, magazines, appointment book, play money, and smocks.

☆ Place the materials in an area where there are several chairs and a table (for receptionist).

☆ Talk with children as they play. Introduce vocabulary to enhance their communication, such as "schedule," "appointment," "blow dry," "hair color," "client," and other appropriate words.

Hat Prop Box

☆ Collect a variety of headwear and pictures of individuals wearing similar headwear. Put in a prop box. Examples of hats include berets, baseball caps, military hats, turbans, parka hoods, sombreros, straw hats, kerchiefs, cowboy hats, fezzes, conductor's hats, and firefighter's hats.

☆ Invite the children to try on the hats. Be sure to include a mirror.

☆ Discuss the hats with children as they explore them. *Who wears this kind of hat? Why do you think this hat has a brim? Why is a firefighter's hat hard?*
Safety Note: Periodically check the hats for cleanliness, especially if there are children in the class who have lice. Clean as needed.

Car Wash

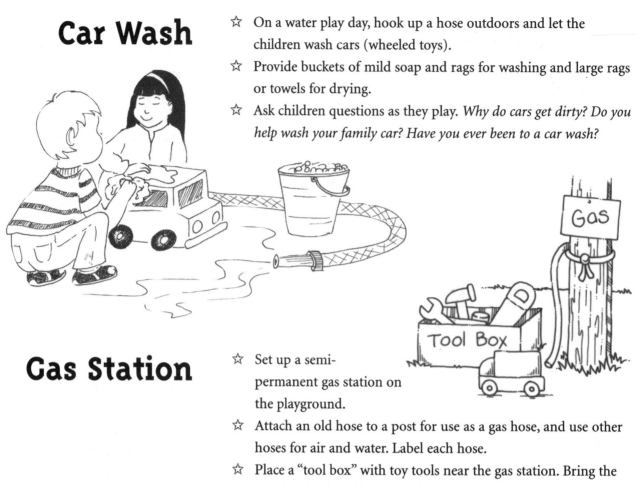

☆ On a water play day, hook up a hose outdoors and let the children wash cars (wheeled toys).

☆ Provide buckets of mild soap and rags for washing and large rags or towels for drying.

☆ Ask children questions as they play. *Why do cars get dirty? Do you help wash your family car? Have you ever been to a car wash?*

Gas Station

☆ Set up a semi-permanent gas station on the playground.

☆ Attach an old hose to a post for use as a gas hose, and use other hoses for air and water. Label each hose.

☆ Place a "tool box" with toy tools near the gas station. Bring the tool box back inside after a day of use.

Tent Town

☆ On hot sunny days, create shade by making tents out of sheets.

☆ Clip a bed sheet (or other large piece of fabric) to a fence with clothespins.

☆ Secure the opposite end of the sheet by placing it under the legs of a picnic table or putting tires or blocks on the edges of the sheet.

☆ An alternate method is to clip the sheet to a fence and tie the opposite corners of the sheet to a tree or a piece of playground equipment.

☆ Put up several tents to develop dramatic play between "neighbors."

Drive-Throughs

☆ Obtain a large appliance box and cut a door and a window in the box to create a "drive-through" grocery store or fast food restaurant.

☆ Place the box in the play yard near the wheeled toy path so the children can "drive" up to order.

☆ For fast food restaurants, provide paper bags for "take-out" orders. Stack them on a small table inside the box.

☆ Provide a cap for the "clerk" to wear. The children can take turns acting as the clerk and serving the "customers" as they drive up.

☆ Suggest that the children draw pictures of things they wish to pick up at the store and then give their "grocery list" to the clerk to use to fill their orders.

Dinner Is Served

☆ Place a tablecloth on a table in the Dramatic Play Center.

☆ Provide dishes and silverware for setting the table.

☆ Cut out pictures of a variety of food from magazines and glue to cardboard to represent serving dishes of food.

☆ Encourage the children to re-play their meal-time experiences.

☆ Talk with children as they play. They may have limited experience with sit-down dinners.

☆ Use this opportunity to discuss table manners. Stimulate appropriate dinnertime conversation by asking questions. *What did you do at school today? What is the best thing that happened to you today?*

Baby Bathtime

☆ Cover a table with towels.

☆ Place a baby tub on the table and fill it about halfway with water.

☆ Provide washable dolls, extra towels, washcloths, a rubber ducky, and mild soap.

☆ Let the children bathe the "babies" and redress them.

☆ Teach the children the following song, sung to the tune of "Rock-a-Bye, Baby."

Evan's Tubtime Song by Richele Bartkowiak
Splishing and splashing
In the bathtub.
When we take our bath
We clean and we scrub.
With our washcloth
And a little shampoo.
And when it's all over
We smell good as new.

Splishing and splashing
That's what we do.
Don't forget Ducky,
He likes it too.
Watching the bubbles
Dance in the tub.
Rub a dub dub.

The Nursery

☆ Provide nursery props, including a rocking chair, diaper bag, stroller, baby bed, baby carrier, blankets, dolls, and doll clothes, for children to use in the Dramatic Play Center.

☆ Teach the children "Rock-a-Bye, Baby" to sing as they rock the babies.

☆ Talk with the children as they play. *How do you pick up a baby? What do babies eat? Why do people use strollers?*

Box House

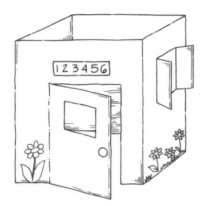

☆ Obtain a large appliance box and cut a door and windows into it to create a playhouse.

☆ Invite the children to paint the outside of the house.

☆ Tape curtains on the windows and glue paper flowers on the outside.

☆ Encourage the children to create situations as they play with the house. Provide suggestions for plots (a visitor is coming, it's laundry day, it's time to redecorate the house, and other ideas).

Box Hideaway

☆ At various times, bring medium to large boxes into the room for children to use as they wish. Boxes should be big enough for children to sit in.

☆ Cut an opening in the top of the box. Cut cellophane panels in different colors to fit the opening.

☆ Place the box in a lighted area.

☆ Encourage the children to crawl inside the box and discover the effect of color on the outside world. Ask children to describe what they see. *What looks different when you view things through the colored windows?*

☆ Change the color panels from time to time for a different view.

Pantry Match

☆ Collect duplicate sets of empty canned goods and food boxes (tuna fish, vegetable soup, shredded wheat, and rice).
Safety Note: Make sure all sharp edges on cans are covered.

☆ Paste one set of containers on a shelf.

☆ Encourage the children to match the second set of containers to the ones on the shelf.

☆ Talk with the children as they work. Ask them how they know which items match. Encourage them to talk about foods they like and don't like as much.

What's in the Trunk?

☆ Place several costumes and costume makings inside an old trunk, suitcase, or box.

Safety Note: Be sure that the trunks or boxes have safety latches and do not lock, and that they can be opened from inside so children cannot be trapped inside.

☆ Be sure to include fun items such as hats, glasses, gloves, beads, ties, petticoats, a variety of shoes, boas, shawls, capes, and masks.

☆ Ask families to contribute interesting items. Garage sales are often gold mines for costumes and unusual clothing.

☆ Encourage the children to explore the items inside the trunk. Challenge them to create wacky outfits, beautiful outfits, funny outfits, and so on.

☆ Children can have their own fashion show or "wacky parade."

Creative Play

Floral Arrangements

☆ Place clay or florist Styrofoam in the bottom of a small box or basket. Secure to the bottom of the container with potter's clay or florist wire.

☆ Provide a variety of plastic or silk flowers and greenery. (See page 64 for additional prop suggestions.)

☆ Encourage the children to arrange flowers in floral designs of their choosing.

☆ Talk with the children about the work of florists. *Why do people order flowers?* Make a list of occasions when someone might use or send flowers.

My Hat

☆ Cut out the center of a paper plate and punch a hole in each side for ribbon ties.

☆ Provide each child with a plate, tissue paper strips, gift wrap bows, and other decorative items.

☆ Ask the children to put glue on their hats and decorate it as desired.

☆ Thread ribbons through the holes to tie the hat under the chin.

☆ Encourage the children to describe their hats. *Where will you wear your hat?*

☆ You may want to read *Jennie's Hat* by Ezra Jack Keats as an inspiration for this activity.

Mad Hatters

☆ Provide a variety of baskets, ribbons, flowers, and beads.

☆ Encourage the children to invert baskets and decorate them to make hats.

☆ Children's interests may be stimulated by reading *Jennie's Hat* by Ezra Jack Keats.

Bakery Goods

☆ Prepare playdough for the children to use to represent bakery items such as cookies, breads, and cakes. (See playdough recipes on pages 46-47 Chapter 1.)

☆ Provide rolling pins for rolling the dough and cookie cutters for cutting "biscuits" and "cookies." Provide baking pans and cookie sheets.

☆ Talk with the children as they work. *What are you making? How will you make it? Who likes to eat it? How much does it cost?*
Holiday Adaptation: Add food coloring to playdough for holiday colors.

Little Designers

☆ In the Dramatic Play Center, place a variety of male and female dress-up clothes (hats, caps, scarves, shoes, belts, ties, costume jewelry, purses, and briefcases).

☆ Also provide a full-length mirror, if available.

☆ Provide enough time for the children to explore all the possible combinations of items until they have developed a pleasurable outfit. The final form may vary a number of times.

☆ Be sure to include a variety of multicultural clothes, such as dashikis, ponchos, saris, and kimonos.

Baubles, Beads, Bangles, and Belts

☆ Provide cardboard tubes, old beads, bits of Styrofoam, old belt buckles, cut pieces of straws, and other things that can be strung.

☆ Cut a necklace (or belt) length of yarn or string. Tie a large knot at one end, and prepare the other end for inserting into decorative items by dipping the end into glue (and letting it dry) or wrapping masking tape around it.

☆ Invite the children to arrange and string materials as desired. The finished product can be used as a belt or a necklace for dress-up.

☆ Encourage the children to describe the item they make. *What stringing pattern did you use? When will you wear your necklace/belt?*

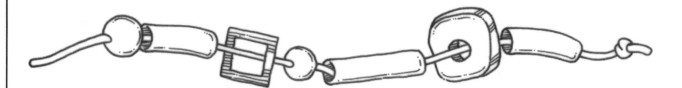

What Is It?

☆ Place a sheet on the wall or use a movie screen.

☆ Create a light source by using a high-intensity lamp or overhead projector.

☆ Place your hands between the light source and the screen and use them to make shadows on the screen. Encourage the children to describe what they see.

☆ Let the children create hand shadows on the wall. Encourage the other children to describe what they see.

Stocking Snakes

☆ Cut off the leg portion from pairs of pantyhose.

☆ Encourage the children to stuff the stocking leg with Styrofoam chips until they have achieved the desired length.

☆ Tie the stocking closed with masking tape or string.

☆ Add eyes, tongue, or stripes using markers.

☆ The end result is a nice wiggly snake to take home.

☆ Encourage the children to name their snakes. Challenge the children who are ready to make up a story about their snake.

Soft Blocks

☆ Provide the children with large, paper grocery bags and a stack of old newspapers.

☆ Have the children crumble newspaper and stuff each grocery sack firmly.

☆ Fold down the tops of the grocery bags, square off, and tape closed.

☆ Children can use the "blocks" to make forts or other structures in the Block Center.
Note: If a structure tumbles down, no one gets hurt by these lightweight blocks.

Let's Pretend

☆ Invite the children to take turns suggesting scenarios for pretend play, such as a clown juggling, a basketball player dribbling the ball, an elephant eating, or a toddler beginning to walk.

☆ Encourage everyone to join in and let each individual do her own interpretation.

Expanding Horizons—Language and Literacy

Overview

Quality literacy programs for young children are rich with activities and experiences that encourage listening, oral language development, phonological sensitivity, letter knowledge and recognition, and print awareness. There is no other time in life when a young child will be more responsive to the acquisition of language than from birth to age five. Their sensitivity is evident in the rapid development of language during these years. The toddler's expression of "Me do!" moves to a far more complex use of language—"*I will do it myself*"—by the time he is five.

The development of oral language includes learning to listen, acquiring new vocabulary, perfecting sentence syntax, extending sentence length, and building clarity in communication. Listening activities include those that require children to pay attention to detail as well as activities that help children utilize their age-appropriate attention span. Vocabulary building requires that children be exposed to new words in a purposeful way. Children are more capable of handling sophisticated vocabulary than we may realize. Sentence length, appropriate syntax, and clarity in communication develop as children actively use language. Since children also learn from modeling, the teacher's use of language becomes a powerful teaching tool. Singing, reading, and discussing are each valuable in developing oral language.

Phonological sensitivity is the "falling in love with language" aspect of early literacy. It occurs when children are allowed to play with language and to listen to language in a variety of formats, such as poems, stories, songs, fingerplays, tongue twisters, and so on. Phonological sensitivity includes the ability to hear rhyming words, to use **onomatopoeia** (words that sound like their meaning, such as "pitter patter," "swoosh," "moo, "swish"), and to recognize **alliterative** sounds (words that begin with the same letter or sound, such as "Peter Piper picked a peck of pickled peppers"). Phonological sensitivity helps children develop an ear for sound. At the preschool level it does not include the drill and practice of sound-symbol relationships (phonics).

Letter knowledge and recognition is the ability to recognize letters of the alphabet. It occurs in conjunction with print awareness. Most four-year-olds are capable of visually recognizing all the letters of the alphabet in both upper- and lowercase. The more experiences children have with the alphabet (learning its sequence, learning it out of sequence, moving it around, saying it backwards), the better they will be at using it later in ways that do not include having to recite it by rote memory in order to alphabetize a list of names.

Print awareness occurs when children experience a print-rich environment, in which print is used in its natural context. Items in the classroom are labeled, books are available and read daily, lists are used when appropriate, children's names are visible on their materials and possessions, and lessons and activities include calling attention to the functions of print, its directionality, and its value. Print awareness does not include teaching young children to write in a formal way. Writing is a skill that will emerge after children have had a plethora of experiences that develop the muscles in their fingers, hands, and wrists, and the coordination of their eyes with the movement of their hands.

Comprehension is the internalization of communication and story concepts. It is developed when children have the opportunity to retell stories, act out stories, and listen to stories without illustrations. It is supported by questioning strategies that require children to make applications, and to analyze and evaluate information. Children demonstrate comprehension skills when they can identify which parts of a story are real and which are make believe, when they can choose a character in the story that they would like to portray and explain why they chose that character, or when they can describe how a story might change if one character in the story is removed or one event in the story is altered.

Language and literacy development includes mastering a number of discrete skills that are integrated into the development of oral language, phonological sensitivity, letter knowledge and recognition, and print awareness. On the next page is a list of literacy skills with definitions. It includes both the discrete skills and the larger umbrella skills.

Alliteration—the repetition of the same sound or letter at the beginning of a word.

Auditory discrimination—the ability to recognize and identify sounds, to hear likenesses and differences.

Auditory memory—the ability to remember sounds after they have been heard.

Classification—the ability to categorize items or objects by like or common criteria.

Comprehension—the internalization of concepts expressed through both written and oral language.

Hand-eye coordination—synchronizing the movement of the hand and the eyes.

Left-to-right progression—the natural eye sweep needed for reading.

Onomatopoeia—a word that sounds like its meaning.

Oral language—the ability to use language for self-expression.

Phonological awareness/sensitivity—an "umbrella" term encompassing the sounds of language from babbling and cooing to phonics.

Print awareness—the understanding that symbols communicate thoughts and feelings. It is also the understanding that print takes many forms, such as lists, letters, storybooks, labels, signs, and so on.

Rhyme—to match the ending sound of a word.

Visual discrimination—the ability to see likenesses and differences.

Visual memory—the ability to remember what is seen and to identify items missing from what has been seen.

Vocabulary development—the discovery of the meaning of words and the identification of new words.

Whole/part relationships—the ability to understand that parts make up a whole, for example, several letters make a word, or several pieces make a complete puzzle.

Listening

"Go-fers"

☆ Select a child to be the "go-fer" and give him directions that contain two requests, for example, "Take the book to the table and pick up the scissors."

☆ If the child can handle two-part directions, give him three-part directions. "Take the cup to the shelf, close the drawer, and bring a spoon to Quinn."

☆ Increase the difficulty of the directions as long as the child is able to comply.

Listening Walk

☆ Encourage the children to help brainstorm a list of sounds they might hear on a listening walk. Place the list on a clipboard.

☆ Take the children on a walk. Instruct them to be very quiet and to concentrate on using their ears more than their eyes.

☆ Place a check next to the sounds on the list as the children report hearing them.

Sound Canisters

☆ Fill film canisters or potato chip cans with small items that will make a distinct sound, such as paper clips, jingle bells, buttons, or gravel.

☆ Make two canisters for each sound-producing item. Glue lids on securely.

☆ Encourage the children to shake the canisters and match the pairs that sound the same.

Where's the Sound?

☆ Ask the children to close their eyes, or wait for an opportunity when they are out of the room.

☆ Hide a music box or a ticking clock.

☆ Invite the children to find the item by listening for the sound.

Follow the Sound

☆ Have the children close their eyes.

☆ Ring a bell and ask the children to walk toward the sound.

Mystery Sounds

☆ Collect items that make a distinct sound, such as an alarm clock, rhythm band instrument, music box, and a service bell.

☆ Ask the children to close their eyes. Make sounds with the items one at a time.

☆ Challenge the children to guess the item by the sound it makes.

Musical Hot and Cold

☆ Select a child to be IT.

☆ Ask IT to leave the room. While the child is out of the room, hide a beanbag.

☆ When IT returns to the room, explain that you and the children are going to sing a song.

☆ When he is close to the hidden beanbag, you will sing loudly. When he is not close to the item, you will sing softly.

☆ After the child finds the beanbag, select a new child to be IT and play again.

Gossip

☆ Sit in a circle with the children.

☆ Start the game by whispering a word or phrase to the child next to you.

☆ That child repeats the word or phrase by whispering it into the ear of the child on the other side of him.

☆ Continue until the word or phrase gets back to you (or whoever starts the game).

☆ Tell the group if the word or phrase is indeed the word with which you started the game.

☆ Continue the game, letting the children take turns starting the game.

Ears Up

☆ Select one child to be the leader.

☆ Ask the leader to give directions to the group.

☆ The group follows only those directions preceded by the words "ears up." For example, "Ears up, touch your toes." If the leader says, "Touch your toes," the children do not touch their toes.
Variation: Alter this activity by inserting a new signal word, such as "blinking eyes" or "snapping fingers."

Which Instrument Do You Hear?

☆ Place rhythm band instruments on the floor in front of you.

☆ Ask the children to close their eyes.

☆ Play an instrument.

☆ Challenge the children to guess which instrument they are hearing.

Do You Hear What I Hear?

☆ Have the children sit in a circle.

☆ Place three rhythm band instruments in the center of the circle.

☆ While the children have their eyes closed, one child makes a sound on each instrument in an order of his choice.

☆ Ask the other children to open their eyes. Select a child to repeat the order of sounds.

☆ To increase the level of difficulty, increase the number of instruments.

The Sound of Silence

☆ Ask the children to sit as quietly and still as possible for one minute.

☆ Tell them that during this time, they should listen carefully for any sounds that occur, such as a door opening, a car passing, someone speaking in another classroom, the air or heat running, and so on.

☆ Place a one-minute timer in front of you and turn it on.

☆ At the end of a minute, invite the children to list any sounds they may have heard. Record their answers on chart paper.

☆ Discuss sounds that occur in the environment all the time but are seldom noticed because of all the other sounds that drown them out. Tell the children that some people call this noise "background noise" and others call it "white noise."

I've Got Rhythm

☆ Encourage each child to create a rhythmic clapping pattern, for example, *clap, snap, clap, snap, clap, snap;* or *clap, rest, rest, clap, rest, rest.*

☆ Record each child's clapping pattern on an audiotape. Play the tape for the children and challenge them to identify their own clapping pattern.

☆ Replay the tape and encourage the children to identify their classmates' clapping patterns.

Sound Makers

☆ Provide the children with three or four cans with lids (potato chip or coffee cans) and a box of objects that can fit into them.

☆ Invite the children to put objects into the cans.

☆ Encourage the children to shake the cans to determine which cans make the loudest sound, and which cans make the softest sound.

☆ If appropriate, ask them to order the cans from softest sound to loudest sound.

Taped Directions

☆ Tape record directions for different learning center activities. Following is an example.

☆ Beforehand, prepare bubble liquid by mixing 1 cup of water, 3 tablespoons of detergent, and 6 tablespoons of tempera paint. Make a variety of colors and put in different containers.

☆ Record the following directions on a tape recorder:
   ★ Put the straw in the colored liquid you wish to use.
   ★ Blow into the straw until bubbles stand above the top of the container.
   ★ Place your paper on top of the bubbles and press down.
   ★ Turn your paper over and take a look.

☆ The children follow the taped directions to create a design on a sheet of paper.

☆ This activity is great for teaching prepositions and concepts of position.

I Spy

☆ Select a child to be IT.

☆ IT starts the game by saying, "I spy…" and describes someone in the class. "I spy someone who is wearing red shoes and green pants."

☆ The rest of the children attempt to guess who IT is describing. If there is not enough information, the child who is IT gives another clue.

☆ The first child to guess the correct person becomes the next IT.

Listening Stories

☆ Make up short stories with the children.

☆ Select a special word in the story for children react to. For example, if your story is about a car, the children might say, "beep, beep," when the car is mentioned. If your story is about a dog, the children might bark when the dog's name is mentioned.

Simon Says

☆ Have the children stand in a line.

☆ Ask them to follow your directions, but only when the direction is preceded by the phrase, "Simon Says."

☆ Begin giving directions slowly. Stress the words "Simon Says" at the beginning of the game. After you play for a while, stop stressing the words.

☆ When the children follow a direction that is not preceded by "Simon Says," they have to sit down and wait for a new game to begin.

☆ The last child standing is the winner.

Twin Tunes

☆ Ask half of the class to sing "Twinkle, Twinkle, Little Star" while the other half listens.

☆ Then ask the half who are listening to sing the "ABC Song."

☆ Alternate singing and listening.

☆ Have both sides sing at the same time, noting that the tunes are the same.

Listening Tunes

☆ Sing songs that encourage listening. Following are two songs to get you started.

Come and Listen (Tune: "Are You Sleeping?")

Come and listen
Come and listen
To my song,
To my song.
Happy children listening
Happy children singing
Sing along, sing along.

This Is the Way (Tune: "Here We Go 'Round the Mulberry Bush")

This is the way we use our ears,
Use our ears, use our ears.
This is the way we use our ears
To listen to our story. (…our teacher, and so on)

Clapping Names

☆ Invite the children to clap the syllables in their names.

☆ Ask them to listen closely as a child says his name.

☆ Repeat the child's name slowly making sure to emphasis each syllable. Say the name again and clap on each syllable in the name as you say it.

☆ Have the children say the name and clap the syllables with you.

☆ Encourage the children to clap the syllables in the days of the weeks, months of the year, seasons, and so on, as appropriate.

The Long and the Short of It

☆ Talk with the children about long words and short words. If there are children whose names are shortened forms of a more formal long name, use their names ("Tom" for Thomas or "Sue" for Susan).

☆ Create a list of long and short words prior to this activity. Write each word individually on pieces of poster board. Place a stack of long words and a stack of short words in front of you, face down.

☆ Draw a word from each stack and say each word to the children without showing them the words. Challenge the children to identify the long word and the short word just by listening.

☆ Say each pair of words. Ask volunteers to tell you which word is long and which is short.

☆ After the child has made a choice, show him the words. Hold the cards one above the other so the children can see difference in length.

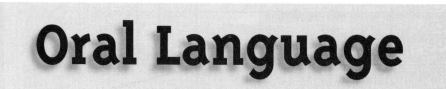

Oral Language

Reading Vocabulary

☆ Before reading a storybook, preview it for words that might be new vocabulary for the children.

☆ Introduce the new words before reading the book. Stop when you get to those words in the story and ask the children to tell you the meaning of the word.

☆ You may want to keep a chart paper list showing all the new vocabulary words learned each week.

Singing Vocabulary

☆ Discuss words in songs that may be new vocabulary for children. Children often sing words in songs without knowing what those words mean. For example, many children sing the song, "Itsy Bitsy Spider" but only a handful know what a "waterspout" is.

☆ Use songs to teach vocabulary. Changing a descriptive word or words in a song often helps clarify word meaning. Using "Itsy Bitsy Spider" as an example, you might change "itsy bitsy" to "big gigantic" or "teeny tiny." Both examples not only introduce new vocabulary but also clarify the original words.

Word of the Day

☆ Select one word every day to be the "word of the day." You might choose a word related to the current classroom theme or classroom project. Don't be afraid of big words. Children often catch on to them faster than adults do.

☆ Write the word of the day on an index card and place it in the Writing Center. Print the word on chart paper and post it in the circle area.

☆ Use the word as many times as possible during the day.

☆ Encourage children to use the word as often as possible and praise their effort when they remember to use the word.

A Picture's Worth a Thousand Words

☆ Take photos of the children doing classroom activities. Encourage them to describe the activities depicted in the pictures.

☆ Develop a file of pictures of different items from magazines.

☆ Let the children take turns choosing pictures and describing how items are used (chairs are for sitting, trees are for climbing, cars are for driving, and so on).

Baggie Book Photo Album

☆ Staple six plastic zipper-closure bags together at the bottom of the bags and put a strip of masking tape or colored tape over the staples to form the spine of the book.

☆ Cut pieces of tagboard or construction paper to fit into each plastic baggie.

☆ Invite the children to bring a photo of their family to school. Place the photos in the Baggie Book Album. The plastic sleeves will protect the photos from getting damaged.

☆ Encourage the children to talk about the photos. *Who are the people in the picture? Are your brothers older or younger than you are? When was the picture taken?*

☆ Change the photos from time to time. Other photo ideas include baby pictures, birthday party pictures, pictures taken on a field trip, and pet photos.

Vocabulary Fun

☆ After reading a story, choose a word or two to extend through discussion.

☆ For example, "In the story, Jerry sat on a stump." *What is a stump? Do we have one in our room? Where might we find a stump?*

Shopping Fun

☆ During group time, put several grocery store items in the middle of the circle.

☆ Hand a basket to one of the children and ask him to find the item named in the following rhyme:

(Child's name) *goes around, around*
Until he finds the (grocery item).
(Child's name) *goes around, around*
Can he find the (grocery item)?

☆ Select another child and repeat the activity until all the items are gone.

Sequencing Concrete Objects

☆ Read the story of "The Three Little Pigs." Discuss the materials that the pigs used to build their homes.

☆ Provide a twig, a small bundle of straw (dried grass), and a brick. Ask the children to sequence the materials in the order they appear in the story.

☆ Read the story of "The Three Bears." Discuss the order that Goldilocks encounters items that belong to the bear family (porridge bowls, chairs, and beds).

☆ Give the children a bowl, a small chair, and a small bed. Ask them to sequence the items in the order they appear in the story.

☆ Provide bowls, chairs, and beds in three sizes and have the children arrange the items in the order that Goldilocks approaches them in the story.

In the Bag

☆ Put several items into a purse, briefcase, or bag.

☆ Encourage the children to look in the purse or bag and describe the items they find.

☆ After the children are experienced with the activity, let them take turns describing an item without letting the other children see it. The other children try to guess what the item is.

Note: This activity offers a great opportunity for teachers to expand the language of the children by asking questions about each item.

Positional Words

☆ Give each child a beanbag.

☆ Ask the children to put their beanbags *on* their shoulder, *under* their chin, *beside* their shoe, *on top of* their head, and so on.

☆ Use other spatial words to reinforce positional vocabulary.

Opposites

☆ Gather several items that are opposites, for example, a big and little block, a tall and short glass, and a soft and hard doll.

☆ Encourage the children to pair items that are opposites.

☆ For additional practice teach the children the following song.

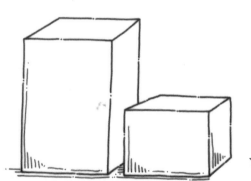

Sing a Song of Opposites by Pam Schiller
(Tune: "Mary Had a Little Lamb")
This is big and this is small,
This is big; this is small,
This is big and this is small,
Sing along with me.

☆ Other verse possibilities:

This is tall and this is short...
This is up and this is down...
This is in and this is out...
This is happy and this is sad...
This is soft and this is hard...
This is fast and this is slow...
This is here and this is there...

Opposites Hunt

☆ Challenge the children to go on an "Opposites Hunt."
☆ Ask them to search the room for pairs of opposites (open and closed windows, big and small blocks, and so on).

Sign Language Vocabulary

☆ Teach the children some basic sign language. Check out a sign language book from the library that illustrates some of the basic signs.
☆ You can also find basic signs on the Internet. Try this site: http://www.masterstech-home.com/ASLDict.html

Show-and-Tell

☆ Show-and-tell gives children their first opportunity to deliver an oral report.
☆ Invite the children to bring an item from home to show to their friends.
☆ Encourage them to describe their item. Ask questions to help them organize their thoughts. *Austin, where did you get the truck? What do you like to do with the truck? Is this one of your favorite toys? Why is it one of your favorite toys?*
☆ You don't want every child in the class to bring something to share on the same day. Develop a schedule that keeps the number of children reporting to no more than three so the children's ability to pay attention is not exhausted.

Ticklers

☆ Have the children lie on the floor on their backs with each child placing his head on another child's stomach.
☆ Tell the children to laugh.
☆ Let two or three children describe how it felt when everyone was laughing.

Deluxe Show-and-Tell

☆ Ask the children to bring in an object from a family member's workplace or from home. Encourage them to talk to their family about the use of the object.

☆ At Circle Time, let the children take turns demonstrating and describing the item and its use. One child might say, "My daddy is a barber. He uses these clippers to cut hair." Or, "My mother is a doctor. She uses this stethoscope to listen to hearts."

String a Story

☆ While holding a ball of yarn in your hands, tell the children a story starter, for example, "Yesterday I saw a green monster at the grocery store. He was…"

☆ Holding the end of the yarn, pass the ball to a child who then adds a line to the story.

☆ When that child is finished, he passes the yarn to another child.

☆ Continue until all of the children have added a line to the story.

Nursery Rhyme Pantomimes

☆ Make a pretend candle using an empty toilet tissue roll and yellow tissue paper.

☆ Ask a few children to jump over the candlestick to interpret "Jack Be Nimble." Don't tell the rest of the children which nursery rhyme they are interpreting.

Jack be nimble, Jack be quick,
Jack jump over the candlestick.

☆ The rest of the group guesses which nursery rhyme is being demonstrated.

☆ Continue with "Little Jack Horner" and a pretend pie, "Little Bo Peep" and her lost sheep, and so on.

Magic Mirror

☆ Ask the children to sit in a circle.

☆ Pass around a hand mirror.

☆ Encourage each child to make a statement about what he sees in the mirror.

☆ After each child has had a turn, encourage the children to draw self-portraits.

Magic Pebble

☆ Show the children a pebble. Tell them to pretend it is magic and can grant wishes.

☆ Let each child hold the pebble and make a wish. Encourage them to use complete sentences.

Magic Wand

☆ Provide each child with a scarf to use as a "magic wand."

☆ Begin playing music.

☆ Direct the children to wave their "magic wands" *over* their head, *under* the table, *between* their legs, *beside* a chair, and so on.

☆ Use other spatial words to reinforce positional vocabulary development.

Sally Sad and Harry Happy

☆ Glue two paper plates to separate craft sticks. Draw a happy face on one ("Harry") and a sad face ("Sally") on the other.

☆ Let the children take turns holding the plate faces and giving reasons for why "Sally" is sad and "Harry" is happy. "I'm Sally Sad, and I'm sad because…," and "I'm Harry Happy, and I'm happy because…"

Puppet Party

☆ Provide children with paper plates, paper, crayons, glue, and tongue depressors.

☆ Invite the children to draw faces on the plates and decorate them to create a puppet face. Show them how to glue on tongue depressors for handles.

☆ Encourage the children to form pairs and present a puppet show for the group.

☆ Be aware that young children may not be capable of creating a plot, so any dialogue created is acceptable. Remember that all interaction builds language concepts.

The Instant Curriculum

What Do You Know About This?

☆ Bring in an interesting object to stimulate descriptions, statements, and questions, such as a butterfly in a box, a stuffed animal, or a goldfish or gerbil.

☆ Encourage the children to talk about the object. Ask open-ended questions (questions that require more than a "yes" or "no" response).

☆ Extend the children's statements. If a child says, "The fish is swimming," you might add, "Up and down in the bowl."

Posing Questions

☆ Ask the children open-ended questions that allow them to fully describe circumstances, events, and thoughts.

☆ Examples of questions that require higher-level thinking can be found on page 117 (Questioning Strategies).

Recipe Dictation

☆ Create a recipe book of children's favorite food items.

☆ Ask the children to name their favorite foods that someone cooks for them.

☆ Ask them how the food is made. Transcribe their descriptions exactly how they say it. Fight the urge to edit.

☆ This makes a great gift for someone special.

Flannel Board Stories

☆ Provide opportunities for the children to retell stories using flannel board characters.

☆ If commercial flannel board characters are unavailable, make your own using images in coloring books.

Expanding Story Concepts

☆ Read a book that ends with something that provides a springboard for expanding the story, such as *David's Father* by Robert Munsch or *Imogene's Antlers* by David Small.

☆ Invite the children to tell how they think the story might continue.

Word Police

☆ Read familiar poems or rhymes to the children. As you read, occasionally mix up or add new words.

☆ Challenge the children to catch your mistakes. Ask them to put on their "Word Police" ears.

☆ Read "Jack and Jill" and change "up the hill" to "down the hill"; read "One Potato, Two Potato" and skip the fifth and sixth potato; change Mother Hubbard's dog to a cat; make Mary's lamb's fleece as white as "coal" and have it follow her to the "mall."

Phonological Awareness

Hicky Picky Bumblebee

☆ Teach the children the following rhyme:

Hicky Picky Bumblebee
Hicky picky bumblebee (clap in rhythm)
Won't you say your name to me? (point to a child)
Carmella. (child says his or her name)
Carmella. (teacher repeats the name)
Let's clap it. Car-mel-la. (clap the syllables in Carmella)
Let's snap it. Car-mel-la. (snap the syllables in Carmella)
Let's tap it. Car-mel-la. (tap the syllables in Carmella)

☆ Say the rhyme again, pointing to a different child. Continue until everyone's name has been used.

Clapping Words

☆ Collect several small objects (pencil, block, paintbrush, crayon) and put them in a box or basket. Select items that differ in the number of syllables in their name.

☆ Invite a child to select an item from the basket and identify it, using a full sentence. "This is a crayon."

☆ The rest of the children repeat the name of the object and clap the syllables in the object's name.

Silly Sentences

☆ Create a series of silly rhyming sentences for children to repeat.

☆ Examples include:

I know a lady with knobby knees
Who's always eating cheddar cheese.
I like ice cream in my soup
By myself, or in a group.

Tongue Twisters

☆ Teach the children some of your favorite tongue twisters.
  ★ Peter Piper picked a peck of pickled peppers.
  ★ Six sneezing sneetches.
  ★ Twenty twirling twigs.

☆ Say the sentence two or three times slowly and then try speeding it up.

☆ Ask the children what sound they hear repeated in the sentence. It is not necessary for them to name the letter that makes the sound. At the preschool stage, the important thing is their ability to hear the repetitive sound.

Alliteration Fun

☆ Give alliterative names to classroom activities, such as "Tall Towers" for block building or "Pink Paint" for easel painting with the color pink.

☆ Do the same thing for snacks. Milk might become "Mighty Milk," hot dogs might be "Diggety Dogs," and bananas might be "Batty Bananas." Be creative!

Alliterative Songs

☆ Sing songs that have alliteration in them such as "Tiny Tim," "Doodle-li-do" or "Miss Mary Mack."

☆ Alter other songs to include alliteration. The "Itsy Bitsy Spider" might become the "Teeny Tiny Spider" or "Five Speckled Frogs" might become "Five Freckled Frogs."

☆ Talk about **alliteration** (see the definition on page 79) and provide examples.

☆ Write alliterative words on chart paper so the children can see the repetitive letter.

☆ Knowing that the sound they hear in the group of words is the same is more important at this stage than actually identifying the letter sound (more important than sound/symbol relationship). This activity is a listening and phonological sensitivity activity.

The Sounds of Rain

☆ Obtain a spray bottle of water with an adjustable nozzle.
☆ Provide a variety of surfaces for the children to spray—a cookie sheet, shower curtain, piece of cardboard, and newspaper.
☆ Encourage the children to experiment spraying the different surfaces with the different force of sprays available. Encourage them to describe the different sounds the water makes.

Onomatopoeia Songs

☆ Sing songs that have onomatopoeia words in them such as "Old MacDonald's Farm," "The Wheels on the Bus," or "Five Little Ducks."
☆ Onomatopoeia words are words that sound like the sound they are trying to describe (washers go "swish," horns go "beep," and a cow says "moo").
☆ Teach the children the word **onomatopoeia** (see the definition on page 79). They will love it and you will be surprised how easily they can learn the word and how much fun they will have saying it.

Name Game

☆ During the day when it's necessary to call a child's name, turn it into a teachable moment for children to learn rhyming sounds. *Would the child whose name rhymes with "ham" get in line?*
☆ Pam or Sam or any other person with a name that rhymes with "ham" responds to the request.

Pick-a-Pair

☆ Place several rhyming pairs of objects in a basket (sock/rock, cat/hat, and bead/seed).
☆ Encourage the children to put the objects into rhyming pairs.

Rime Time

☆ Teach the children the following rhyming word song:

Rime Time (Tune: "The Adam's Family Theme")
Rime time, (click, click) rime time, (click, click)
Rime time, rime time, rime time. (click, click)

There's can and there's pan.
There's fan and there's ran.
There's man and there's tan.
The "an" family.

☆ Additional rhyming groups include:
pet, jet, vet, net, let, set...
like, hike, bike, mike, trike, pike...
pot, dot, hot, not, lot, got...
ball, call, hall, fall, tall, mall...

Rhyme or Reason

☆ Ask the children to sit in a circle.
☆ Start the game by saying a word to the child sitting on your right. The child must either say a word that rhymes with your word or change the word to a new word that is related to your word.
☆ For example, if you start with the word "ball," the child next to you might say "fall" to rhyme with "ball" or "bat" because it is related to "ball."
☆ The child sitting to this child's right now says a word that rhymes with or relates to "fall" or "bat."
☆ Continue the game until everyone has had a turn.

Rhyming Game

☆ Provide the children with a box of small toy objects.
☆ Ask the children to name each object.
☆ When you are certain the children can correctly identify each object, ask them to find objects with names that sound alike (cake and rake, boy and toy, and so on).

Fill-In Nursery Rhymes

☆ Select Mother Goose rhymes from nursery rhyme books.
☆ Read nursery rhymes out loud. Stop at the ending rhyming word and let the children supply it. For example:

Jack be nimble,
Jack be quick.
Jack jumped over the _____.

Rhythmic Nursery Rhymes I

☆ Chant individual lines of nursery rhymes, putting equal emphasis on each word.
☆ Invite the children to repeat lines in the same rhythm.
☆ Add claps on specific words, such as those at the end of each line.
Teacher: *Ma-ry had a lit-tle* **lamb.**
Child: *Ma-ry had a lit-tle* **lamb.**
☆ You can change the rhythm by putting emphasis on every other syllable:
Ma-ry had *a* **lit-tle lamb.**

Rhythmic Nursery Rhymes II

☆ Accompany chanted nursery rhymes with a tambourine or drum.
☆ Alternate chanted lines between boys, girls, and the entire group. For example:

Group: *Jack and Jill went up the hill to fetch a pail of water.*
Boys: *Jack fell down and broke his crown.*
Girls: *And Jill came tumbling after.*

Whispered Rhymes

☆ Read familiar nursery rhymes, whispering the words that rhyme.
☆ Next, read familiar nursery rhymes in a whisper and speak the rhyming words out loud.

Rhyme in a Can

☆ Place several rhyming objects in a can—sock, lock, and rock.
☆ Encourage the children to make up a story that includes all the items.

Say and Touch

☆ Teach the children the following rhyme:

Say and Touch
Say, "pup," now stand up.
Say, "go," now touch your toe.
Say, "neat," now touch your feet.
Say, "real," now touch your heel.
Say, "laugh," now touch your calf.
Say, "bee," now touch your knee.
Say, "high," now touch your thigh.
Say, "paste," now touch your waist.

☆ For children who are more experienced with rhyming words, give a clue and let the children fill in the blank. Say, "Neat, now touch your _____ ."

Letter Knowledge and Recognition

What's Missing?

☆ Provide the children with a box of small objects, for example, a crayon, scissors, glue bottle, block, and book.
☆ Let the children select four items.
☆ Ask the children to close their eyes, and then remove one of the items.
☆ Challenge the children to tell you what's missing.
☆ Continue the game, changing the items.

Whoops!

☆ Draw a number of large objects or people on a piece of chart paper. On each picture, leave out a major feature (a leg from a table, an eyebrow from a face, or a wheel from a car).

☆ Ask the children to describe what is missing.

☆ As they become more proficient, increase the complexity of the missing feature (a button from a shirt, a lace from a shoe).

☆ This type of activity prepares children for noticing details. When proficient, they will be able to see the small differences between "b" and "d" and "p" and "g."

What's the Order?

☆ Collect three or four items from around the classroom, such as a block, crayon, book, and doll. As a variation, use flannel board cutouts.

☆ Arrange the items in a specific order.

☆ Ask the children to close their eyes.

☆ Change the order of the items.

☆ Ask one child to put the items back in the original order.

☆ This activity sharpens children's ability to pay attention to detail—a necessary skill when learning the differences in letter shapes.

Variation: Do this activity with objects that focus on an area of study.

Can You Remember?

☆ Have the children sit in a circle and close their eyes.

☆ Ask them questions about the room. *What color is the bathroom door? What did we tape on the window yesterday?*

☆ This activity sharpens children's ability to pay attention to detail.

Wallpaper Lotto

☆ Cut 18 different patterns of wallpaper into duplicate 2" squares.

☆ Cut out two 6" squares of cardboard. Section them off into nine 2" squares to create lotto boards. Glue nine 2" wallpaper squares on the lotto boards. Reserve the duplicate squares for playing cards.

☆ Two children may play the game. Provide each child with one of the lotto boards.

☆ Turn the wallpaper lotto playing cards face down.

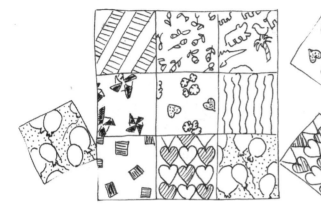

☆ Each child takes a turn drawing a card and attempting to match the squares on his lotto board. Matches are placed on the board, non-matches are turned face down and used when the first stack of cards runs out.

☆ The game ends when both children cover their lotto boards completely.

☆ When children become proficient matching designs, create a new game using letters.

Alphabetical Order

☆ Teach the children the alphabet in its normal sequence.

☆ Sing "The Alphabet Song," and then sing it backwards.

The Alphabet Forward and Backwards
(Tune: traditional ABC song)

A B C D E F G
H I J K L M N O P
Q R S T U V
W X Y and Z
Now, I've said my ABC's.
Next time sing them backwards with me.

Z Y X W V U T
S R Q P O N M
L K J I H G
F E D C B A.
Now, I've said my ZYX's,
Bet that's not what you expected!

Which Letter Is Missing?

☆ Place four consecutive alphabet cards on the floor. Have the children say the letters.

Note: Use commercial alphabet cards or make a set by printing each letter of the alphabet on a 5" x 7" index card.

☆ Ask the children to hide their eyes, and remove one of the letters.

☆ The children open their eyes and identify the missing letter.

Gel Bags

☆ Place ½ cup of hair gel in a zipper-closure plastic bag. Glue the bag shut.

☆ Invite the children to use their index fingers to write letters on the bag.

Playdough Letters

☆ Make playdough using a playdough recipe on pages 46-47.

☆ Encourage the children to form alphabet letters with the playdough.

☆ For a variation, the children can make the letters on top of alphabet cards.

Pretzel Letters

☆ Prepare pretzel dough by mixing the following ingredients together:

1 ½ cups warm water
1 envelope yeast
4 cups flour
1 teaspoon salt

☆ Give each child enough dough to shape into the first letter of his name.

☆ Brush dough letters with a beaten egg and sprinkle with coarse salt. Bake at 425° for eight minutes.

Thumbprint Letters

- ☆ Print several alphabet letters on 4" x 6" index cards, one letter per card.
- ☆ Provide a stamp pad.
- ☆ Invite the children to press their thumbs on the ink pad and then make fingerprints on top of the lines of the letters on the cards.

Freckle Names

- ☆ Write each child's name on separate pieces of construction paper. Use an uppercase letter for the first letter of each child's name and lowercase letters for the remaining letters.
- ☆ Ask the children to outline their names on their paper with glue.
- ☆ Give each child a handful of hole punches from the collage box to sprinkle over the paper. Shake off the excess onto a newspaper.

Letter Tracing

- ☆ Write familiar vocabulary words on 4" x 6" index cards using bold print.
- ☆ Cover each card with tracing paper, using paper clips to secure the paper to the card.
- ☆ Provide large pencils or crayons and encourage the children to trace the words.

Letter Matching

- ☆ Write several letters on index cards.
- ☆ Give the children magnetic letters.
- ☆ Ask them to place each magnetic letter on top of the matching letter written on the index cards.
- ☆ Write a word on chart paper and encourage the children to copy it using magnetic letters.

Pair, Think, and Share

☆ Ask the children to select a partner.
☆ Assign each pair of children a letter of the alphabet. Challenge them to think of a way they can form the letter using their bodies.
☆ Let each pair share their idea about forming the letter.
☆ Have the rest of the group identify the letter.

Circle the Letter

☆ Use a copier to enlarge a page of print from a newspaper or magazine.
☆ Print a letter on an index card.
☆ Invite the children to circle all the letters on the page that look like the letter you have printed on the index card.

Letter Tic Tac Toe

☆ Encourage the children to play "Tic Tac Toe" using two different letters of the alphabet instead of the standard X and O.

Sand Writing

☆ Fill a shallow cake pan with sand.
☆ Encourage the children to create designs using their fingers.
☆ Provide word or letter cards as examples.

Sand Letters

☆ For each child, draw one large alphabet letter on a 5" x 7" index card.
☆ Give the children a squeeze bottle of glue to use to outline the letter.
☆ Have the children sprinkle sand over the glue and shake off the excess.
☆ This creates a tactile letter for children to use and re-use for letter recognition.

Finger Writing

☆ Invite the children to use their index finger to make letters in a tray of sand.
☆ As a variation, use shaving cream, hair gel, gravel, or ice cream salt instead of sand.

Tactile Letters

☆ Cut out letters from sandpaper and glue them to individual index cards.

☆ Invite the children to trace the letters with their fingers. They can also place drawing paper over the letters and rub with a crayon to create a letter rubbing.

☆ You can also cut tactile letters from burlap, corrugated cardboard, or textured wall paper.

Tablecloth Lotto

☆ Tape butcher paper to a table and print the alphabet on it.

☆ Make a set of matching alphabet index cards by writing a letter of the alphabet on separate 4" x 6" index cards.

☆ Challenge the children to match the cards to the letters on the tablecloth.

Lucky Letters

☆ Write a different alphabet letter on large cards. Make a matching set of smaller cards.

☆ Place the 26 large cards on the floor in a circle, alphabetically or randomly. (You may want to start with alphabetical order and then change to random order at a later date.)

☆ Play music and have the children walk around the circle of cards.

☆ When the music stops, each child picks up the letter card closest to him.

☆ Hold up one of the small alphabet cards. The child who is holding the large letter that matches the small letter you are holding identifies the letter. (If you hold up an H, the child with an H in his hand identifies the letter.)

☆ Continue the game until the children tire of it.

Bingo

☆ Prepare bingo game boards labeled with letters. Provide buttons for markers.

☆ Randomly draw letters from a bowl. (Use Scrabble tiles, or write letters on small squares of poster board.)

☆ Show the letter and announce it to the group. The children with the letter on their bingo cards use buttons to cover that letter.

☆ The game ends when one child covers all of his letters on his bingo card.

Scrabble Letters

☆ Provide Scrabble letters and encourage the children to find the letters that spell their name.

☆ As children become familiar with other sight words, they can use the letters to spell those words as well.

E-I-E-I-O

☆ Sing "Old MacDonald Had a Farm."

☆ Write the letters "E," "I," and "O" on a piece of chart paper. Point to the letters as you sing them.

☆ Sing the song again, changing the letters to three other letters. How does it sound?

Mail Call

☆ Print each child's name on an envelope and place in a bag.

☆ Write each child's name on an index card, and give it to the child.

☆ Ask the children to sit in a circle and hold up their name cards.

☆ Let the children take turns delivering the "mail" (matching the envelopes to the name cards).

☆ For added fun, place surprise gifts such as stickers or pictures in the envelopes.

The Instant Curriculum

Manual ABC's

☆ Teach the children the manual alphabet (finger spelling) using "Where Is Thumbkin?"

Where is A? Where is A? (make the letter "A" with your right hand and keep your left hand behind your back)
Here I am! Here I am! (bring left hand from behind your back and make the letter "A" with your left hand)
How are you today, A? (shake right hand)
Very well, I thank you. (shake left hand)
Run away. (return left hand to position behind your back)
Run away. (return your right hand to position behind your back)

☆ Continue singing the song, moving through the alphabet.
☆ Directions for the manual alphabet can be found on several websites. Here are web addresses for two sites:
http://www.deafblind.com/card.html
http://where.com/scott.net/asl/abc.html

Print Awareness

Top, Middle, and Bottom

☆ Fold sheets of drawing paper into thirds and open back up. Give each child a sheet of paper.
☆ Ask them to draw a picture.
☆ When they have finished their drawings, encourage them to show their pictures to their friends and describe what is at the top of their paper, the middle of their paper, and the bottom of their paper.
☆ Show the children print on the page of a book. Point out that the print starts at the top of the page and ends at the bottom of the page.

More Top, Middle, and Bottom

☆ Sing "Head, Shoulders, Knees, and Toes" with the children.
☆ Ask the children to identify which body parts are at the top of their body, which are in the middle, and which are at the bottom.
☆ Show the children print on the page of a book. Point out that the print starts at the top of the page and ends at the bottom of the page. *What is in the middle?*

Left to Right

☆ Make a grid with 16 squares.
☆ Encourage the children to make an ABC-ABC-ABC pattern on the grid using three different colors of buttons (red button, blue button, green button; red button, blue button, green button).
☆ Ask them to work from left to right and top to bottom. The pattern will have to wrap around the grid the second time it is repeated.
☆ Show the children print on the page of a book. Point out that the print starts at the top left of the page and moves to the right all the way to the bottom of the page.

Cozy Comics

☆ Cut out comic strips from the Sunday newspaper and bring them to class.
☆ During times when you can work with children individually or in small groups, read the comics to children.
☆ Point out the left-to-right order of the pictures as you read the comics.

"Reader Wiggle"

☆ Teach the children "The Reader Wiggle" to the tune of "The Hokey Pokey."

The Reader Wiggle

When I read a book (hold hands out with palms up as if reading)

I start from left to right, (shake left hand and turn the right hand palm up)

And I do the very same thing (shake finger as if saying, "I told you so")

When I want to write. (shake left hand and turn the right hand palm up)

I do the Reader Wiggle (put hand over head and shake, wiggle hips)

And I turn myself about. (turn around)

That's how I read and write! (shake finger as if saying, "I told you so")

I do the R-e-a-d-e-r Wiggle, (hold hands overhead, wiggle fingers, and turn around)

I do the R-e-a-d-e-r Wiggle, (repeat actions)

I do the R-e-a-d-e-r Wiggle,

That's how I read and write! (shake finger as if saying, "I told you so")

When I read "The Three Bears" (hold hands out with palms up as if reading)

I move from left to right. (shake left hand and turn the right hand palm up)

I go from word to word, (point finger as if moving word to word)

And I know I've got it right. (point to self—shake your head "yes")

I do the Reader Wiggle (put hand over head and shake, wiggle hips)

And I turn myself about. (turn around)

That's how I read and write! (shake finger as if saying, "I told you so")

I do the R-e-a-d-e-r Wiggle, (hold hands overhead, wiggle fingers, and turn around)

I do the R-e-a-d-e-r Wiggle, (repeat actions)

I do the R-e-a-d-e-r Wiggle,

That's how I read and write! (shake finger as if saying, "I told you so")

☆ Encourage the children to make up their own movements for the "Reader Wiggle."

Name
Puzzles

☆ Write each child's name on a large card.

☆ Cut the card into puzzle pieces, making each letter a puzzle piece.

☆ Invite the children to put the letters back together to spell their names correctly.

☆ Make the name cards self-correcting by making each cut between letters different.

Letter
Puzzles

☆ Write a word on a 3" x 8" strip of poster board, leaving enough space between letters to make a puzzle cut line.

☆ Cut the letters apart to make puzzle pieces.

☆ Invite the children to put the puzzles together. *What word does the puzzle spell?*

☆ Show the children print on the page of a book. Point out that letters go together to form the words. Explain that the space between words is a signal that a new word is beginning.

String a
Letter

☆ Cut 3" diameter circles from construction paper or poster board. Print letters on the circles and laminate them. Punch holes in the circles.

☆ Provide laces or strings.

☆ Encourage the children to string letters together to make a word.

Cereal Box
Puzzles

☆ Cut off the front panels from cereal boxes. Cut each panel into puzzle pieces.

☆ Encourage the children to put the puzzles together.

☆ Discuss the relationship between the *pieces* of the puzzle and the *whole* puzzle. Explain that the puzzle is made up of many pieces, which are each important to the whole picture.

The Instant Curriculum

Labels

☆ Label objects and areas in the room (Library Center, door, sink, block, and so on).

☆ Labeling helps develop the concept that written symbols represent spoken words.

Note: Limit the number of labels. Too many labels will go unnoticed.

☆ You may want to let the children help decide which items in the classroom should be labeled. Rotate labels periodically.

Nametags

☆ As each child arrives in the room, ask his name and write it on a self-adhesive nametag.

☆ Let the children watch as you transcribe their spoken name into a written name. Say the letters as you print them on the nametag. Use an uppercase letter for the first letter and lowercase letters for the rest of the letters.

☆ Have the children wear their nametags all day.

☆ On another day, do the same activity using first and last names.

Grocery Put Away

☆ Obtain empty food cans and boxes. Make sure you have at least two of each item.

☆ Place one set of cans and boxes on a shelf or table. Place the matching items inside a grocery bag.

☆ Have the children put the groceries away by matching the items in the bag to the items on the shelf or table.

Funny Funny Papers

☆ Cut out comic strips from the newspaper. Cover the words in the strips. (White correction fluid works well.) Give one to each child.
☆ Encourage the children to create their own version of the story using the pictures as clues.
☆ Write the children's dictated stories over the covered words to help them develop the concept that writing is a symbol for talk.

Story Dictation

☆ Select a topic and encourage the children to dictate a story about it. Write down the children's words.
☆ Encourage them to illustrate their story.

Experience Charts

☆ Encourage the children to describe their experiences or feelings about different experiences.
☆ Write the children's descriptions on a chart as they talk. For example:

We went to the barn.
We saw cows and horses.
We played in the hay.
The hay smelled good.

☆ Use as many opportunities as possible for children to describe events and see them transcribed into written form.

Classroom Pen Pals

☆ Keep a supply of envelopes readily available.

☆ Encourage the children to draw pictures that tell their friend something or to use inventive spelling to convey a message. Children can also have you or another adult write their words.

☆ Let the children put their completed letters into envelopes and deliver them to their friends' cubby.

☆ Remind the children that print is used to communicate information to our friends.

Rebus Charts

☆ Write tongue twisters, songs, rhymes, and the experiences of children on chart paper.

☆ Add drawings beside or over some of the nouns. For example: "I went to the rodeo and wore my hat (drawing) and my new boots (drawing)."

☆ Encourage the children to help you "re-read" what was written.

Rebus Treasure Hunt

☆ Create picture clues for finding a treasure. Arrange the clues in a left-to-right and top-to-bottom order.

☆ Divide the class into two groups and give each group a set of picture clues.

☆ Encourage them to search for treasure using the clues!

☆ The first group to find the treasure is the winning group.

Rebus Recipes

☆ Challenge the children to use rebus directions for making a simple snack.
☆ Friendship Mix on page 54, Purple Cow Shakes on page 51, and Shake-a-Puddin' on page 54 all work well as rebuses.

Nursery Rhyme Fill-Ins

☆ Write a simple nursery rhyme on a piece of chart paper.
☆ Use rebus illustrations where possible in the nursery rhyme.
☆ Introduce the illustrations and then invite the children to read the rhyme with you.

Writing Rhymes

☆ Read several simple rhymes to the children. Nursery rhymes are a good example of simple rhymes.
☆ Make up simple rhymes with the children and write them on a flip chart. For example:

Jogging is fun
If you like to run.

Walking is great
But don't be late.

Story Starters

☆ Give the children a story starter and encourage them to dictate a story to you.
☆ Here are a few good starters:
   ★ When I looked out my window I saw a dog chasing a pig down the street.
   ★ The best present I received on my birthday was _____.
   ★ Yesterday I met a funny-looking man who said he was from another planet.

Wordless Books

☆ Gather some wordless books and show them to the children. Good ones to use are *Pancakes for Breakfast* by Tomie dePaola, *The Snowman* by Raymond Briggs, or *Good Dog, Carl* by Alexandra Day.
☆ These books provide the plot, characters, and themes, and let readers supply the words.

The Instant Curriculum

Baggie Books

☆ Invite the children to use pictures to create a story.

☆ Staple six baggies together at the bottom of the bags and put a strip of masking tape or colored tape over the staples to form the spine of the book.

☆ Cut pieces of tagboard or construction paper to fit into each baggie.

☆ Encourage the children to dictate and illustrate a story to go on the pages and then place them in proper sequence inside the baggies.

☆ Use stick-on notes across the bottom of the page to use as a place to write the dictated story.

☆ Change stories easily by removing current pages and replacing with a new story.

☆ Let children use popular books as models to imitate. For example, *Brown Bear, Brown Bear* by Bill Martin, Jr. may become *Black Cat, Black Cat.*

Lists

☆ Create lists for classroom activities when appropriate.

☆ Typical opportunities include making a list of sounds you expect to hear on a listening walk, brainstorming a list of possible names for a classroom pet, and brainstorming a list of ideas for where to go on a field trip.

☆ Making and using lists help children become familiar with one of many ways print is used for written communication.

Journal Writing

☆ Take several sheets of white paper and one piece of colored construction paper, fold them in half, and staple at the fold (make sure the colored piece of paper is on the outside) to make a journal. Or, have children bring a spiral notebook to school.

☆ Each day, ask the children to write or draw on a page of their journal. They can draw a picture for the day or use "make believe" letters to write down their thoughts for the day.

☆ Provide an opportunity for children to "read" a journal page to someone else.

☆ What they write is not important; it is the concept that should be stressed.

Note: This activity helps children understand that their thoughts can be communicated through symbols.

Pen Pal Buddies

☆ Find a class at another school or center that will participate in exchanging letters from time to time.

☆ Letter writing is one of the many ways print is used in written communication.

News Events

☆ Have the children ask their parents to help them find a simple news article in the newspaper and cut it out.

☆ Ask them to bring their article to class.

☆ Briefly share the primary information in each article with the children. Focus on the concept that print is used to communicate news events to the world.

Comprehension

Story Detectives

☆ After reading a story to the children, ask multiple-choices questions.

☆ For example, read *Little Red Riding Hood.* Then, ask the children to select the right answer to this question: *"What was Little Red Riding Hood carrying to her grandmother's house?"* (briefcase, purse, basket, or box)

Note: One or two questions of this type after a story help children become familiar with this type of questioning strategy.

True/Not True

☆ Present children with pairs of sentences—one that is true and one that is untrue.

★ Everyone in this classroom is a boy.

★ This class is made up of girls and boys.

☆ Ask the children to select the true statement.

☆ After the children are confident in selecting this type of categorical statement, present sentence pairs in which one sentence is partially true and the other sentence is completely true.

Questioning Strategies

☆ Ask questions that require the children to stretch their thinking and comprehension skills. Ask questions that use all the levels of thinking described by Benjamin Bloom (Bloom's Taxonomy): recall, comprehension, application, analysis, synthesis, and evaluation.

☆ For example, if you have just read *The Little Red Hen,* here are some questions that will use all the levels of thinking:

★ **Recall:** *What was the Little Red Hen trying to do?*

★ **Comprehension:** *Who did she ask to help?*

★ **Application:** *Can you think of a time someone asked you to help with something and you didn't want to help? What did you do?*

★ **Analysis:** *Which parts of the story could actually happen? Which parts are only make-believe?*

★ **Synthesis:** *How would the story have been different if the animals had helped the hen bake her bread?*

★ **Evaluation:** *Do you think it is okay that the Little Red Hen didn't share her bread with the animals that didn't help? Why?*

Story Map

☆ Make a Story Map for stories that you read to the class. See the example below for a suggested form to use.

TITLE

AUTHOR

THEME

PLOT

CHARACTERS

SETTING

CONFLICT

RESOLUTION

The Instant Curriculum

Word Webs

☆ Write a word related to the current classroom theme in the center of a piece of chart paper. If the children are studying pets, for example, you might write "cat" in the center of the paper.

☆ Circle the word. Ask the children to tell you everything they know about cats. Write one word descriptions from what they say all around the word "cat." Draw lines from the circled word to the descriptions to create a word web.

☆ For younger or less experienced children, you can do this activity in a more concrete way. Place a plastic, stuffed, or picture of a cat on the floor and make a circle of yarn around it. Write the descriptive words that children tell you about cats on index cards and place them on the floor around the circled cat. Use yarn to create lines from the cat to the index cards.

Story Re-Enactments

☆ Make a masking tape "bridge" on the floor.

☆ Tell the story of *The Three Billy Goats Gruff*. Have three children act out the goats walking over the bridge and another child act out the troll under the bridge.

☆ Let the children take turns acting out the parts.

☆ Use this activity with the game, "Who's That Traipsing on My Bridge" on page 191 to extend comprehension.

☆ Tell the story of *Goldilocks and the Three Bears*.

☆ After telling the story, place three bowls on a table, three chairs against the wall, and three sheets on the floor (representing beds).

☆ Retell the story, letting the children take the parts of the three bears and Goldilocks.

☆ Encourage the children to insert their own dialogue at critical points in the story. ("It's too hot!" "It's too cold!" "It's just right!")

 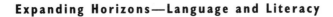

Story Pantomime

☆ Read a story, such as *The Snowy Day* by Ezra Jack Keats or another favorite story.

☆ Have one (or more) child pantomime the activity of the lead character as he looks for the snowball in his pocket, makes angels in the snow, and so on.

☆ Tell the story again and let another child or a few children interpret the story.

Action Stories

☆ Use action stories with the children.

☆ Action stories allow children to become physically involved in the story, which helps them internalize the story. "Going on a Bear Hunt" (see pages 127-128) is a good example of an action story.

☆ Following is another action story the children will enjoy.

Old Gray Cat
The old gray cat is sleeping, sleeping, sleeping.
The old gray cat is sleeping in the house.
(one child is the cat and curls up, pretending to sleep)

The little mice are creeping, creeping, creeping.
The little mice are creeping through the house.
(the other children are mice creeping around the sleeping cat)

The old gray cat is waking, waking, waking.
The old gray cat is waking through the house.
(the cat slowly sits up and stretches)

The old gray cat is chasing, chasing, chasing.
The old gray cat is chasing through the house.
(the cat chases the mice)

All the mice are squealing, squealing, squealing.
All the mice are squealing through the house.
(the mice squeal; when the cat catches a mouse, that mouse becomes the cat)

The Instant Curriculum

First Things First—
Making Math Meaningful

Overview

Math for young children must be concrete, hands-on, meaningful, developmental, filled with play and exploration, and taught with consistent terminology. When manipulating materials, children internalize the patterns inherent in math. Through hands-on experiences, they learn that there is often more than one solution to a problem.

Rote counting to 10 does not mean that a child understands the meaning of ten. If children count 10 marbles and put them into a tall, slender glass, and then count 10 more marbles and put them into a small shallow bowl, they will tell you that there are more marbles in the tall, slender glass. So take time to develop concepts thoroughly. Don't rush. Children will learn to count as counting becomes meaningful to them. They will learn to count to four and at the same time understand what four represents much better when they count four candles on their birthday cake than they will by counting four marbles into a jar.

This chapter is organized by developmental sequence. Following a developmental sequence when teaching math allows children to build each new concept on previously learned concepts. It is important that young children truly understand foundation concepts before moving on to more abstract operations such as addition and subtraction. Using a developmental sequence for teaching math helps children gradually build their understanding. For example, children need to be able to recognize and name attributes (free exploration) and understand positions of items (spatial relationships) before they are able to classify items (classification) into groups. They must be able to see the likenesses and differences between materials in order to classify. When they look at materials to classify them, it prepares them to be able to identify, create, and extend patterns (which are made up of likenesses and differences). By adhering to this sequence and providing children with a

Brain Fast Facts

☆ Mathematical acuity peaks in early adolescence.

☆ Mathematical, musical, and spatial skills are related to one another. They are each wired in approximately the same location in the brain.

☆ When children are able to see patterns in mathematical activities (for example, counting is the systematic addition of one set member at a time, numbers progress in an odd/even arrangement, and so on), they will develop a more rational understanding of math.

☆ Math concepts taught by rote memorization result in the information being stored in the lowest functioning part of the brain.

multitude of opportunities for practicing and internalizing math, you are preparing them for more complex activities when they are introduced later.

Make math fun. Use play and exploration opportunities. Sing math-related songs, play math-related games, and insert math into daily activities, such as counting the number of children on the playground or how many times a ball is bounced. Be intentional and purposeful in your teaching. Stop and discuss the number "five" when reciting "Five Little Monkeys Jumping on the Bed."

Be consistent with your terminology when teaching math. A group of items is a *set*, so use the word "set." When doing fingerplays and singing songs that reduce the number in the set from five to none ("Five Little Pumpkins," "Five Little Ducks"), don't teach the concept as "take away." Teach the concept as "one less." The phrase "Take away" is only one way to separate sets when using subtraction. It doesn't hold true in all subtraction problems.

The following is a list of math concepts and definitions. The list also represents an appropriate developmental sequence for introducing each concept. It begins with the first math skill the child needs to internalize and then follows with consecutive skills, each built on the understanding of the preceding skill.

Attributes—descriptive words that define objects, for example, *red* blocks, *square* blocks, and so on.

Counting—the systematic addition of one set member at a time.

Free exploration—the investigation of items, such as buttons, corks, washers, blocks, and jar lids, to become familiar with their attributes.

Spatial relationships—the understanding of terms, such as *up*, *down*, *over*, *under*, *in*, and *out*, used to describe positions and directions.

Classification—the process of grouping or sorting objects into classes or categories according to a systematic characteristic, criteria, or principle.

Patterning—the process of creating repetitions of symbols or objects based upon likenesses and differences, such as red circle, blue triangle; red circle, blue triangle; and so on.

One-to-one correspondence—the process of pairing or matching items or objects, for example, one napkin for each person.

Ordering and sequencing—the process of ordering relationships, for example, from smallest to largest, lightest to heaviest, or least to most.

Numeration—the ability to recognize numerals and place a correct numeral with a given number of objects. "Three" is a number; "3" is a numeral.

Measurement—the comparison of items by a standard unit.

Addition—the joining of sets.

Subtraction—the separation of sets.

Graphing—the process of classifying data.

Fractions—a method of dividing items.

Using "teachable moments" is valuable in teaching math. Count boys in the line and then girls in the line. Count the number of jumping jacks during exercise and the number of cookies during snack. This is using math and counting in the meaningful context of everyday experiences.

Free Exploration

Junk Boxes

☆ Collect items to place into "junk" boxes (size of the box depends on the size of the items). Select items that children will enjoy exploring, such as keys, empty spools, buttons, nuts and bolts of all sizes, corks, bottle lids, and other interesting items.

☆ Invite families to help you collect these items.

☆ Place the boxes on a low shelf in your Math Center.

☆ Encourage the children to explore the materials. Talk with them as they handle the various items. Help them develop language that serves to describe the items (naming attributes).

Naming Attributes

☆ Explain to the children that *attributes* are words that describe someone or something.

☆ Demonstrate the concept using the children as examples. Point out that some of the children have blue eyes and others have brown. Call attention to different hair colors and heights.

☆ Select an item in the room, such as a rug or table, and help the children make a list of the attributes that describe the item. For example, attributes of a table might be four legs, smooth surface, big, square, and beige.

I Spy

☆ Play "I Spy" with the children.

☆ Pick an item in the room and give an attribute description of the item to the children. "I spy something that is red, soft, and square."

☆ Let the children take turns guessing what item you are describing.

☆ When they become more skilled in naming attributes, you can let them take turns providing clues for something they spy.

Can You Find It?

☆ Hide an item in the classroom before the children arrive.

☆ Give the children clues that describe the hidden item. Challenge them to find the item.

☆ If they are unsuccessful, offer additional clues or provide information that reduces the space in which they are looking.

Tree Tag 1

☆ Encourage the children to help make a list of words that could be used to describe a tree (tall, short, green leaves, no leaves, rough trunk, smooth trunk, and so on).

☆ Take the children to the playground or to the local park.

☆ Describe a tree. "I see a tree that is not very tall. It has a smooth trunk and leaves that are orange and red."

☆ As soon as the children determine which tree you are describing, they run to the tree and tag it.

The Instant Curriculum

Tree Tag II

☆ Gather streamers of different colors.

☆ Tie a different colored streamer around each of several trees that are fairly close together.

☆ Choose a color and say the color name. The children must run to a tree with that color of streamer.

☆ Say another color and the children must run to a tree with that color of streamer.

☆ Continue until the children grow tired of the game.

Hand Match-Up

☆ Invite the children to match their hand size with the hand size of their friends.

☆ Encourage them to find a friend with larger hands, smaller hands, and hands that are the same size as theirs.

Descriptive Vocabulary

☆ Gather several items that are opposites, for example, a big and little block and a tall and short glass.

☆ Ask the children to pair the items that are opposites.

☆ Have the children describe which attribute makes the objects opposites.

More Vocabulary

☆ Gather several objects from the classroom and place them in a bag or a box.

☆ Remove the items from the bag, one at a time, and encourage the children to provide as many descriptive words for the item as they can.

Spatial Relationships

Top, Middle, and Bottom

☆ Fold a piece of drawing paper into three equal parts. Give a sheet of folded paper to each child.

☆ Ask the children to draw a self-portrait on their folded paper. Ask them to draw their head in the space at the top of the paper (within the fold) and their legs in the space at the bottom of the paper. Have them fill in the middle space by drawing their torsos and arms. *What is funny about your drawing?*

☆ Encourage the children to show their portraits to their friends and describe which section each of their body parts are in. **Home Connection:** Send self-portraits home. Write "Lesson in Spatial Relationships" on the back of each portrait. Suggest that the children talk with their families about the arrangement of their body on the paper.

Little Box Surprises

☆ Wrap small jewelry boxes or other similar boxes with contact paper.

☆ Place a button inside each box and give a box to each child.

☆ Ask the children to take the button out of the box and place it *on top of* the box, *beside* the box, *under* the box, and *in* the box.

☆ Let them choose a place to put their button in relation to the box and then describe to you and their friends where they have chosen to place their button.

Inside Outside

☆ Provide a beanbag and a box. Use masking tape to identify a throw line.

☆ Encourage the children to stand behind the throw line and toss the beanbag into the box.

☆ Ask them to describe where the beanbag lands each time, inside the box or outside the box.

☆ Divide a piece of paper into two columns. Draw a simple picture to represent *inside the box* at the top of one column and a picture to represent *outside the box* at the top of the second column.

throw line

bean bags

☆ Encourage the children to record the results of their throws by placing a tally mark in the appropriate column each time they throw.

Over and Under

☆ Make a weaving loom by running yarn horizontally around an empty Styrofoam meat tray. Cut small slits in the sides of the tray to hold the yarn in place.

☆ Provide pipe cleaners, strips of ribbons, and lace. Encourage the children to use these items to weave a design on their looms.

☆ Encourage them to say "over" and "under" as they maneuver the pipe cleaners or ribbons through the yarn on the loom.

Where's the Button?

☆ Select a child to be IT and ask her to leave the room. Hide a button in the circle area.

☆ Give IT clues as to where the button is. Call attention to the use of spatial relationship words used to help provide the clues.

☆ When IT finds the button, play the game again. Let IT select a child to become the new IT and have the previous IT hide the button.

"Going on a Bear Hunt"

☆ Teach the children the following action chant, "Going on a Bear Hunt."

☆ Ask the children to identify the spatial relationship words in the chant.

Going on a Bear Hunt
We're going on a bear hunt. (leader says the first verse alone)
Want to come along? (children answer "yes")
Well, come on then. Let's go! (pat thighs with alternating hands in a walking pattern)

(continued on the next page)

Look! There's a river. (children echo)
Can't go over it. (children echo)
Can't go under it. (children echo)
Can't go around it. (children echo)
We'll have to go through it. (children echo)
(pretend to walk into river, through the water, and onto other bank; make a splashing sound, then resume patting thighs in a walking pattern)

Look! There's a tree. (children echo)
Can't go under it. (children echo)
Can't go through it. (children echo)
We'll have to go over it. (children echo)
(pretend to climb up and over tree, then resume patting your thighs in a walking pattern)

Look! There's a wheat field. (children echo)
Can't go over it. (children echo)
Can't go under it. (children echo)
Can't go around it. (children echo)
We'll have to go through it. (children echo)
(brush hands together and make a swishing sound, then resume patting thighs in a walking pattern)

Look! There's a cave. (children echo)
Want to go inside? (children answer "yes")
Ooh, it's dark in here. (children echo)
(look around, squinting)
I see two eyes. (children echo)
Wonder what it is. (reach hands to touch)
It's soft and furry. It's big.
It's a bear! Let's run! (retrace steps, pat thighs in a running pace)
(Repeat actions in a backwards sequence—wheat field, over the tree, across the river, then stop.)
Home safely. Whew! (wipe brow)

The Instant Curriculum

Circle Commands

☆ Have the children stand in a circle.

☆ Give them directions to follow, using spatial words. "Place your hands *on* your hips." "Put your foot out *in front of* you." "Put your elbow *on* your knee."

Twister

☆ Play a game of Twister with the children.

☆ If you don't have a commercial game, create your own game by cutting out yellow, blue, and red circles from contact paper and placing them on a shower curtain liner that has been cut in half.

☆ Cover a square 3" x 3" box (a one-half pint milk carton with the top folded down works well) with white paper to make a die. Draw a pair of red hands on one side, yellow hands on another, and blue hands on a third side. Draw a pair of red, yellow, and blue feet on the remaining three sides.

☆ Two children can play the game at one time. They take turns rolling the die to determine their move.

☆ If the die lands on red hands the child must put her hands on a red circle on the mat. If it lands on blue feet, then she must put her feet on a blue circle on the mat. The game continues until one of the children loses her balance.

☆ Discuss the spatial relationship vocabulary used when playing this game.

Classification

Classmate Classifications

☆ Place a strip of masking tape on the floor.
☆ Choose a boy to stand on one side of the tape line and a girl to stand on the other side.
☆ Ask the class what is different about the two children.
☆ When someone identifies the distinguishing characteristic of boy/girl, ask another child to come up. Ask the children where he or she should stand.
☆ Give each child a turn.
   Note: Continue this activity from time to time using other classification criteria, such as type of shoes worn or color of clothing.
☆ Use everyday activities to reinforce classification, for example, "All the children with white shoes may go to the snack table."

Classification Books

☆ Staple several sheets of construction paper together to make a book.
☆ Encourage the children to look through old magazines and newspapers for pictures of items they can classify into groups. For example, they might have a page dedicated to people, another to animals, and another to food.

Button Match

☆ Collect several different types of buttons (two holes, four holes, red, black, round, and so on).
☆ Glue one button to the inside of each section of an egg carton.
☆ Encourage the children to sort the remaining buttons into the sections according to an established criterion, such as number of holes, color, and shape.

Shoes, Shoes, Shoes

☆ Ask the children to take off their shoes.
☆ Encourage them to classify the shoes according to type (tennis shoes, dress shoes, oxfords) or according to how the shoes fasten (buckle shoes, tie shoes, slip-ons, Velcro-clasp shoes).

Eyes Open, Eyes Shut

☆ Give each child a handful of wiggle eyes. Ask them to drop the eyes into a box.
☆ Encourage them to sort the eyes into "eyes open" (those that land facing up) and "eyes shut" (those that land facing down).
☆ When children become more skilled, encourage them to match the eyes using one-to-one correspondence to see if more eyes are open or shut.

Classifying Snacks

☆ Provide several different types of fruit for snack.
☆ Invite the children to try each type of fruit and choose their favorite.
☆ Make a floor graph of their choices. Place a red construction paper square on the floor to represent apples, a purple square to represent grapes, an orange square to represent oranges, and a yellow square for bananas.
☆ Ask the children to stand in a line behind the square that represents the fruit they have chosen as their favorite.
☆ Explain that they have created a human graph. Give each child a construction paper square to represent her choice. Ask the children to put their square in the spot where they are standing. Now they can actually see the graph.
☆ Ask questions. *Which fruit got the most votes? Which got the least? Were any of the votes equal?*
☆ When children become more skilled at making graphs, give them a piece of paper divided into grids and let them color the square to match the squares on the floor. This will be a symbolic representation of the graph that was at first a human graph, and then a graph made of concrete representations.

Classifying by Color

Stringing Bead Sort
☆ Give the children stringing beads and ask them to sort the beads by color.
☆ Invite the children to find other things in the classroom and sort them by color.

Fabric Sort
☆ Provide a box of fabric or paper scraps.
☆ Encourage the children to sort the fabric or paper by color.
☆ Create a special category for mixed colors.

Eyes of All Colors
☆ Have the children look in a mirror to determine their eye color.
☆ Designate a place in the room for each eye color and ask the children to go to the area that represents their eye color.

Classifying by Shape

Shape Match
☆ Place 3' strips of masking tape on the floor to create four columns. Place a different shape—square, circle, triangle, or rectangle—at the top of each column.
☆ Cut out a variety of sizes of colorful circles, triangles, rectangles, and squares.
☆ Ask the children to place the shapes in the corresponding column.
☆ Progress to more difficult shapes—rhombus, octagon, and trapezoid—as the children are ready.

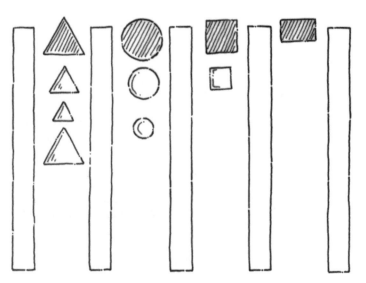

The Instant Curriculum

Adaptations: Use the same chart format, but create new categories, such as facial expressions, leaf shapes, and types of animals.

Block Cleanup

☆ Discuss the arrangement of blocks as the children put them away. "All the rectangles go here. The squares go on the top shelf."

Cracker Snackers

☆ Provide shape crackers for snack.
☆ Ask the children to classify the crackers by shape before eating them.

Cookie Cutter Shapes

☆ Provide shape cookie cutters and playdough (see recipes on pages 46-47).
☆ Have the children cut out cookie shapes and place them on cookie sheets according to their shape.

Shape Step

☆ Cut out several different shapes in several different colors and lay them on the floor.
☆ Play music and let the children dance.
☆ Stop the music and ask each child to step on a shape.
☆ Ask the children to name the shape they are standing on.
Home Connection: Suggest that the children look for shapes on their way home from school. Be sure to ask them the next day what shapes they saw.

Classifying by Size

Big and Little

☆ Provide a box of big and little items. Try to use pairs of objects with an obvious difference in size, such as a big book and a little book, a big ball and a little ball, and a big glove and a small glove.
☆ Encourage the children to sort the items into categories of *big* and *little*.
☆ Challenge the children to look for big and little items in the classroom.

☆ Ask them to brainstorm other words used to designate size (large and small, enormous and tiny).

☆ Say the following action rhyme with the children to reinforce the concept of size.

Big and Small
I can make myself really big (stand up on toes)
By standing up straight and tall.
But when I'm tired of being big,
I can make myself get small. (stoop down)

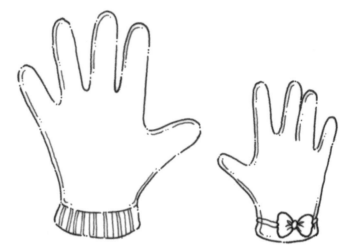

Short and Tall

☆ Provide a box of short and tall/long items. Try to use pairs of objects where the difference in size is fairly obvious, such as a tall and short glass, a long and short straw, a tall and short plant, and a long and short shoelace.

☆ Encourage the children to sort the items into categories of *short* and *tall* or *long*.

☆ Challenge the children to look for short and tall/long items in the classroom.

Long and Short

☆ Provide a box of long and short items. Try to use pairs of objects where the difference in size is fairly obvious, for example, a long and short shoelace, a long and short pencil, a long and short stick, and so on.

☆ Encourage the children to sort the items into categories of *long* and *short*.

☆ Challenge the children to look for long and short items in the classroom.

The Instant Curriculum

Classifying Using Senses Other Than Sight

Hard and Soft

☆ Provide different textures of fabrics for the children to classify.

☆ Ask them to sort the fabrics into categories of *soft* and *rough*.

☆ Encourage the children to look for additional hard and soft items in the classroom.

Loud and Soft

☆ Provide a basket of small items—some of which will make a sound when dropped (a button, washer, small block) and some of which will not (a cotton ball, feather, piece of fabric).

☆ Invite them to drop the items from the basket onto a cookie sheet to determine whether they make a sound when dropped. Ask them to classify the items into the categories of *loud* or *soft* depending on the sound they make when they hit the cookie sheet.

☆ Challenge the children to create a list of other items that make loud or soft sounds.

Sweet/Not Sweet

☆ Give the children several items to taste, some of which are sweet and some of which are not sweet (milk chocolate morsels, raisins, popcorn, and pretzels).

☆ Invite the children to sample each item and classify it as *sweet* or *not sweet*.

☆ Challenge the children to brainstorm a list of other foods that are sweet and a list of other foods that are not sweet.

Nice Smell?

☆ Dampen a few cotton balls with extracts, oils, perfumes, and spices and place them on a tray.

☆ Encourage the children to sniff each ball and classify it as a scent they like or don't like. They may not always agree. This is okay because we don't all have the same opinion regarding scents and aromas.

Safety Note: Make sure that none of the children in the class have allergies to any of the scented materials.

Open-Ended Classification

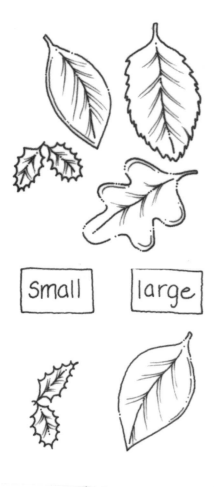

Things That Are…, Things That Are Not…

☆ Put several items in a zipper-closure bag, such as a pipe cleaner, paper clip, crayon, penny, and clothespin.

☆ Let the children classify the items in the bag according to their own established criteria, but using the phrase, "Things that are…; things that are not…"

☆ For example, a child might place the pipe cleaner, paper clip, and clothespin into one pile, and the remaining items into another pile and say, "Things that are fasteners; things that are not fasteners."

Note: This type of classifying allows children to see multiple attributes of an item and also increases the child's awareness of how to develop classifying criteria.

Leaf Sorting

☆ Pick a variety of leaves from trees and bushes (large leaves, small leaves, shiny, dull, rough edges, and so on).

☆ Put the leaves into one pile and ask the children to decide on a characteristic for sorting (large leaves and small leaves) and put the leaves into two piles based on their selected characteristic.

☆ Now ask the children to sort the two piles into two more piles (for a total of four). Continue this process for as long as the children are able to think of ways to classify the leaves.

☆ This activity may be done outside. Draw chalk circles around each new group of leaves so that the children can see how the piles of leaves have developed. If the activity is done inside, the same pattern can be created on butcher paper.

☆ See if the children can reverse the process to get the leaves back into one pile.

Book Classification
- ☆ Ask the children to help classify several books from the Library Center.
- ☆ They can sort them by themes (animals, transportation, bugs), or they might choose to classify them into fiction and non-fiction categories. Other possible categories include paperback and hardback books or big books and small books.
- ☆ Let the children decide their own criteria as they sort. Be sure to ask them to explain which criteria they are using.

Classification Applications

Questions
- ☆ Ask children questions that require them to use their classification skills. *What kind of story do you most enjoy listening to? How do you arrange your clothes at home?*
- ☆ Ask questions that require children to make choices. Classify their choices.

Real Life Uses
- ☆ Discuss real world uses of classification, such as books in the library, groceries in the store, and items in the kitchen at home.
- ☆ Explain that classification helps keep us organized. It is a pattern we can count on when we are looking for something.
- ☆ Take a walk to the office, kitchen, or library. Ask the people who work there to show you some of the ways they classify items they use in their job.

    Home Connection: Ask the children to look for things at home that are classified (silverware, food in the pantry, and so on). Discuss the items when they return to school the next day.

Patterning

People Patterns

☆ Seat (or stand) six children in a line, alternating the direction they are facing.

☆ When the class has identified the pattern (facing front, facing back, …), have each child in turn continue the pattern by sitting in the correct direction.

☆ Verbalize the pattern as children sit facing front, back, front, and so on.

Note: Another time, assist the children in creating other people patterns (stand/sit, arms up/arms down, and other patterns).

Object Patterns

☆ Place common objects such as plastic forks, jar lids, or cups on a table.

☆ Create a pattern by placing the objects into a repetitive sequence, for example, cup/jar/lid/fork, cup/jar/lid/fork.

☆ Encourage the children to first copy the pattern, and then create their own.

Paper Patterns

☆ Cut out circles, squares, and triangles that are all the same color.

☆ Let the children create patterns with the geometric shapes.

☆ After exploring various patterning possibilities, the children may glue their favorite pattern on paper.

Crayon Patterns

☆ Empty several boxes of crayons onto the table or floor.

☆ Encourage the children to create a pattern with the crayons—two red crayons, one purple crayon, two red crayons, and so on.

138

The Instant Curriculum

Paper Chains

☆ Cut sheets of colored paper into 1" x 9" strips. Use at least two colors but not more than three colors.

☆ Ask the children to glue strips of paper to form a color-patterned chain.

☆ Use the chains as necklaces, bracelets, or room decorations.

Set Patterns

☆ Provide the children with small counters (buttons, poker chips, and so on).

☆ Work with the children to create patterns (one counter, two counters; one counter, two counters). Let children create their own patterns of number sets.

Block Patterns

☆ Demonstrate how to create patterns using various shaped blocks in the Block Center.

☆ When the children build structures, ask them to identify the patterns that occur.

Fruit Kabobs

☆ Provide fruit (strawberries, grapes, chunks of pineapple) and wooden skewers (craft sticks).

☆ Let the children place the fruit on their sticks in a pattern.

Vertical Patterns

Up and Down

☆ Show the children how to use color tiles or beads to create a pattern that runs from top to bottom in a vertical line.

☆ Give the children colored straws and encourage them to create patterns in a vertical line. Can they make the same pattern in a horizontal line?

☆ Point out vertical patterns in the environment, such as steps, blinds, and articles of clothing.

Tube Bands

☆ Give children empty paper towel tubes and thin and fat rubber bands (or colored rubber bands).

☆ Ask the children to place rubber bands on the tube in a pattern with the tube standing up vertically.

☆ Ask them to lay the tubes horizontally. *Do the rubber bands still make a pattern?*

Balls in a Tube

☆ Obtain a tall plastic cylinder (tennis ball can) or make your own by cutting a 1" strip from one side of an empty paper towel tube and wrapping it in plastic wrap. Close one end with tape.

☆ Give the children two colors of playdough (see pages 46-47 for recipes).

☆ Have them roll playdough balls and drop them into the tube in a pattern.

☆ Ask the children questions. *If you turn the tube on its side, do you still have a pattern? If you turn the tube upside down, do you still have a pattern?*

Stacking Cans

☆ Provide empty vegetable cans. Make sure that several have the same label.

Safety Note: Make sure any sharp edges on the cans are covered.

☆ Invite the children to stack the cans in a pattern.

The Instant Curriculum

Circular Patterns

Around We Go

☆ Give each child a paper plate and squares of colored construction paper. Have them create a pattern around the edge of the paper plate.

☆ Point out that there are circular patterns in the environment—the numbers on a clock, circular brick driveways, and although less obvious, days of the week and seasons of the year.

☆ Read books with circular patterns. Good choices are *If You Give a Mouse a Cookie* by Laura Joffe Numeroff and *Why the Chicken Crossed the Road* by David Macaulay.

Stringing Beads

☆ Ask the children to string beads in an AB (two attribute) pattern (red/yellow, red/yellow, and so on).

☆ After they have completed several repetitions of the pattern, help them tie the beads in a circle. *What happens to the pattern?*

Paper Clip Chains

☆ Give the children two colors of paper clips.

☆ Ask them to string the paper clips in an AB pattern (red clip/yellow clip, red clip/yellow clip).

☆ When they have completed several repetitions of the pattern, help them clip their chain together to make a circle. *What happens to the pattern?*

Variation: Make paper chains using an AB pattern.

Home Connection: Encourage the children to take their chains home and point out the pattern in their chains to their families.

Wrap-Around Patterns

Around the End and Back Again

☆ Cut paper into 8" x 8" squares and draw sixteen-square grids on them.

☆ Give each child a square and red, yellow, and green crayons. Help them color the squares red, yellow, and green in a pattern that begins with the square at the top left of the grid and ends at the right bottom square on the grid.

☆ Call attention to how the pattern wraps around the lines on the grid.

Pegboard Patterns

☆ Provide a pegboard and three colors of pegs.

☆ Ask the children to create an ABC (three-attribute) pattern using the pegs.

☆ Because most children think patterns only occur in straight lines, they may need help in turning the corner and continuing the pattern on the second row of the pegboard.

Movement Patterns

Footprint Patterns

☆ Place a long sheet of butcher paper on the floor.

☆ Fill two large cake pans with two different colors of tempera paint and place them at one end of the paper. Place a tub of soapy water and a towel at the opposite end.

☆ Instruct the children to remove their shoes and socks and place one foot in one color of paint and the other foot in the other color of paint. Help them walk the length of the butcher paper. (Use caution because the paint may be slippery.)

☆ When they reach the end of the paper, help them step into the soapy water to remove the paint.

☆ Ask them to describe the pattern they made with their feet.

Jumping Jack Patterns

☆ Ask the children to do jumping jacks in a pattern. Have them alternate jumping once with their arms overhead and then jumping with their arms out in front of them.

☆ Try making patterns with other exercises. For example, when doing toe touches, children can alternate touching their toes and then the floor.

Musical and Sound Patterns

Head, Shoulders, Knees, and Toes

☆ Sing "Head, Shoulders, Knees and Toes" with the children. Ask the children to identify the pattern in the words and movements of the song.

☆ Sing other songs with an identifiable pattern ("This Old Man," "Here We Go 'Round the Mulberry Bush," and "Go In and Out the Windows"). Be sure to ask the children to identify the pattern in each song.

Sound Patterns

☆ Invite the children to make auditory patterns.

☆ Encourage them to make a series of sounds in a pattern, for example, click their tongues, blow through their teeth, click their tongues, blow through their teeth, and so on.

Clapping Patterns

☆ Encourage the children to make up clapping patterns (clap three times quickly and then two times slowly, three times quickly and two times slowly).

☆ Provide a tape recorder for children to record their patterns. Play the recording and see if they are able to recognize the pattern they created.

Predictable Language Patterns

☆ Point out the predictable lines in story books and explain to the children that they are a pattern.

☆ Traditional tales, such as "The Little Red Hen," "The Three Little Pigs," and "The Three Bears," often have easy-to-identify, predictable language patterns.

Cultural Patterns

Days of the Week

☆ Discuss cultural patterns with children. Cultural patterns are things that remain consistent within a given culture, such as number sequences, alphabet sequence, months of the year, days of the week, and seasons.

☆ Read books built around the sequence of the days of the week, such as *The Very Hungry Caterpillar* by Eric Carle or *Tuesday* by David Wiesner.

☆ Teach the children the following song to the tune of "The Addams Family."

Days of the Week
Days of the week. (snap, snap)
Days of the week. (snap, snap)
Days of the week, days of the week,
Days of the week. (snap, snap)

(continued on the next page)

There's Sunday and there's Monday,
There's Tuesday and there's Wednesday,
There's Thursday and there's Friday,
And then there's Saturday.

☆ Point out that the days of the week are also circular.

Months of the Year

☆ Discuss the months of the year as both a cultural and circular pattern. The months always remain in the same order.

☆ Read *Chicken Soup With Rice* by Maurice Sendak or other books that are based on the months of the year.

☆ Flip through a calendar and have the children say the months with you. Make sure you go past December to January so that they see the full cycle.

☆ Sing the following "Months of the Year" song with the children to the tune of "Bumping Up and Down in My Little Red Wagon."

Months of the Year
January, February, March, April,
May, June, July, August,
September, October, November, December.
Then you turn around.

Sun	Mon	Tue	Wed	Thu	Fri	Sat
			1	2	3	4
5	6	7	8	9	10	11
12	13	14	15	16	17	18
19	20	21	22	23	24	25
26	27	28	29	30	31	

..*December:*.*.*

Seasons

☆ Discuss the seasons as a circular pattern. The seasons never change places with one another, although some parts of the world experience more subtle seasonal changes than other parts.

☆ Read *The Tortilla Factory* by Gary Paulsen or another book that is based on seasons and shows the seasons as both circular and cultural.

Environmental Patterns

Pattern Hunt

☆ Take the children outdoors to search for patterns.

☆ Call attention to patterns in windows, bricks, roads, landscaping, spider webs, and so on.

☆ When you return to class, make a list of all the patterns that you found.

The Instant Curriculum

Pattern Rubbings

☆ Give the children paper and crayons.

☆ Take them outdoors and encourage them to make rubbings of patterns, such as on bricks or tree bark.

☆ Help the children describe the patterns they find.

Clothing Patterns

☆ Ask the children to look for patterns in their clothing (stripes, floral prints, dots, plaids, and so on).

☆ Have children wearing different types of patterns stand up, or ask children wearing plaids to stand up, or children wearing stripes to stand up, and so on.

One-to-One Correspondence

Equal Sets

Partner Match

☆ Ask the children to choose partners. If there is an extra child, include yourself in the game.

☆ Point out that there is an *even* match. Each person is matched with another person and there is no one left to match.

☆ Let the partners play You Can't Make Me Laugh. The children take turns trying to make their partner laugh.

One Pebble for Every Child

☆ Bring a sack of pebbles or marbles to the circle. Give each child a pebble.

☆ Tell the children that they are going to see if all the children who are in the circle now will be in the circle after bathroom break, center time, or outdoor play—whichever fits the schedule.

(continued on the next page)

☆ Have the children put their pebble back in the sack when they leave the circle.

☆ When the circle reconvenes, hand each child a pebble and then show the children that the sack is empty.

☆ Repeat the phrase, "One child for every pebble and one pebble for every child" several times throughout the activity.

Note: The phrase "one *pebble* for every *child* and one *child* for every *pebble*" helps children conceptualize one-to-one matching.

On With the Show

☆ Ask the children to stand between a light source (overhead projector, lamp, or strong flashlight) and a wall to create a shadow. Encourage the children to do something funny and watch their shadow copy.

☆ Point out that there is one *child* for every *shadow* and one *shadow* for every *child*.

Sock Match

☆ Place a basket of unmatched, patterned socks on the floor. Ask the children to locate the match for each sock.

☆ Discuss other clothing items that have a match, such as shoes and mittens.

Ice Cream Cones

☆ Cut out ice cream cones from brown construction paper. Cut out "scoops" of ice cream from brightly colored construction paper.

☆ Ask the children to match a scoop of ice cream to each cone. Encourage the children to glue their cones and scoops on paper when they have finished.

☆ Make up other similar games such as matching hats to heads or dogs to bones.

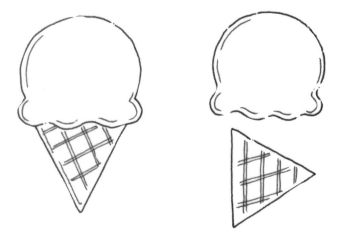

Penny Match

☆ Trace pennies on ten index cards: one circle on the first card, two circles on the next, three on the next, and so on.

☆ Ask the children to match pennies to circles: one penny for each circle, one circle for each penny.

Rings and Fingers

☆ Give the children plastic rings and let them match the rings to their fingers.

☆ Recite, "One *ring* for every *finger*, one *finger* for every *ring*."

Pompoms to Suction Cups

☆ Obtain a rubber bath mat that has suction cups on the bottom.

☆ Give the children small pompoms (available in craft stores) to place on the suction cups.

☆ Provide an equal number of pompoms to the number of suction cups.

One-to-One Correspondence

Unequal Sets

Today's Helpers

☆ Let the children take turns passing out napkins, cups, books, cookies, and other items to their classmates.

☆ This kind of activity provides firsthand experience with matching items one-to-one. Less experienced children will keep passing out items until they are all gone, instead of realizing they should stop when everyone has one.

Note: You may want to begin by making sure that the number of napkins and the number of children are equal, but eventually you will want to use unequal sets. Practice develops understanding.

One Left

☆ Give children one more napkin and one more cup than needed when they are distributing napkins and cups for snack.

☆ After one napkin and cup have been given to each child, ask the servers how many napkins they have left and how many cups they have left.

☆ Point out that the sets are uneven.

Musical Chairs

☆ Play Musical Chairs with the children. Discuss the match of one child for each chair and one chair for each child. *Are the sets equal?*

☆ Point out that the game is played with unequal sets. There is always one more child than there are chairs available.
Safety Note: If you are concerned about the safety of children while playing this game, play it by having them place a beanbag in the chair or simply touch the back of the chair.

More or Less

☆ Play More or Less. Ask the children to choose a partner and give each pair a box containing nine buttons.

☆ Each child takes a few buttons and places her hands (with the buttons) behind her back.

☆ The children count to three and then hold out their hands to their partners. Using one-to-one correspondence, the children determine who has more and who has less buttons. *Does anyone have equal sets in their hands?*

☆ Children return the buttons to the box and play again. Continue until they tire of the game.

☆ Be sure they state each time which child (set) has more, which has less, and when appropriate, when the children have the same number of buttons (sets are equal).

Who Has the Most?

☆ Arrange the children in groups of three. Give each child in the group a handful of small hard candies and a round plate. Make sure that one child has significantly more candy than the others.

☆ Tell the children that the plate is a "birthday cake" and they are to decorate it with their candy. When the children are finished, let each group decide which of the three cakes they would most like to eat. They will probably choose the one with the most candy,

The Instant Curriculum

relying on their visual assessment. Ask why they chose as they did and how they know which cake has the most candy.

☆ The children will decide who has the most candy by visual assessment. Ask them how they can find out who has the most candy for sure without counting.

☆ Encourage each group to match the candies one-to-one to determine which cake has more candy.

Ordering

Ordering by Height

Friends in a Row

☆ Arrange four children in a row, starting with the tallest child and ending with the shortest child.

☆ Show the same arrangement with classroom materials, such as blocks, pencils, and books.

Books on a Shelf

☆ Invite the children to help arrange the library books on a shelf from left to right and from the tallest book to the shortest book.

☆ Ask the children if they can think of other ways to arrange the books.

Tube Towers

☆ Provide empty paper towel, wrapping paper, and toilet paper tubes.

☆ Cut some of the tubes into smaller sections.

☆ Encourage the children to arrange the tubes from tallest to shortest in a standing position.

☆ Ask them to place the tubes on the table on their sides and repeat the activity.

Ordering by Length

Caterpillar Line-Up

☆ Cut egg cartons into different lengths to make "caterpillars."

☆ Encourage the children to decorate them with paper scraps, if desired.

☆ Have the children arrange the caterpillars in order from longest to shortest.

Go Fishing

☆ Cut out different lengths of cardboard fish and attach a paper clip to each.

☆ Make a fishing pole by tying a fishing line or string to a dowel. Attach a magnet to the end of the string.

☆ Make a pond using blue construction paper pond and place it on the floor. Add fish to the pond.

☆ Encourage the children to catch fish by touching the magnet to the paper clip. As they catch the fish, have them arrange them from smallest to largest.

Variation: Have the children catch only five fish. If they catch a fish that is the same length as one they already caught, they put it back into the pond. When each child has caught five fish, see who has caught the longest line of fish by placing all the fish in a row, tail to mouth.

The Instant Curriculum

Ordering by Weight

Egg Weigh

☆ Collect plastic eggs and place small items (pebbles, spool of thread, paper clips, and so on) inside them.

☆ Let the children take turns placing the eggs in order from heaviest to lightest.

☆ Extend this activity by using more eggs, or by asking the children to pair eggs that seem to weigh the same.

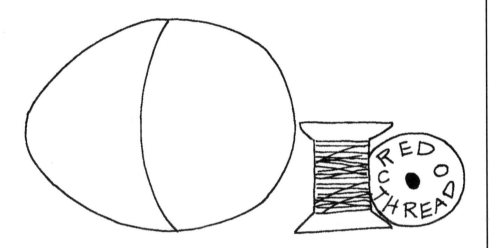

Bell Envelopes

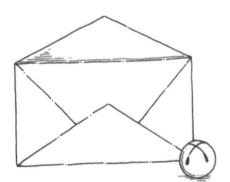

☆ Place jingle bells in five small envelopes. Place one bell in the first envelope and seal it, place two bells in the next envelope and seal it, three in the next, and so on.

☆ Encourage the children to arrange the envelopes in order from the lightest to the heaviest.

☆ Next ask them to arrange the envelopes in order from the one that makes the smallest sound to the one than makes the loudest sound. Does anyone notice that the order is the same in both activities?

Ordering by Liquid Measurement

Water Play

☆ Provide a tub of water with measuring cups and containers for exploration.

☆ Encourage the children to experiment with the measuring cups to determine which cups hold more water.

Most to Least

☆ Fill four jars with ¼ cup, ⅓ cup, ½ cup, and 1 cup of water respectively.

☆ Encourage the children to arrange them in order from the jar with the most water to the jar with the least water.

Tone Bottles

☆ Make a set of tone bottles by varying the amount of liquid in six bottles.

☆ Have the children arrange the bottles in a least to most arrangement.

☆ Provide a wooden stick and encourage the children to explore the tones that result from tapping the bottles. Do they notice the relationship between the amount of water and the depth of tone?

Ordering by Position and Size

First, Next, Last

☆ Give children directions using the terms *first*, *next*, and *last*. "Juan, *first* I would like you to take your coat to your cubby, *next* pick up a book from the Library Center, and *last* come to the circle area and sit down."

☆ Record directions for an art project with first, next, and last steps explained on the audiotape. Have the children follow the directions on the tape.

Top, Middle, Bottom

☆ Invite the children to make cracker and cheese sandwiches.

☆ Discuss the position of the ingredients with the children as they make the sandwiches. *What goes on the bottom? What is in the middle? What goes on top?*

☆ Repeat this activity with other appropriate snacks. Another good snack idea is to make a layered banana pudding with cookies on the bottom, pudding in the middle, and bananas on the top.

cheese

cracker

Tree Surprise

☆ Provide the children with paper baking cups (for cupcakes).

☆ Ask them to arrange the baking cups in horizontal lines starting with one cup at the top, two underneath, then a row of three, and so on (like a tree).

☆ Staple the baking cups to a bulletin board, if desired.

☆ Ask the children to identify the resulting shape.

Block Pyramids

☆ Demonstrate how to make a pyramid out of the blocks.

☆ Place five blocks side by side on the floor. Stack four blocks side by side on top of the five blocks. Make a layer of three blocks, then two blocks, and then one block.

☆ Encourage the children to copy the pyramid and experiment with making their own pyramids.

Concentric Circles

☆ Cut out various sizes of circles from wallpaper scraps and construction paper.

☆ Sort the circles by size to aid the children in the visual discrimination of different sizes.

☆ Ask children to create *concentric* circles in designs of their own choosing by gluing smaller circles on top of larger ones.

☆ Explain to the children that they will lay the circles on top of each other, starting with the largest circle and layering the remaining circles from largest to smallest.

☆ Use size-comparative terms as you work with the children (small, smaller, smallest; big, bigger, biggest).

Ordering by Comparing Sets

Least to Most

☆ Cut out five gingerbread men from brown construction paper and laminate them.

☆ Decorate the "cookies" with small candies as the children watch. Use four or five pieces of candy on the first cookie, and then add two more to the second cookie, then two more to the third cookie, until finished.

(continued on the next page)

☆ When you finish, rearrange them out of order. Ask the children to help you put them in order from the cookie with the fewest candies to the cookie with the most candies.

☆ When the children feel that they have visually determined the correct order, check the arrangement using one-to-one correspondence.

Dot Order

☆ Cut out five 3" x 3" squares of paper.

☆ Using stick-on dots, place one dot on the first square, two on the second, three on the third, and so on.

☆ Challenge the children to arrange the squares from the fewest dots to the most dots.

Numeration

Math Number Bags

☆ Place three washers in a zipper-closure plastic bag. Make one for each child.

☆ With a marker, write the number "three" on the bottom of the bag. Draw a vertical line down the middle of the bag.

☆ Let children explore the bags. Encourage them to move the washers from one side of the line to the other, leaving washers on either side of the line.

☆ Help them understand that the total number of washers in the bag always remains the same. They may manipulate the washers to see combinations that make three—two washers on one side of the line and one washer on the other, three washers on one side and no washers on the other, and so on.

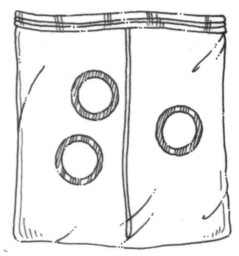

☆ As new numbers are introduced, make number bags for each number.

Beanbag Throw

☆ Place a box or basket in an open space.

☆ Make a masking tape line on the floor, 6' to 8' away from the box.

☆ Have the children stand behind the line and take turns throwing beanbags into the box. Let each child have four to five throws.

☆ Help each child make tally marks to represent the number of beanbags in the box.

☆ They can match tally marks one-to-one to determine the winner.

☆ This is a great activity to use as an introduction for the purpose of numerals.

Number Cards

☆ As children begin to work on new number concepts, create a numeral card to represent that number.

☆ Write the numeral on a 5" x 7" index card.

☆ Encourage the children to press their thumbs on an ink pad and trace over the numerals with their thumbprints.

☆ After the children complete their thumbprints, ask them to draw (or cut and paste) the appropriate number of objects on the paper, such as buttons, stickers, or pieces of ribbon.

Note: This is a good activity to send home. Write "Numeral Recognition" on the bottom of the paper to communicate the idea with parents. Send one card at a time as the children learn about each number. You may even want to ask the children to place objects on the paper at home with a family member's help.

The Shape of Things

☆ Cover a shoebox with contact paper or construction paper. Cut out a hole on two sides of the box, large enough for a child's hands to enter and manipulate objects.

☆ Place three to six wooden or plastic numerals in the box.

☆ Encourage one child at a time to reach in through the sides of the box, feel the shapes of the numerals, and arrange them in numerical order (left to right).

☆ Upon completion, the child verifies her arrangement by removing the lid of the box. If the order is incorrect, encourage her to feel the shape of each numeral and try the process again. **Note:** You can also do this activity using larger numerals. Put large numerals on a table and drape them with a tablecloth.

Number Clips

☆ Write the numerals 1 to 10 on index cards (one numeral per card).

☆ Provide the children with paper clips and the numbered index cards and ask them to attach the number of clips on each card to correspond with the printed numeral.

Counting Patterns

☆ When children become proficient in counting to ten, teach them to count to ten in patterns.

☆ Have them count: one, two, clap; three, four, clap; five, six, clap; seven, eight, clap; nine, ten, clap.

☆ On another occasion have them count a different pattern: one, two, three, clap; four, five, six, clap; seven, eight, nine, clap; ten.

Pasting Sets

☆ Prepare a number chart as shown below.
☆ Cut out a variety of colorful circles or squares.
☆ Help the children paste the correct number of circles next to each numeral on the chart.
☆ Progress to higher numbers as the children are ready.

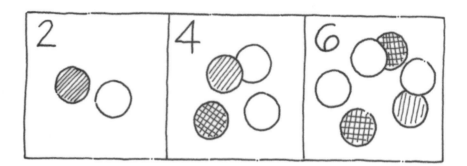

Plates and Clips

☆ Write the numerals 1 through 10 on paper plates (one numeral per plate).
☆ Hook paper clips together into sets (for example, hook three clips together to make a set of "three").
☆ Help the children match the paper clip chains to the numerals on the plates.
Note: For a variation, create sets by putting reinforcement stickers on index cards or by punching holes in index cards.

Mix It Myself Snack

☆ Put a variety of snack mix items, such as miniature marshmallows, raisins, peanuts, and sunflower seeds, into separate bowls.
Safety Note: Be certain that none of the children are allergic to peanuts.
☆ Provide the children with numeral cards that indicate the number of items they should count into their own snack cups.
☆ Children create their own snack by counting, for example, five raisins, four marshmallows, six sunflower seeds, and four peanuts into a cup.

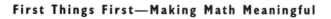

Piggy Banks

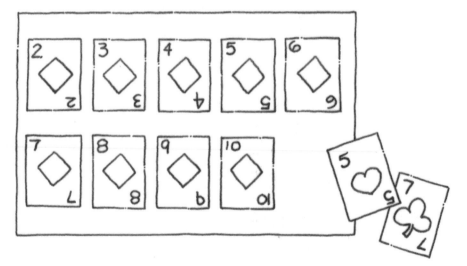

☆ Cut a slit in the lids of five re-sealable plastic containers. Make sure the slits are large enough for pennies to fit through.

☆ Write the numerals 1 through 5 on the containers.

☆ Give the children some pennies and ask them to drop the appropriate number of pennies into each "piggy bank."

☆ Ask the children questions. *How many pennies will you put into this bank? Which bank has the most money? Which bank has the least money? Could you put the banks in order from fewest pennies to most pennies?*

Card Match

☆ Use an old deck of cards to create a matching game. Glue one set of cards (2 through 10) in one suit (hearts, spades, etc.) on a folder or piece of poster board.

☆ Use the remainder of the deck (minus the face cards and aces) as matching cards.

☆ Remind the children to match the loose cards to the set that has been glued on the folder.

☆ Remind the children to look at the numbers, not the hearts, spades, diamonds, or clubs when matching the cards.

Musical Numbers

☆ Write numerals on large and small cards.

☆ Place the large numeral cards on the floor in a circle and have the children walk around the circle while music plays.

☆ When the music stops, each child puts her toe on a numeral card. Hold up a small numeral card, call out the number, and the children check if they are standing by the corresponding large numeral card.

☆ Start the music and the children walk around the circle again.

Circle 'Round the Zero

☆ Teach the children how to play Circle 'Round the Zero.

☆ Ask them to stand in a circle. Point out that the shape of the circle is the same shape as a zero.

☆ Explain that *zero* represents the absence of numbers. It is what is used when there is nothing in a set.

☆ Show the children the symbol for zero.

☆ Select a child to be IT.

☆ IT walks around the circle as the children chant the following rhyme:

Circle 'round the zero (IT walks around the circle)
Find your lovin' zero (IT selects a friend and stands behind her)
Back, back, zero. (IT stands back to back with her friend)
Side, side, zero. (IT moves to the side of her friend)
Front, front, zero. (IT moves to face her friend)
Tap your lovin' zero. (IT tapes her friend on the shoulder)

Number Bingo

☆ Cut out 5" x 5" squares and divide them into 1" squares to make bingo cards.

☆ Create a free space on each card and randomly number the other squares 0-5, using some numerals more than once.

☆ Give each child a bingo card and some bingo markers (buttons or pennies).

☆ Hold up a large numeral. Ask the children to find the matching numeral on their card and cover with a button or penny. Continue until a child fills her card.

My Number Book

☆ Staple five pint-size zipper-closure plastic bags together along the bottom. Cover the staples with a strip of vinyl tape to create a book spine. Cut white poster board or tagboard to fit inside each bag. Make one for each child.

☆ Print "My Number Book" on one sheet of paper and insert it into the first bag to be the book cover.

☆ Write one numeral on each of the other sheets and insert them into the remaining bags back to back.

☆ Encourage the children to paste stickers, stamps, or cutout magazine pictures on each page to correspond with the numeral on that page.

Golf Tee Combinations

☆ Write the numerals 1 through 5 on five margarine tub lids (one number per tub).

☆ Punch the same number of holes in each lid as the number written on it (five holes for the #5 lid).

☆ Place twice the number of golf tees in each tub as indicated on the lid, half one color and half a second color. For example, if the number on the lid is 5, place five white tees in the tub and five red tees in the tub.

☆ Help the children make combinations for the number on the lid using both colors of tees. For example, for the number four tub:
four red + zero blue
three red + one blue
two red + two blue
one red + three blue
zero red + four blue

Living Sets

☆ Encourage the children to create sets using their classmates as set members.

☆ For example, if the children are learning about the number five, ask them to create variations of that number by arranging classmates in sets of five (two girls and three boys, one boy and four girls, or zero girls and five boys).

Washer Drop

☆ Spray paint one side of ten 1" washers. Place the washers in a small container.

☆ Let the children drop the washers on a table.

☆ Ask them to count the washers that land colored side up and colored side down to see combinations that make a complete set.

☆ Begin with three painted washers and three unpainted washers; increase the number of washers as the children increase their understanding.

Candy Sets

☆ Give each child a bag of multi-colored candies. Ask them to separate the candy into sets by color.

☆ Ask them how many green, orange, yellow, red, light brown, and dark brown candies they have.

☆ Extend this activity further by asking the children to count the candies into sets. *How many light brown and yellow candies do you have? How many green and red ones?*

Crunchy Sets

☆ Give each child a handful of different shaped crackers.

☆ Ask them to separate the crackers into sets by shape and count the number of crackers in each set.

Mud Cakes

☆ On a warm, sunny day, plan an outdoor activity in the sandbox.

☆ Provide small buckets of water to make mud cakes and sticks (or real candles) to use as birthday candles.

☆ When the children have each made a mud cake, ask them to place three candles on their cake.

☆ Ask them to add one more candle. *Now how many do you have?*

☆ Continue adding candles when the children are ready.
Variation: Cut out a cake and candles from felt and let the children do the activity on a flannel board.
Home Connection: Cut out a cake and candles from construction paper. Have the children do the activity on a piece of construction paper and paste into place. Write "The Number Three" on the back of each child's paper.

And One More

☆ Encourage the children to act out stories that add characters to the story one at a time (*The Gingerbread Man* and *The Great Big Turnip*).

☆ After each new character is added, ask the children how many people or animals are in the story now.

Egg Carton Shake

☆ Using a marker, place one to five dots in each section of an egg carton.

☆ Put two buttons, pennies, or other appropriate item in the bottom of the carton.

☆ Close the lid and shake the carton.

☆ Then open the lid and have the children count the dots together in the sections where the two buttons have landed.

Target Practice

☆ Cut off the tops of milk cartons on an angle at different heights and then staple the sides of the cartons together. This forms a "target" with three or four sections. Print numerals on each section.

☆ Have the children toss a yarn ball or bounce tennis balls into the target sections and add up the points.

Subtraction Action

☆ Sing songs and do fingerplays with the children that subtract characters one at a time ("Five Little Speckled Frogs" or "Five Little Monkeys" …teasing Mr. Alligator).

☆ Always let the children act out the songs as fingerplays so they can visually see the results of one being eliminated.

☆ Use correct terminology. Instead of teaching subtraction as "take away," say, "less one" or "minus one."

In the Bag

☆ Number small paper lunch bags from 1 to 10.

☆ Place objects in each bag to correspond with the numeral on the outside of the bag.

☆ Write -2, -3, and -4 on small index cards.

☆ Place one card, number side down, in front of each bag. Be sure the card has a numeral smaller than the one on the outside of the bag.

☆ Encourage the children to turn over a card, remove the number of objects from the bag, and count how many are still in the bag.

The Instant Curriculum

Shapes

Cookie Cutter Shapes

☆ Use one of the playdough recipes on pages 46-47 to mix a batch of playdough.
☆ Provide shape cookie cutters.
☆ Encourage the children to roll the dough and cut out shapes.
☆ Discuss the shapes with the children. Ask them to name the shapes and count the sides of each.

Shape Construction

☆ Cut yarn into 24" long pieces and tie the ends together to form a circle. Give one to each child.
☆ Demonstrate how to manipulate the yarn to form various shapes.
☆ Encourage the children to make shapes with their yarn as you call out different shapes.

Playdough Shapes

☆ Give the children playdough (recipes on pages 46-47).
☆ Encourage them to form shapes with the playdough.

Shape Hunt

☆ Cut out two circles, two squares, two triangles, and two rectangles.
☆ Hide one set of shapes somewhere in the room (each shape in a different place).
☆ Give a child one shape at a time and have her try to find the matching shape until all four are found. Give each child a turn. **Variation:** Cut out several shapes and hide them around the room, some in sight, and some out of sight. Tell the children to be on the lookout for shapes as they play. As children find the shapes during the day, place them in a box. At the end of the day, invite the children to sort the shapes.

Musical Shapes

☆ Cut out several squares, circles, triangles, and rectangles from poster board or contact paper.

☆ Place the shapes on the floor in a circle.

☆ Play a favorite CD or tape and have the children walk around the circle until the music stops.

☆ When the music stops, the children put their toe on the shape closest to them.

☆ Ask each child to name the shape her toe is touching.

Squares and Rectangles

☆ Draw the outline of a 3" x 2" rectangle. Cut out six 1" squares from colored paper.

☆ Ask the children to fit the squares into the rectangular space, pasting them so the entire rectangle is filled.

Triangles and Rectangles

☆ Cut out two 4" x 2" rectangles, one white and one colored, for each child.

☆ Cut the colored rectangle into four triangles of equal size.

☆ Give each child a white rectangle and four triangles.

☆ Ask them to fit the triangles into the rectangle and paste in place.

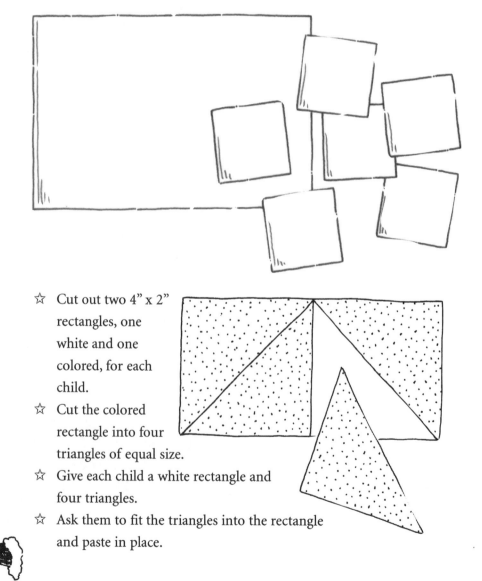

Measurement

Linear Measurement

Hand Match
☆ Ask the children to match their hands to their friends' hands until they find a friend with a hand size that matches theirs.
☆ Suggest they find someone with hands smaller than theirs and someone with hands larger than theirs. *Who has the largest hands? Who has the smallest?*

Four Hands High
☆ Challenge the children to use their hands to find something in the room that is "four hands high."
☆ *Can you find something that is one hand high?*
☆ Suggest they find something that is taller than four hands high.

Who Is the Tallest?
☆ Ask the children to look at their classmates and visually predict who is the tallest and who is the shortest.
☆ Record two or three predictions.
☆ Line up the children. Ask one child to step out of the line and look at the others.
☆ Let that child find the shortest child by picking a child and comparing that child to the others. After the first child gets the line started, have another child take over.
☆ When the line is correctly arranged from shortest to tallest, let each child take a turn stepping out of the line and looking at the results.

Chain Links
☆ Give each child six paper clips that have been hooked together.
☆ Challenge them to find items in the room that are the same length as their chain.
☆ Ask them to find objects that are smaller than their chains, then ask them to find objects that are larger than their chains.

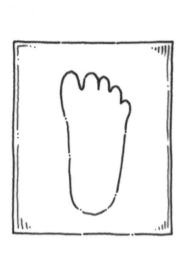

A Yard Long

☆ Give each child a piece of yarn that is one yard long.

☆ Encourage them to try to find something in the room that is the same length as their piece of yarn.

Two Feet Long

☆ Help each child trace around her foot on a piece of cardboard.

☆ Show the children how to use their own foot to measure the length of the room, the art table, and so on.

Inch by Inch

☆ Tape or paint lines on a classroom table 1" apart.

☆ Label the lines 1", 2", 3", and so on.

☆ Provide a variety of objects that are exact in inch measurements, such as a 5" straw, 4" comb, 3" tube, and so on.

☆ Encourage them to match objects to lines to compare lengths.

Foot Lengths

☆ Paint and number lines at 1' intervals on the sidewalk or bike path.

☆ Encourage the children to measure objects or themselves. They can also use the number lines for jumping lines.

☆ Use the lines for stopping points when sharing riding toys. "Austin, when you get to ten, it's Evan's turn to ride."

Big Steps, Small Steps

☆ Have children count baby steps between the Block Center and Art Center (or any two locations that are close together).

☆ Now have them count the giant steps between the same two spots. *Which steps resulted in the highest number?*

Weight Measurement

How Much Do I Weigh?

☆ Weigh each child at the beginning of the school year and then again at the end of the year. *Is the number larger at the beginning of the year or the end of the year? Why?*

Using Scales

☆ Give the children a basket of items to weigh with a balance scale. *Which object is the heaviest? Which object is the lightest?*

The Instant Curriculum

Capacity Measurement

Temperature Measurement

How Many Children Can Sit in a Dinosaur's Footprint?

☆ Explain to the children that a typical dinosaur's foot was about 3' in diameter.

☆ Use masking tape to construct a 3' diameter circle on the floor.

☆ Have the children sit inside the resulting "dinosaur footprint" until it is full. *How many children can sit in a dinosaur's footprint?*

How Many?

☆ Provide a tub of water and several measuring utensils, including measuring cups and spoons, larger containers such as plastic liter soda bottles, and funnels.

☆ Let the children experiment to see how many cups of water it takes to fill the larger container or how many tablespoons of water it takes to fill a cup.

Coolest to Warmest

☆ Give the children three glasses of water: one cold, one room temperature, and one warm.

☆ Invite the children to arrange the glasses from the coolest to the warmest temperature.

Temperature Experiment

☆ Fill two plastic glasses with tap water. Ask the children to check each glass to determine that they are the same temperature.

☆ Place one glass in the sun and one glass in the shade.

☆ After a couple of hours, ask the children to feel the two glasses of water. *Are they still the same temperature? Which is cooler? Which is warmer?*

Temperature Indicators

☆ Teach the children strategies for determining what the temperature is outdoors.

☆ Show them how to feel a window pane to determine if it is warm or cool outdoors. Explain that glass gets cold when the weather is cold and warm when the weather is warm. Glass is a *conductor* of both hot and cold conditions.

(continued on the next page)

☆ Teach the children the value of looking out the window to determine the temperature. Ask them to look out a window where other people can be seen, if possible. *What do you think the weather is like if you see people wearing coats? How can you tell if the wind is blowing?*

Time Measurement

Morning and Night

☆ Discuss morning and night with the children. Talk about things they do in the morning and things they do at night.

☆ Invite the children to help make a list of activities for both categories.

☆ Give each child a sheet of paper. Ask them to draw a moon on one side of the paper and a sun on the other side.

☆ Encourage them to draw pictures of things they do during the morning on the sunshine side of their paper and things they do at night on the moon side of their paper.

Daily Schedule

☆ Discuss classroom routines. Print your daily schedule on a large sheet of paper.

☆ Children understand beginning concepts of time in terms of what comes next. Use colored stick-on dots on the daily classroom schedule to indicate what time important parts of the day occur, such as story time, lunch, recess, and dismissal time.

☆ Place corresponding small colored stick-on dots on the class clock.

Yesterday and Tomorrow

☆ Hang a calendar in the room. Talk about the passing of one day to the next.

☆ Talk about things that happened yesterday and things that will be happening tomorrow. Encourage them to share information about yesterday and to think about things that will be doing tomorrow.

November						
Sun	Mon	Tue	Wed	Thu	Fri	Sat
	1	2	3	4	5	6
7	8	9	10	11	12	13
14	15	16	17	18	19	20
21	22	23	24	25	26	27
28	29	30				

Into the Future

☆ Make calendars to mark the days until a special event.

☆ Let the children remove the markers each day and count the days remaining until the upcoming event.

☆ Help build the joy of anticipation. Learning to wait patiently and with increasing expectation and joy is becoming a lost art.

Graphs

Brothers and Sisters

☆ Make a simple graph with one column for "yes" and one column for "no."

☆ Ask the children if they have a brother or sister, and mark the graph in the appropriate column according to their answers.

☆ Count the marks in each column. Ask the children if more classmates have a brother or a sister or don't have a brother or a sister.

My Favorite Juice

☆ Prepare two types of juice and let the children choose which juice they want for snack.

☆ Ask the children which type of juice they chose and let them mark the column on a graph that corresponds to their answers.

Color of the Day

☆ Cut out six 4" squares of construction paper in red, orange, yellow, green, blue, and purple. You will also need small wooden cubes in the six colors.

☆ Place the six colored squares on a table. As the children come into the room, ask them to pick the cube of their favorite color and place it on the matching square of construction paper.

☆ If there is already a cube on their favorite color, then ask them to put their cube on top of that one, as if making a tall building.

☆ After all the children have participated in this activity, discuss which "building" is the tallest (which has the most cubes). The answer is the "color of the day."

Popular Pets

☆ Poll the children about their pets. (You may want to have children with more than one pet limit their contribution to one pet only.)

☆ Tally the results in a simple table. Be sure to include a "no pet" category. For example:

Horse	II	Cat	IIIII II
Fish	III	Dog	IIIII IIII
Mouse	II	Guinea pig	I
Turtle	I	No pet	IIII

More Popular Pets

☆ Give each child a plastic dog, cat, fish, or other pet to represent the pet she has at home. Give children without pets a small plastic basket to represent an empty pet bed.

☆ Write the types of pets on a previously prepared graph form. Ask the children to place their plastic animals or baskets on the graph under the appropriate heading.

☆ Use the graph for counting and comparing activities. *How many children own cats? Dogs? Fish? Do more children own cats than dogs? How many fewer cat owners are there than dog owners? Are there more children with pets or without pets?*

From Pictorial to Symbolic

☆ Many science and social studies projects offer the possibility of a *pictorial* or *symbolic* presentation of data. Following is a simple example developed from a study of peanuts.

☆ Draw peanuts containing one, two, or three kernels on small cards. Make a few of each. Make a chart with three columns: one kernel, two kernels, or three kernels.

☆ Give each child a peanut to open, and have her count the number of kernels inside.

☆ Ask the children to find the card showing a peanut shell with as many kernels as their peanut has. The children then place the card in the column marked with a similar picture.
Safety Note: Check for allergies to peanuts before allowing the children to eat or touch the peanuts. If any of the children are allergic to peanuts, use a material other than peanuts (such as peas in a pod) for the activity.

How Do I Get to School?

☆ Prepare a graph with columns for each type of transportation children may use to travel to school—bus, car, or walking.

☆ Ask the children to place a mark in the column that applies to them.

☆ Evaluate the data with the children. *How many children walk to school? How many children ride the bus? How many ride in a car?*

My Favorite Fruit

☆ Put out a choice of three types of fruit during snack time. Prepare a graph with columns for each type of fruit.

☆ Let the children choose which fruit is their favorite and mark it on the graph.

☆ With the children, evaluate the data. *Which fruit was the most popular? Which was the least popular?*

Let's Vote

☆ Display three CD or audiocassette tape covers.

☆ Give each child a small removable stick-on note.

☆ Encourage the children to vote for the music they want to listen to at center time by placing their stick-on note on the CD or audiocassette cover of choice.

☆ Count votes. The CD or audiocassette with the greatest number of stick-on notes wins.

Fractions

The Same Amount for Everyone

☆ Put out a large chocolate bar and ask the children how it can be divided fairly.

☆ Children will mention the already existing lines.

☆ Break the chocolate bar on the lines and count the number of pieces.

☆ Explain to the children that *fractions* are used to divide things fairly.

Safety Note: Check for allergies and be aware of cultural and religious food limitations when planning any activity that involves children touching or eating food.

What Is a Half?

☆ Tell the children that *one-half* means to divide something into two equal parts.

☆ Illustrate this concept by cutting apples or paper in half, and pouring a full glass of water partially into a second glass so that each glass is half full.

☆ As each item is divided, ask the children one at a time which part they would want. The children should notice that it doesn't matter.

☆ Cut the paper or apple into unequal portions and ask the same question.

The Universal Language—Music and Movement

Brain Fast Facts

☆ Singing increases our oxygen level, which increases our alertness.

☆ Singing increases endorphins in our blood stream. Endorphins act as memory fixatives.

☆ Music, math, and spatial abilities are wired in the same location in the brain.

☆ Dances help children develop an understanding of patterns.

☆ Singing and music and movement activities provide experiences with a variety of patterns, language, meter, tone, and tempo.

Overview

Children develop confidence in their musical abilities, and in themselves, by singing, playing rhythm instruments, moving to music, listening to a variety of music, and being encouraged to experience music from the inside out, internalizing the meter, tempo, beat, and feel of the music. Music is a valuable asset because it provides opportunities to reinforce all areas of the curriculum—literacy, physical development, mathematical skills, social skills, and thinking skills.

Movement activities such as marching, walking, bending, hopping, galloping, swaying, and dancing develop muscles and coordination. Creatively moving like an elephant and a rabbit helps children internalize the differences in the movements of each.

In addition to curriculum support, music provides opportunities for self-expression. Planning time for children to move freely to music allows them to individualize their responses and be creative in their physical movements. The sheer joy of moving to music allows children to experiment with a variety of tempos, rhythms, sound levels, and forms of music.

Music and movement activities can also be used for transitions. Asking children to move in imaginative ways from one area of the classroom to another appeals to their creativity, while also functioning as a method to help them focus on the next activity as opposed to a request for change.

Routine musical cues can be established as transition points throughout the day, such as clean-up time, getting ready for lunch, and other transition times. Using non-verbal directives help children "tune in" to what is expected and view the change as a playful activity.

This chapter is filled with songs, chants, rhymes, games, dances, and creative movements to help develop all aspects of curriculum content and skills important in the lives of preschool children.

Songs

Happy Birthday

☆ When children have a birthday, include musical activities that relate to their years of age.

☆ Have a birthday choir. When a child has his fifth birthday, for example, he selects five people to stand and sing, "Happy Birthday."

☆ Another musical birthday activity is the "cymbal salute." The child tells the class how old he is by "clanging" the correct number with the cymbals.

Variations of Old-Time Favorites

☆ Adapt familiar songs to make them appropriate for your teaching objectives or to individualize them for your classroom.

☆ For example, to practice gross motor skills you might adapt "Here We Go 'Round the Mulberry Bush" to "Touch and Stretch":

Touch and Stretch
This is the way I touch my toes,
Touch my toes, touch my toes.
This is the way I touch my toes,
And that's the way it goes.

☆ Make up additional verses, such as "stretch up high" and "touch the sky."

Different Voices

☆ To let the children hear their voices sound differently, ask them to put their hands over their ears while they sing.
Variation: Ask the children to put a hand, or both hands, up to their mouths and cup their hands while singing.

Sing and Listen

☆ Tape record the children singing.
☆ Replay the song for them to hear.
☆ Add interest by having each child say his name into the recorder before singing the song.

Crescendo

☆ Use word cues as the children sing a song (sing softly, sing a little louder, and so on). Lead them through a song, singing from very softly to softly to moderately loud to loud.
☆ Using the same cues, lead them back down from loud to soft.
☆ Reinforce word clues with facial expressions and by widening or diminishing space between your hands.

Do As I Do

☆ Play singing games that allow individual interpretation and opportunities to lead, such as "Did You Ever See a Lassie?"

Did You Ever See a Lassie?
Did you ever see a lassie, a lassie, a lassie,
Did you ever see a lassie go this way and that?
Go this way and that way, and that way and this way,
Did you ever see a lassie go this way and that?

☆ Invite the children to take turns demonstrating a movement, such as patting their head, jumping, and bending. The group follows with the same action.

Circle Songs

☆ Ask the children to form a circle and move in a circular fashion around the room while singing a favorite song.
☆ After a while, stop the music and have the children change the direction of their circle.
Variation: Use two circles of children, one smaller circle inside a larger circle. Or use several smaller circles of four to five children all singing and moving at the same time.

Roofs and Windows

☆ Ask the children to pick partners and form a double circle. The partners make "roof peaks" by facing each other and holding up joined hands.

☆ Choose one child at a time to go under all the "raised roofs" (under the arms). The child walks or skips under the raised pairs of arms while the children sing the following song.

☆ When the music stops, the child stands still and the pair of children lower their arms and enclose him. The child picks another child to walk under the arms.

☆ Use the following song, "Go In and Out the Windows" with this activity.

Go In and Out the Windows
Go under the raised arms. (child walks around circle, weaving in and out underneath the arms)
Go under the raised arms,
Go under the raised arms
As we have done before.
(The children form a single circle, hold hands, and raise their arms.)
Go in and out the windows. (child walks around circle, weaving in and out between children)
Go in and out the windows,
Go in and out the windows,
As we have done before.

Additional verses:
Stand and face your partner…(child chooses a partner)
Now follow her/him to London… (child and partner weave through circle)
Bow before you leave her/him… (child leaves partner [new IT] and joins circle)

Hummin'

☆ Use a tape recorder to record the children humming a variety of familiar songs.

☆ Play the songs back for the children to identify.

☆ Encourage the children to begin singing the words as they identify the familiar melody.

"If You're Happy and You Know It" Variations

☆ Customize the lyrics to fit your needs.

☆ Invite the children to sing "If You're Happy and You Know It."

☆ After the children sing the first verse change the lyrics to one of the suggestions below or to one of your own creation:

If you're happy and you know it point to something red…
If you're happy and you know it point to a friend…
If you're happy and you know it point to your ear…

☆ Continue singing new verses. Make them up to fit your curriculum or the personality of the children in your class.

"Itsy Bitsy Spider" Variations

☆ Sing "Itsy Bitsy Spider" and change the movements from fine motor to gross motor.

☆ Ask the children to stand and move like spiders as they sing.

☆ Make sure to teach the lesson that goes with this song: persistence and determination.

"Twinkle, Twinkle, Little Star" Variations

☆ Sing "Twinkle, Twinkle Little Star."

☆ As you sing the song change the description of the star from "little" to "gigantic" and adjust your voice to reflect the difference in the size of the star.

☆ Sing the song again, changing the description again. Sing about a "silent" star, "tiny" star, and "blinking" star.

☆ Encourage the children to name other kinds of stars they want to sing about.

Singing Discussions

☆ Try having "singing discussions." Ask questions in a singing voice and encourage the children to answer in a singing voice. Any tune will do. *What did you learn today?*

Chants

Who Took the Cookie?

☆ Play the rhythmic chanting game, "Who Took the Cookie From the Cookie Jar?"

Who Took the Cookie From the Cookie Jar?
Who took the cookie from the cookie jar?
(Name) *took the cookies from the cookie jar.*
Who, me?
Yes, you.
Couldn't be.
Then who?
(Different child, chosen by first child accused) *stole the cookie from the cookie jar.*
Who, me?
Yes, you.
Couldn't be.
Then who?

☆ Pat your thighs and snap in a rhythmic motion as you say the chant.

☆ Continue until everyone has been accused. End by accusing the cookie monster.

The Instant Curriculum

Giant Stomp

☆ Invite the children to do the "The Giant Stomp." This is a great activity to do as an extension to a story about a giant, such as "Jack and the Beanstalk," *David's Father* by Robert Munsch, or *Abiyoyo* by Pete Seeger.

The Giant Stomp
"Fee, Fi, Fo, Fum," said the giant.
"Fee, Fi, Fo, Fum," said the giant.
"Fee, Fi, Fo, Fum," said the giant.
"Fee, Fi, Fo, Fum." (stomp, stomp)

"I smell the feet of an Englishman!" (repeat two times)
Said the big, tall giant. (sniff, sniff)
"Be he here or be he there, (shrug shoulders, repeat two times)
I'll find him anywhere!" (stomp, stomp)

☆ This chant and movement activity is also a great reinforcement for the concept of *large* and *small*. For contrast, you may want to have the children do the following song, "The Flight of the Fairies."

"The Flight of the Fairies"

☆ Invite the children to dance to "The Flight of the Fairies." This is a good follow-up activity to any stories that include fairies or wishes.

The Flight of the Fairies
"Tweedli-reedily-ree," whispers the fairy with glee.
   (sway left and right)
"Tweedli-reedily-dee," responds her sisters three.
   (sway with hands over head)
"Tweedli-reedily-di," they all say with a sigh. (gracefully curtsy)
"We do so love to fly." (pretend to fly)

Swirl and twirl and swish (turn twice)
We're here to grant a wish. (curtsy)

Swirl and twirl and swish (turn twice)
Please tell us what you wish. (hold hands to ears)
(children close their eyes and make a silent wish)

"Oni Woni"

☆ Teach the children the following action chant "Oni Woni."

Oni Woni
Oni Woni Woni, Wah Wah.
Oni Woni Woni, Wah Wah.
Eye Eye Eye yippee Eye Eye.
Eye Eye Eye yippee Eye Eye.
Eye Eye.
Eye Eye.

☆ The hand movements are: tap your own knees, then the knees of the person to your right, then your own knees, then the person to your left, and continue from the beginning.

☆ Have the children say the chant several times before adding the hand motions. You may want to just have them tap the knees of the child on their right. After they are comfortable with this move, you can teach them to alternate right and left knee taps.

Creative Movement

Giants and Elves

☆ Beat a drum loudly and then softly while children walk around the room.

☆ Encourage the children to tiptoe like elves to soft music, and walk like giants to loud music.

Olympic Streamers

☆ Roll newspaper into a 6" long tube and tape in place.

☆ Tape a long, thin strip of crepe paper to the end to make a "wand."

☆ Play music and encourage the children to make circles and other figures with the streamers as they move rhythmically around the room.

The Instant Curriculum

Preschool Fitness

☆ Put on lively music and have the children do a variety of large muscle exercises, such as marching, reaching, flapping their arms, and bowing.

Around the Chairs

☆ Place a line of chairs in the center of the room.
☆ Put on music and invite the children to move around the chairs in different ways, such as walking, hopping, skating, galloping, or skipping (if appropriate for the group).

Butterfly Wings

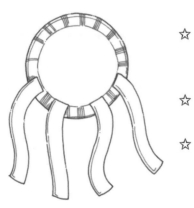

☆ Tape four or five 10" streamers to the edge of a paper plate. Make two for each child.
☆ Ask the children to hold one plate in each hand.
☆ Play music and encourage the children to move around the room, fluttering their "wings."

Cool Music

☆ Teach the children how to make a fan by pleating an 8 ½" x 11" piece of paper. Bring pleats together at the bottom of the paper to form a handle, and spread out the top part.
☆ After making the fans, put on music and let children fan to the rhythm of the music being played.
☆ Encourage them to fan each other, fan their feet, fan their face, and fan you.

Circles to Music

☆ Provide each child with paper and crayons.

☆ Play music.

☆ Ask the children to make circles on their paper to the rhythm of the music. Intermittently stop the music and ask the children to change to another color of crayon.

☆ The children will create a design of colorful circles, with a variety of interpretations.

Friendship Circles

☆ Spread a long (10' to 15') sheet of butcher paper on the floor.

☆ Have the children sit on both sides of the paper, each facing another child. Provide a variety of crayons for each child.

☆ Play slow music. Tell the children to make big, slow circles to the music with their crayons.

☆ Change the tempo by playing faster music and have them color faster.

Note: Since two children will be using the same general space to color on the paper, they will have an interesting problem-solving situation. They can synchronize their circular movements, or they can adapt their coloring movements to a smaller space.

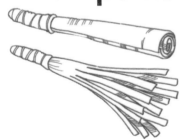

Pompoms

☆ Prepare pompoms by rolling half sheets of newspaper into stick shapes. Tape the bottom half to form a handle and cut the top half into strips.

☆ Play music with varying rhythms from marches to waltzes.

☆ Encourage the children to "swish" their pompoms as they move to the rhythm of the music.

Freckles and Stripes

☆ Provide each child with a variety of crayons and paper.

☆ Play music with a fast tempo and have children make dots on their paper in time with the music.

☆ Play music with a slow tempo and have them make stripes with the sides of their crayons.

☆ Continue by playing both types of music, having children listen and decide whether it's freckle or stripe music before they use their crayons.

Hi-Low

☆ Play a xylophone and encourage the children to respond descriptively with their bodies to the pitch of the music.

☆ They can put their arms up for high notes, and their arms down to their ankles for low notes.

☆ They can stand up for high notes and sit down for low notes.

☆ Have them walk on tiptoes to your continuous playing of high notes, and bend over for your continuous playing of low notes.

Ball Roll

☆ Place the children in two rows about 4' apart.

☆ Let them roll a ball back and forth between the rows as they sing a favorite song.

"Hey! My Name Is Joe"

☆ Teach the children the following movement chant, "Hey! My Name Is Joe."

Hey! My Name Is Joe
Hey, my name is Joe
And I work in a button factory.
I've got a wife and a dog and a family,
One day the boss came up to me and said,
"Hey Joe, are you busy?" I said, "No."
He said, "Turn the button with your _____
    (left hand, right hand, left foot, right foot, head)
Hey, my name is Joe
And I work in a button factory.
I've got a wife and a dog and a family,
One day the boss came up to me and said,
"Hey Joe, are you busy?" I said, "YES!"

"Tooty-Ta"

☆ Teach the children the following action chant, "Tooty Ta." Suit the actions to the words.

Tooty Ta

Tooty ta, tooty ta, tooty ta, ta.
Thumbs up.

Tooty ta, tooty ta, tooty ta, ta.
Elbows back.

Tooty ta, tooty ta, tooty ta, ta.
Feet apart.

Tooty ta, tooty ta, tooty ta, ta.
Knees together.

Tooty ta, tooty ta, tooty ta, ta.
Bottoms up.

Tooty ta, tooty ta, tooty ta, ta.
Tongue out.

Tooty ta, tooty ta, tooty ta, ta.
Eyes shut.

Tooty ta, tooty ta, tooty ta, ta.
Turn around.
Tooty ta, tooty ta, tooty ta, ta.

☆ Change beginning consonants to any letter, depending on your needs ("tooty ta" can be "mooty ma," for example). Change the letters from time to time. This is a great phonological awareness activity.

"Metamorphosis"

☆ Teach the children the following action rhyme, "Metamorphosis."

Metamorphosis
I'm an egg (curl up in fetal position)
I'm an egg
I'm an egg, egg, egg!

I'm a worm (open up and wiggle on the ground)
I'm a worm
I'm a wiggly, humpty worm!

I'm a cocoon (curl up in a fetal position with hands over the face)
I'm a cocoon,
I'm a round and silk cocoon!

I'm a butterfly (stand and fly around using arms for wings)
I'm a butterfly
I'm a grand and glorious butterfly!

The Instant Curriculum

Moving Freely

Deejay for the Day

- ☆ Have the children take turns bringing in their favorite CD or tape from home.
- ☆ Invite the child to be the "Deejay" for the day. Let him lead the children in moving freely in response to the music.

On Stage

- ☆ Use masking tape to define an area that can serve as a stage.
- ☆ Ask the children to sit in front of the stage like an audience at a concert.
- ☆ Invite four to five children to come on "stage" and put on a show while music is played. They can move to the music, sing, or play rhythm band instruments as a back-up band.
- ☆ When the first group has finished, invite another group to perform.
- ☆ Props such as microphones, guitars, and costumes add to the fun.

Music Makers

Tabletop Band

- ☆ Provide children with several objects, such as pencils, straws, and newspaper pompoms (see "Pompoms" on page 182 in this chapter). Encourage them to tap the objects on a table in rhythmic response to music.
- ☆ For the children to experience the variety of sounds made by the different "instruments," first ask them to tap only pencils, then straws, and finally, pompoms. If desired, you can even ask them to play their fingertips!
- ☆ For the *finale* (end of song), let the children choose their instrument and everyone plays together.

Leader of the Band

☆ Let the children take turns leading a class rhythm band. Encourage them to march around the room to music.

☆ To make a "baton" for the leader to use, provide a rhythm stick or rolled-up newspaper.

☆ If desired, provide a smaller "baton" such as a coat-hanger tube for children to lead a seated rhythm band.

Bottle Maracas

☆ Make a maraca by placing coarse sand or gravel in an empty, clear plastic shampoo or detergent bottle. Glue the lid on for safety.

☆ Invite the children to use the maracas along with other rhythm band instruments.

Drum and Sticks

☆ Use an empty gallon can with a plastic lid for a simple drum. Encourage the children to tap it with the eraser end of a pencil or with a stick that has a ball of cloth tied on the end.

☆ Make rhythm sticks for children by cutting dowel sticks into 10" to 12" lengths or use wooden kitchen spoons or coat-hanger tubes.

☆ Invite the children to play the sticks by tapping them on the floor or table or by tapping the sticks together.

Body Rhythms

☆ Create a rhythm by playing a drum.

☆ Encourage the children to pick up the rhythm by "playing the table" with cupped hands.

☆ Other children can respond rhythmically by clapping hands, slapping thighs, stomping feet, clicking tongues, or snapping fingers.

Bottle Band

☆ Give each child a clean, empty, ½ liter plastic bottle. Demonstrate how to blow in the bottle to create a sound.

☆ Play some music and invite the "bottle band" to play along.

Homemade Music Makers

☆ Encourage the children to choose an instrument from a box of homemade music makers, such as empty paper towel tubes for horns, pan lids for cymbals, rubber bands around empty cereal boxes for guitars, gravel in empty chip cans for maracas, and empty coffee cans with plastic lids for drums.

☆ Play some background music and invite the children to play along.

Dances

Scarf Dancing

☆ Provide each child with a scarf or long piece of lightweight cloth.

☆ Play music.

☆ Encourage the children to wave their scarves to the rhythm of the music and move to the music.

☆ If scarves or cloth are not available, use crepe paper streamers.

Paper Plate Flying

☆ Provide each child with two paper or plastic plates.

☆ Play some "flying" music (many classical music pieces are suitable, or use "Flight of the Bumblebee").

☆ Encourage the children to wave their plates to the rhythm of the music and pretend to fly. They can pretend to be birds, bumblebees, fairies, fireflies, or airplanes.

Shadow Dancing

☆ Place a sheet on the wall or use a movie screen.

☆ Create a light source by using a high intensity lamp or projector light.

☆ While playing music, invite the children to take turns dancing creatively in front of the light source.

☆ Challenge the children to make animal shadows, scary shadows, and funny shadows.

Preschool Limbo

☆ Stretch a broomstick across two chairs.

☆ Play some music with a limbo or Caribbean melody.

☆ Encourage the children to move rhythmically around the room in a line, taking turns going under the broomstick.

☆ Children should bend forward, instead of backward, for safety.

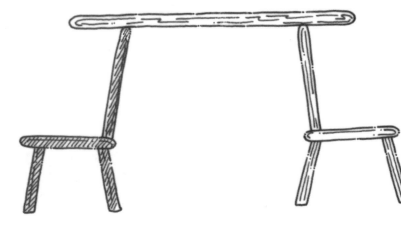

Swish and Sway

☆ Provide each child with a "grass" skirt made from newspaper.

☆ Make a "grass" skirt by cutting whole sheets of newspaper into strips, leaving a waistband at the top. Tape the skirt together at each child's waist with masking tape.

☆ Play some tropical/Hawaiian music.

☆ With your back to the children, show them how to do the dance. Move both arms to the right at shoulder height while side-stepping with feet in the same direction. Hands and arms make slight wave-type motions, hips sway in the same direction.

☆ Repeat arm, feet, and hip movement to the left.

☆ Continue alternating left and right, several steps each way.

☆ Emphasize the "swishing" of the skirts, and encourage the children to say "swish, swish, swish" as they dance. **Note:** The hula dance is a traditional Hawaiian dance, an important part of the Hawaiian culture. While Hawaiians are familiar with the hula, not every Hawaiian person dances the hula.

Pick Your Partner

☆ Let the children choose a partner. Arrange them in parallel lines with partners facing each other. Use masking tape to designate lines.

☆ Invite the children to follow these simple steps:

"Bow to your partner." (Partners bow.)

"Swing your partner." (Partners lock arms and spin around twice.)

"Do-si-do." (Partners fold arms across their chest and "back" around their partner.)

"Promenade." (Partners hold hands, right and left hands together, and walk.)

Dance, Thumbkin, Dance

☆ Teach the children the following finger dance, "Dance, Thumbkin, Dance."

Dance, Thumbin, Dance

Dance, ye merrymen, everyone. (dance all fingers)

For Thumbkin, he can dance alone,

Thumbkin, he can dance alone.

Dance, Foreman, dance: (dance index finger around, moving and bending)

Dance, ye merrymen, everyone. (dance all fingers)

For Foreman, he can dance alone,

Foreman, he can dance alone.

Dance, Longman, dance: (dance middle finger around, moving and bending)

Dance, ye merrymen, everyone. (dance all fingers)

For Longman, he can dance alone,

Longman, he can dance alone.

(continued on the next page)

Dance, Ringman, dance: (dance ring finger around- he won't bend alone)

Dance, ye merrymen, everyone. (dance all fingers)

For Ringman, he cannot dance alone,

Ringman, he cannot dance alone.

Dance, Littleman, dance: (dance little finger around, moving and bending)

Dance, ye merrymen, everyone. (dance all fingers)

For Littleman, he can dance alone,

Littleman, he can dance alone.

Games

Musical Beanbags

☆ Give each child a beanbag.

☆ Play music and invite the children to move around the room with the beanbag on their head, on their shoulder, or on their elbow.

☆ When the music stops, the children "freeze," holding the position they are in until the music resumes.

Variation: Play the game again, but have the children close their eyes. What happens to the speed of the game?

Pass the Beanbag

☆ Seat children in a circle.

☆ Provide a beanbag for the children to pass around.

☆ As you beat a drum, ask the children to pass the beanbag to the tempo of the music. Alternate between slow and fast music.

☆ When the music stops, the child who has the beanbag stands and takes a bow.

Freeze

☆ Play music and invite the children to dance freely.

☆ Tell the children that when the music stops, they should "freeze" in place.

☆ Start the music again and the children dance again.

The Instant Curriculum

Who's That Traipsing on My Bridge?

- ☆ Make a bridge with blocks or butcher paper.
- ☆ Select a child to be the "troll." The troll sits by the bridge with his eyes closed.
- ☆ Select a child to walk over the bridge. The child says, "Trip-trap, trip-trap," and walks across the bridge as you beat the rhythm on a drum.
- ☆ The troll say "Who's that traipsing on my bridge? Get off, get off, get off, I say."
- ☆ The child who is crossing the bridge answers back, "It is only I."
- ☆ The troll tries to guess the name of the trespasser. If he is able to name the trespasser within three guesses, the trespasser becomes the troll and the troll returns to the group. If the troll cannot guess correctly, he must play the troll again.
- ☆ When the children are able to identify their classmate's voices, encourage them to disguise their voices.

Cooperative Musical Chairs

- ☆ Play a game of Cooperative Musical Chairs. This game is a variation of Musical Chairs.
- ☆ Make a circle on the floor with masking tape.
- ☆ Play music. Encourage the children to walk around the circle until the music stops. When the music stops, everyone steps into the circle.
- ☆ The idea is for all the children to get inside the circle so everyone wins. Continue playing for as long as the children are interested.

Snack Pass

- ☆ Provide a straw for each child and any snack that has a good-size hole in the center, such as crackers, pretzels, and "O"-shaped cereal.
- ☆ Play some music and have the children stand in a circle and pass one of the snacks around using only the straw to pass and receive. No hands allowed.

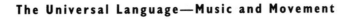

Hopscotch

☆ Draw a hopscotch pattern with chalk or make one with masking tape.

☆ Give each child a beanbag.

☆ The children toss the beanbag into a different box each turn, following the numerical sequence, and hop through the pattern without stepping into the box with the beanbag.

☆ The first child to complete the sequence is the winner.

☆ For young children, just making it through is winning. If children don't know how to hop they can jump on the squares.

Variation: Make triangles or circles instead of squares for the hopscotch board.

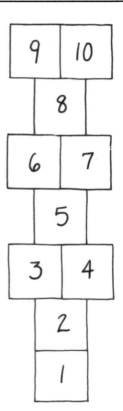

Paper Chase

☆ Give each child a sheet of newspaper or tissue and have him wad it into a ball.

☆ Challenge them to toss the paper balls into the air and keep them aloft using their hands, head, knees, and other body parts.

Inchworm Race

☆ Demonstrate for the children how an inchworm moves. Even better, let an inchworm do its own demonstration.

☆ Use masking tape to create a start line and a finish line about 12' apart.

☆ Have the children select a partner and race from the start line to the finish line moving like an inchworm. Play slow music for this activity.

Building Muscle Mastery— Physical Development

Overview

Physical development encompasses both fine motor and gross motor activities. In early childhood, it is equally important to both cognitive development and social-emotional development. As children explore physical space, they begin to understand how their bodies function in space. They become more skilled and expressive in their movements from one point in space to another through running, hopping, jumping, twisting, turning, tumbling, and skipping.

Fine Motor: Fine motor activities develop the small muscles of the hand and enable children to develop competence in manipulating materials in their environment and, ultimately, to master the skill of writing in the primary school years.

Materials, equipment, and activities that require the child to manipulate with her fingers and hands, make precise movements, and use dexterity will develop the small muscles of the hand. Puzzles, string beads, interlocking toys, and playdough are examples of these materials. All cutting, coloring, drawing, and folding activities contribute to competence in this area. Cleaning tables with sponges, playing with sand, folding napkins, buttoning coats, and lacing shoes are routine activities that also contribute to fine motor development.

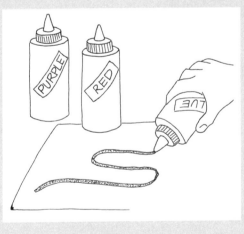

Gross Motor: Gross motor activities develop the large muscles of the body, the arms, legs, and torso, and enable children to develop mastery of body movements. Children's self-esteem increases as they develop mastery over their bodies. Early experiences with gross

Brain Fast Facts

☆ Motor development is wired during the first two years of life and refined between ages three and five. This means that children need plenty of freedom and plenty of room to move during the first five years of life. This is when they are best able to perfect their coordination, balance, and control of body muscles.

☆ Practicing a specific skill such as catching a ball or holding a crayon makes a big difference in later performance.

☆ Movement awakens and activates the brain. Movement provides sensory stimulation and feeds the brain information. It helps the brain focus more clearly on what is being learned. In turn, our movements help us express our knowledge. It both initiates and supports mental processes.

motor activities lay a foundation for a lifetime commitment to physical fitness.

In order to develop their large muscles, children need balls to throw, ropes to jump and climb, tricycles to ride, wagons to pull, as well as swings, slides, and climbing apparatus. Activities like marching, scarf waving, bending, bowing, and dancing all contribute to the development of the whole body. The playground is a major component of the gross motor development program, providing space for children to run and play.

A playground with space and equipment and a classroom with developmentally appropriate materials will provide the setting for children to develop fine and gross motor skills. This chapter describes activities that encourage the development of children's mastery of their bodies. Through movement of the body and manipulation of materials children are also learning spatial concepts and developing hand-eye coordination. Fine and gross motor skill development is a critical component of the early childhood curriculum.

Gross Motor

Obstacle Course

☆ Arrange an obstacle course in the room that includes a "tightrope" to walk across (a tape line), a table to crawl under, chairs to crawl around, a book to jump over, and a box to crawl through.

☆ Following the leader, children walk, crawl, and jump through the course. This is a good activity for a rainy day.

Big Steps, Giant Steps

☆ Have the children walk the perimeter of the playground taking baby steps and then giant steps. *Which steps get you around the playground in the least amount of time? Which steps are the most fun to take?*

Variation: Have the children walk around the playground backwards.

Home Connection: Suggest that children count the baby steps from their bedroom to the bathroom at home.

Hula Hoop Toss

☆ Tape a hula hoop between two adult-sized chairs or hang from the ceiling.

☆ Let the children take turns throwing beanbags, stocking balls, or paper balls through the hoop. (See "Homemade Balls" on page 197 in this chapter.)

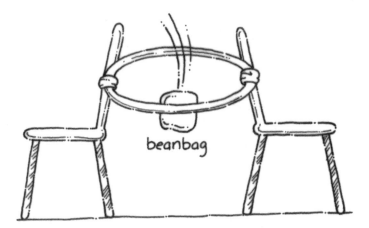

beanbag

Musical Cues

☆ Teach the children how to skip and gallop. Use "skipping music" to skip and "galloping music" to gallop.

☆ Tape record segments of the two different types of music (for example, "Skip to My Lou" and a cowboy song). Alternate the skipping and galloping music. When the tape is played, children will change from skipping to galloping, and vice versa, as the musical cues change.

Mirror Reflections

☆ Have the children select a partner and stand facing each other.

☆ One child moves very slowly and the second child copies the movement.

☆ Encourage them to use a variety of arm, leg, and face movements.

Amazing Mazes

☆ Create a maze out of classroom items by moving tables and chairs and adding blocks and other classroom materials.

☆ Invite the children to go through the maze on their hands and knees, trying not to touch anything.

Blanket Toss

☆ Invite several children to hold the sides of a blanket (or tablecloth or sheet).

☆ Have them try to move a ball on the blanket without dropping it on the floor.

☆ As they become skilled at working together they can wave the sheet to toss the ball in the air and catch it again.

☆ Add music, if desired.

Homemade Balls

☆ Use masking tape to create two lines on the floor, 4' to 6' apart.

☆ Make balls by wadding up sheets of paper or stuffing pantyhose.

☆ To make stocking balls, begin rolling stockings down from waists. Gather the right leg of the stocking into a ball and then roll into the left leg. Turn the cut toe of the left leg back over the rolled up ball and stitch the ends together.

☆ Encourage the children to stand behind one line and toss the balls over the second line into a bucket or basket.

☆ Children can count their successes and tally them, if desired.

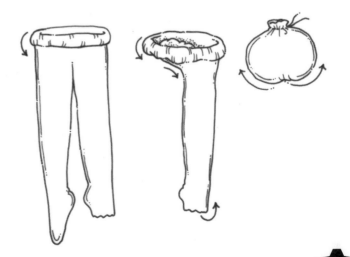

Basket Balance

☆ Display pictures of individuals carrying heavy loads on their heads.
☆ Provide baskets for children to try balancing on their heads.
☆ Use safe, lightweight objects (such as rolled-up socks or wadded paper) to load the baskets.

Walk a Crooked Line

☆ Use masking tape to create a crooked line on the floor. You can use either a wavy line or a zigzag line. You may want to alternate the type of line each time you use this activity.
☆ Encourage the children to walk the line. Ask them to walk the line using baby steps, and then walk backwards.
☆ Provide a beanbag and have them walk the line with a beanbag on their head.

Duck Waddles

☆ Cut out "duck footprints" from orange construction paper and lay them in a trail across the classroom floor.
☆ Encourage the children to waddle like ducks along the trail. *Is it easier to waddle or to walk?*

Spider Walk

☆ Invite the children to walk like a spider by bending at the waist, putting their hands on the floor, and walking using both hands and feet.
☆ Talk with the children about how many legs they are using when walking on both hands and feet. Point out that is more difficult than walking on just two legs.
☆ Ask the children how they think the spiders control all eight of their legs at one time.
☆ When the children become skilled walking like this independently, teach them to walk with a group of three friends. Have a group of four children stand back to back and lock their elbows. Then have the group of four walk in a designated direction. *How difficult is this task? Why?*

 The Instant Curriculum

Back-to-Back Lifts

☆ Ask the children to choose a partner.

☆ Instruct partners to sit back to back on the floor.

☆ On the count of three the partners help each other stand by keeping their backs together and pushing against each other.

☆ Try the activity again. This time have the partners interlock their arms.

☆ Try the activity both ways several times. *Which is easier? Why?*

Tunnels

☆ Collect several cardboard boxes in graduated sizes. The boxes need to be large enough for children to crawl through.

☆ Cut off the sides of each of the boxes to create a tunnel.

☆ Invite the children to crawl through the tunnel.

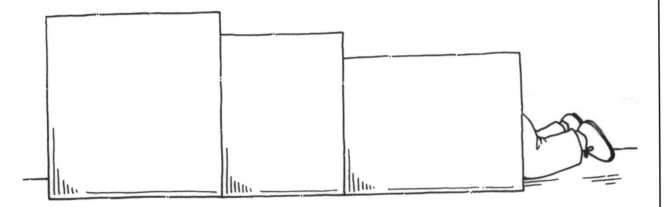

Broad Jumps

☆ Use masking tape to create a start line on the floor.

☆ Have the children take a running start and then jump from the line as far out as they can.

☆ Mark their jump with a piece of tape with their name on it.

☆ Encourage the children to take several turns, trying each time to out jump their last jump.

Home Connection: Suggest that children challenge a family member to a contest of "Who Can Jump the Longest Distance." Be sure to ask the children about the contest later. *Who won?*

Ring That Bell

☆ Use masking tape to create a throw line. Place a service bell approximately 4' from the line.

☆ Give each child a beanbag. Encourage them to toss the beanbag and hit the bell.

☆ When children become proficient at the 4' distance, move the bell to a distance a little further away from the start line.

☆ Ask the children to try throwing both underhand and overhand. *Which type of throw is easier? Which type of throw is more accurate for you?*

Home Connection: Encourage the children to watch for businesses that use service bells while running errands with their family. In a few days, remember to ask children if they have seen service bells anywhere. *What kind of a business needs a bell? How is it used?*

Shovel Pickup

☆ Place plastic eggs or ping-pong balls around the classroom. Give the children a shovel and bucket and challenge them to pick up the balls.

☆ When children become proficient at picking up the eggs or balls, change the item they pick up. You might try Styrofoam chips or small blocks.

Indoor Croquet

☆ Cut both ends off several coffee cans or round boxes, such as an oatmeal box.

☆ Place the cans or boxes on their sides around the room. Number the cans to designate a sequence, if you wish. Provide ping-pong balls and cardboard tubes.

☆ Challenge the children to hit the balls through the cans in random or sequential order.

Log Rollers

☆ Place two 12' strips of masking tape on the floor parallel to each other and about 5' apart.

☆ Have the children lie on the floor between the two lines and roll from one end to the other without rolling outside the lines. *What makes this a difficult thing to do?*

"The Little Ants"

☆ Teach the children "The Little Ants" (sung to the tune of "This Old Man").

☆ It allows children to practice marching, hopping, dancing, spinning, and waving—all important gross motor tasks.

The Little Ants

Little ants marching by,
In a line that's mighty long,
With a hip, hop, happy, hi
Won't you join my song?
Little ants are marching on.

Little ants hopping high,
In a line that's mighty long,
With a hip, hop, happy, hi
Won't you join my song?
Little ants are hopping on.

Little ants dancing by,
In a line that's mighty long,
With a hip, hop, happy, hi
Won't you join my song?
Little ants are dancing on.

Little ants spinning by,
In a line that's mighty long,
With a hip, hop, happy, hi
Won't you join my song?
Little ants are spinning on.

Little ants sneaking by,
In a line that's mighty long,
With a hip, hop, happy, hi
Won't you join my song?
Little ants are sneaking on.

Little ants waving "bye,"
In a line that's mighty long,
With a hip, hop, happy, hi
Won't you join my song?
Little ants are waving "bye."

Fine Motor

Bubbles in My Hand

☆ Provide a tub of soapy water. Use liquid detergent to create the suds.

☆ Teach the children how to soap their hands, touch their index finger to their thumb, and blow bubbles through the resulting hole.

Balls and Cups

☆ Provide the children with playdough (see pages 46-47 for recipes) and a bathtub mat with suction cups.

☆ Challenge the children to make small balls of playdough and place one on each suction cup.

Catch Me If You Can

☆ Blow bubbles (see page 43 for bubble solution recipe).

☆ Challenge the children to "catch" the bubbles with their hands.

Liquid Movers

☆ Give the children a tub of water and a variety of objects that pick up water, such as basters, syringes, and eyedroppers.

☆ Encourage the children to experiment with each item. Help them use tally marks to record how many times each item must be used to fill an 8-ounce cup.

Wire Creations

☆ Give children pipe cleaners.

☆ Invite them to twist the pipe cleaners into any shape they desire.

☆ Let each child describe her creations to her friends.

Note: Wires can be placed in a small amount of modeling clay to make the sculptures freestanding.

Easy Cutouts

☆ Cut out pages from a magazine, a few for each child. Circle some items on each page.

☆ Give each child several pages.

☆ Invite the children to cut out the items by cutting around the circles you have drawn. This is easier and less frustrating than cutting around intricate details.

Nut Sorting

☆ Provide children with tongs, a muffin tin, and several types of nuts in shells, such as pecans, walnuts, and almonds.

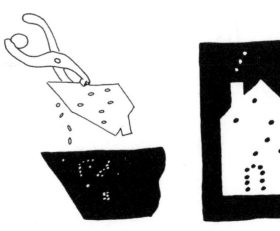

☆ Challenge the children to pick up nuts with the tongs and transfer them to the muffin tin.

Seed Sorting

☆ Provide children with tweezers, a muffin tin, and several types of seeds, such as pumpkin, popcorn, and apple.

☆ Have the children pick up seeds with tweezers and sort into the muffin tin.

Colorful Confetti

☆ Provide the children with half sheets of a variety of colors of construction paper.

☆ Encourage them to punch holes in the paper with hole punchers to make confetti.

Note: Save confetti for art projects.

Clay Letters

☆ Fill an old cookie sheet with a thin layer of modeling clay.

☆ Let the children use a pencil or stick to draw letters or designs in the clay.

☆ When the designs are complete, the children can use their fingers to press the letters or designs out of the clay.

Shaving Cream Designs

☆ Spray a tabletop with shaving cream.

☆ Invite the children to write their names or create designs in the shaving cream, directly on the tabletop.

Tracing Fun

☆ Provide line drawings from coloring books.

☆ Cover drawings with tracing paper, using a paper clip to secure the paper.

☆ Provide large pencils or crayons and encourage the children to trace the drawings.

Tracing Lids

☆ Provide a variety of sizes of plastic lids for the children to trace around with crayons.

☆ Cut geometric shapes into some of the lids an X-acto knife (adult only).

☆ Encourage the children to place the lids on background paper and use crayons to trace the shape inside the lid.

Cookie Cutter Tracing

☆ Provide a variety of cookie cutters for the children to trace around with crayons.

☆ Invite them to add other designs to traced shapes.

Cups of Color

☆ Fill all the cups of a six-cup (or twelve-cup for more variety) muffin tin halfway with water.

☆ Place red, blue, green, and yellow food coloring into four of the muffin cups of water.

☆ Provide eyedroppers and encourage the children to transfer colored water to other muffin cups, thus creating different shades of color.

☆ By combining colors, children can create new colors.

Little Ships

☆ Provide a pan of water, tongs (or meatball press), and a bowl of Styrofoam chips.

☆ Encourage the children to transfer Styrofoam chips from the bowl to the pan of water.

☆ If a water table is available, let several children use tongs to "float chip ships."

Greeting Card Puzzles

☆ Collect used greeting cards.

☆ Make puzzles by cutting the cards in halves, thirds, or fourths, depending on the developmental level of the class.

☆ Let the children work the puzzles.

Home Connection: Have the children paste their card puzzles onto a piece of construction paper and take them home as a personal greeting to share with their family.

Water Transfer

☆ Provide an eyedropper, a cup of water, and a shallow pan or bowl with a sponge in it.

☆ Invite the children to use the eyedropper to remove water from the cup and drop it onto the sponge.

☆ When all the water has been transferred, have the children press the sponge to release the water. They can then use the eyedropper to pick up the water and return it to the cup.

Button Transfer

☆ Cut nickel-size holes into the plastic lid of a margarine tub. Place the lid back on the tub.

☆ Provide tweezers and a container of buttons.

☆ Challenge the children to use the tweezers to transfer the buttons from a cup to the tub.

Torn Paper Creations

☆ Stimulate the children's imaginations by providing a variety of torn paper shapes.

☆ Encourage the children to express what they see—there are no wrong answers!

☆ Invite the children to tear paper into their own designs and use crayons to add details. They can glue their torn paper designs to a background, if desired.

☆ Read *It Looked Like Spilt Milk* by Charles Green Shaw as an introduction to torn paper shapes or as an extension of the activity.

Paper Folding

☆ Demonstrate how to fold paper into a "fan." Regular (9" x 12") construction paper makes a great fan.

☆ Provide paper and encourage the children to fold their own fans by pleating their paper.

☆ As an alternative, give children 1" x 12" strips of green construction paper. Show them how to pleat the strips to make "worms."

Grass Tug of War

☆ Let each child pick a blade of grass and select a friend to be a partner.

☆ Show the children how to loop their pieces of grass through their partner's grass and then pull until one piece of the grass breaks.

The Instant Curriculum

Weaving Variations

☆ Following are several variations of ways to offer weaving activities.

☆ Provide plastic woven laundry baskets and crepe paper streamers. Encourage the children to weave the crepe paper through the holes in the basket.

☆ Take the children on a nature walk to find a small branch that has a fork at one end. Help the children wrap yarn back and forth between the two forked pieces of the branch to create a weaving loom. Provide lace, ribbon, and rickrack to weave through the "nature loom."

☆ Let the children weave crepe paper streamers through the links on a chain link fence.

Home Connection: Suggest that children look for woven items at home. Ask them (with permission) to bring one of the items they find to class to share with the other children.

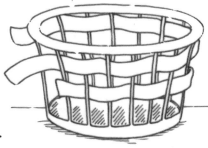

Shadow Puppets

☆ Provide a light source, such as an overhead projector, strong flashlight, or lamp.

☆ Show the children how to make shadow puppets with their hands, using their fingers to make a variety of shapes.

☆ Encourage the children to move their hands to make different shapes.

Home Connection: Have children teach a family member to make a shadow puppet.

Finger Puppets

☆ Make finger puppets for the children to use. You can often use coloring book characters to create finger puppets by removing the legs and cutting holes for children to insert their fingers.

☆ Encourage the children to make their puppets "dance."

Me Puzzles

☆ Take pictures of the children or ask them to bring pictures from home. Make enlarged copies of the photos.

☆ Glue the photos to cardstock and laminate.

☆ Cut the pictures into puzzle pieces.

☆ Invite the children to work their puzzles. Have them exchange puzzles with a friend and work their friend's puzzles.

Napkin Folding

☆ Provide napkins and encourage the children to fold them, noting that there is more than one way to fold.

☆ You may want to draw fold lines on the napkins to simplify this activity.

Paper Cutting

☆ Provide magazines and scissors.

☆ Encourage the children to cut pictures from magazines. For beginners, you may want to draw a circle around the item to cut out.

☆ As children become more proficient, encourage the children to cut freely.

Button Sweeping

☆ Provide a pastry brush, small buttons, a bowl, and a scoop.

☆ Encourage the children to use the pastry brush to sweep the buttons into the scoop and drop them into a bowl.

Playdough Fun

☆ Provide playdough (see recipes on pages 46-47). Playing with playdough is one of the best fine motor activities available to young children. It develops all the muscles in the hands that will later be used for writing. Offer it as an activity as often as possible. Following are several suggestions for creative ways to use playdough.

★ Use cookie cutters to cut shapes from the dough.

★ Roll "snakes" of many lengths. *Who can roll the longest snake?*

★ Create sculptures using beads, pipe cleaners, ribbon, and other miscellaneous items.

★ Mix two colors of playdough. Let the children knead them together to see what third color emerges.

★ Roll balls of many sizes. *Who can roll the largest ball?*

★ Make "jewelry," such as bracelets and necklaces.

★ Use a potato masher or large-holed garlic press to create "hair."

★ Shape into letters.

The Instant Curriculum

The Wonder of Wonder-Science

Overview

Young children are natural scientists. They are eager to discover all they can about the world in which they live. Science for young children allows them to explore, manipulate materials, ask questions, discover cause and effect, project consequences, and solve problems. It encourages them to participate in simple investigations that help them begin to develop the skills of asking questions, gathering information, communicating findings, and making informed decisions. It provides experiences with both living and non-living things.

An effective science program helps children develop reasoning skills. The experiences cultivate children's natural sense of wonder and curiosity, and stimulate them further to find out more about the "why" and "how" of their world. They will learn about both the biological and physical world.

The classroom and playground are natural scientific laboratories when there are enthusiastic adults to guide the learning. The environment should encourage children to ask questions and search for answers. The teacher's role is to guide children to find answers for themselves.

Children should be encouraged to use their senses and follow their inherent sense of wonder and discovery to explore plants, light, water, simple tools and machines, animals, rocks, gravity, and other areas of both life and physical science. In addition, children need opportunities to develop sensitivity to the environment and to understand their role in preserving it.

Scientific principles are not learned in isolation. These principles unfold in the Art Center as children mix paints, in the Music Center as they explore tone bottles, in the Block Center as they build towers and interact directly with balance and gravity, and on the playground as they chase their shadows with a friend. The important aspect of children's learning opportunities is the awareness of the teacher. Scientific principles may go unnoticed without the intervention of a knowledgeable teacher.

The activities in this chapter provide firsthand experiences for children to learn about science. The materials needed to implement the program can be obtained with minimal expenditure of funds. All that is needed is an enthusiastic teacher who is willing to help create a rich environment for scientific thinking and learning.

Definitions

Diffusion—refers to the process by which molecules intermingle as a result of their kinetic energy of random motion, for example, the scattering of light or the mingling of fluid and solids.

Fluid—is a molecular form that is liquid or gas. Fluids are different than solids in that they have a flexible shape. Some objects can float in a fluid.

Force—is defined as a push or pull that can cause an object to move, can slow down an object, can stop its motion, or can change the direction of an object's motion. Since any change in speed (velocity) is considered an acceleration (or deceleration), it can be said that a force on an object results in the acceleration of that object.

Friction—is resistance to motion that is opposite the direction of travel. It is caused when two surfaces are in contact. Since friction acts to slow down a moving object, it is called a resistive force. This is different than active forces that cause objects to accelerate or change direction.

Gas—is an air fluid form that has a flexible shape and will somewhat take the shape of its containers. Liquids can become gases. Evaporation is an example of a liquid becoming a gas.

Gravitation—is an unseen force that attracts objects to each other.

Gravity—is a force that accelerates falling objects.

Kinetic energy—is the energy an object has if it is moving. If there are some constrained or pent up forces preventing the object to move, it is said to have potential energy.

Liquid—is a fluid as opposed to solid. Fluids have a flexible shape and somewhat take the shape of their containers. A liquid is a substance that exhibits a readiness to flow.

Magnetism—is the unseen attraction (force) between certain objects, called magnets.

Motion—what an object appears to have if it changes its position with respect to the observer over a period of time. In other words, if you look at something that is in one position and then see it later in another position, it has moved with respect to you. The distance it went in a period of time is its speed or velocity. The change in velocity over time is its acceleration.

Non-soluble—refers to a fluid's ability to hold its shape, for example, a liquid or a gas that will not diffuse.

Solid—is a body (molecular form) that is so firmly packed that it resists penetration.

Air

Sacks of Air

☆ Give the children lunch-size paper bags to blow up.
☆ Encourage them to feel the sack and observe its fullness.
☆ After blowing up several bags, let the children pop the bags to let the air escape.
☆ Ask them to think of another way to let the air escape.

Air Pushers

☆ Place small items, such as paper, feathers, or Styrofoam packaging chips, inside a circle of masking tape on the floor.
☆ Let the children take turns trying to "squirt" (push with air) the items out of the circle with empty plastic catsup, mustard, or detergent dispensers.

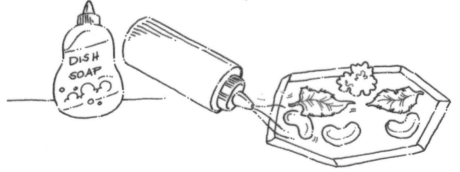

Air Pusher Experiment

☆ Talk with the children about how air moves things. Ask them if they have seen dirt blowing across the playground.

☆ Place loose sand on a tray and level it.

☆ Give the children straws and a paper fan.

☆ Encourage them to test ways to move the sand. Suggest that they blow from different directions and with different amounts of force. *What happens?*

Air Movers

☆ Place a variety of objects, such as paper fans, straws, paper towel tubes, and plastic squirt bottles, on a table for children to explore how to move air.

☆ Provide objects for children to attempt to move such as a ping-pong ball and Styrofoam chips.

Circle Kites

☆ Provide each child with a flat circle (1' in diameter) cut from a paper grocery bag or other paper source.

☆ Let the children glue thin streamers on the circle.

☆ When dry, punch two holes in the circle and insert a string.

☆ Take the children outside and let them run with their circle kites while the streamers ripple in the breeze.

☆ Inside, place a fan in a safe location and let the children "fly" a few kites at a time inside the room. (The children stand near the fan and hold their kites while they "fly." **Safety Note**: Keep children a safe distance away from the fan.)

Bubbles Up

☆ Provide bubble soap (see page 43 for recipe) and wands.
☆ Encourage the children to blow bubbles.
☆ Discuss what makes the bubbles float.

Bubble Machines

☆ Make a solution of soapy water by mixing liquid detergent and water in a small bowl.
☆ Give each child a straw. Let them take turns making bubbles in the bowl by blowing through the straw.
☆ Precede this activity with a lesson on blowing air through the straw as opposed to sucking air into it.

Floaters and Droppers

☆ Provide a basket of items, such as feathers, tissues, buttons, washers, and other assorted items for the children to explore as "floaters" and "droppers."
☆ Ask the children to toss the items into the air one at a time and determine if the item is a "floater" because it floats down or a "dropper" because it drops straight to the ground.

When the Wind Blows

☆ Ask the children to look out the window to discover all the ways they can tell if the wind is blowing (clothing blowing, trees swaying, flags waving, leaves tumbling across the lawn, swings swinging, and so on).
☆ Children have a difficult thing time understanding what they cannot see. The concepts of *air* and *wind* are difficult to internalize.
☆ Following is a poem about the wind by Christina Georgina Rossetti that you may want to share with the children.

Who Has Seen the Wind?

Who has seen the wind?
Neither you nor I.
But when the leaves hang trembling,
The wind is passing through.
Who has seen the wind?
Neither you nor I,
But when the leaves bow down their heads,
The wind is passing by.

Air Conditioning Hoops

☆ Position a small fan in a spot that is safe for the children.

☆ Place the following items on a table: an embroidery hoop with cloth in it, a shallow pan of water, and a towel.

☆ Ask the children to dip the embroidery hoop (with cloth) into the water and place it on the towel to let excess water drip off.

☆ Have them hold the hoops in front of the fan and feel the cool breeze on their faces.

Safety Note: Keep children a safe distance from the fan.

Helicopters

☆ Make "helicopters" for each child. For each helicopter, draw a shape (as shown in the illustration below) on an 8" piece of construction paper. Cut out the shape. Cut along the center line. Fold one strip forward on the dotted line and one strip backwards. Attach a paper clip at the bottom of the helicopter.

☆ Give the children the helicopters and provide a spot where they can stand a little off the ground (perhaps a stool) to drop them. **Note:** The higher a child is when he drops the helicopter, the better the twirl.

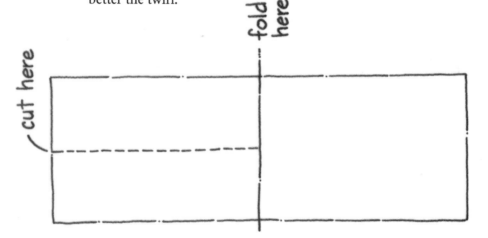

Raisin Elevators

☆ Pour clear, carbonated soda water into a clear, unbreakable glass.

☆ Drop four or five raisins into the glass.

☆ After 40 to 60 seconds, children will observe the raisins moving up and down in the glass.

☆ Help the children to draw the conclusion that air bubbles caused the upward movement.

☆ Have them observe the glass later in the day when the carbonation has ceased. This will reinforce the role of the air bubbles in lifting the raisins.

The Instant Curriculum

Sound: What We Hear When Air Moves

Megaphones

☆ Enlarge the megaphone pattern below on a copy machine. Trace the megaphone on cardboard or tagboard and cut it out to make a pattern.

☆ Let the children trace around the pattern on heavy paper and cut out if they are able.

☆ Help the children roll the megaphones and tape or staple in place.

☆ Bring the children outside and practice "cheerleading."

Safety Note: Caution children against holding a megaphone close to another child's ear.

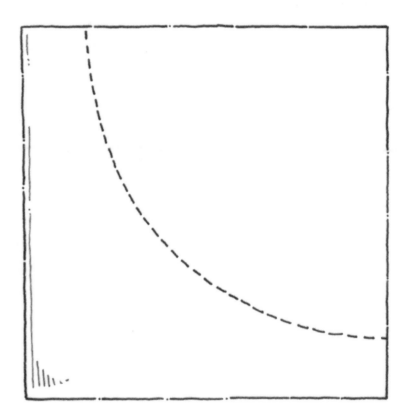

Who's Coming?

☆ Ask the children if they have ever seen a movie in which someone puts his ear to the ground to find out if horses are coming or a train is moving down the track.

☆ Explain that sounds are vibrations that can be felt as well as heard. Sound vibrations travel through the ground and other solid materials, including tabletops. The sound also sounds louder.

(continued on the next page)

☆ Have two children sit at opposite ends of a long table and take turns scratching under the table. One child puts his ear on the table while the other child scratches under the table. They will note how much louder the scratching sound is.

☆ To further demonstrate this concept (and as a good group management technique), have the children put their heads down on the table to listen for your "scratching signal" to go to lunch, go to circle, and so on.

Sound Vibrations

☆ Ask the children to place their hands on their throats and say their name out loud.

☆ Encourage them to describe what they feel.

☆ Now have the children place their hands on their throats and whisper. *What do you feel?*

☆ Point out that the vocal *chords* in the throat open and close to help produce sound. It is their vocal chords that they feel vibrate in their throats.

☆ Introduce "vocal chords" and "vibrate" as new vocabulary words.

Kazoos

☆ Provide empty toilet paper tubes, 6" square sheets of wax paper, and rubber bands.

☆ Help the children make kazoos by wrapping the wax paper around the end of their toilet paper tube and securing it with a rubber band.

☆ Encourage the children to blow their kazoos. Explain that the air pressing through the tube and paper create the special sound. Encourage the children to hum a tune into their kazoos.

The Instant Curriculum

Tuning Fork Exploration

☆ Tap a tuning fork on different surfaces, such as metal, wood, plastic, thick fabric, thin fabric, and water.

☆ Help the children see that the tuning fork produces a richer sound on hard surfaces. The vibration on hard surfaces is greater than on soft surfaces.

Water

Water changes state. For example, an ice cube is *solid* water. When it melts, the water is *liquid.* When it is heated, it changes to a gas (*steam*). Water mixes and spreads into other liquids (*diffusion*). Some things will dissolve in water (*soluble*) and some things will not dissolve in water (*insoluble*). (See the definitions of *diffusion, gas, liquid, insoluble,* and *solid* on pages 210-211 of this chapter.)

Liquid

All Liquids Flow

☆ Draw a line through the middle of paper plates to create equal halves. Give one to each child.

☆ Ask the children to turn their plates so that the line in the middle is horizontal.

☆ Show the children how to put a spoonful of hand lotion, glue, paste, and water on the top half of their plates.

☆ Instruct them to tilt their plates and watch the liquid run down to the other half of the plate. *Which item runs the fastest? Which is the slowest? Are all the substances liquids? Why do some run faster than others?*

☆ Explain that all liquids run (flow), but the *thickness* or *viscosity* of the liquid determines how fast it runs. Introduce the word "viscosity" as a new vocabulary word. Viscosity is the tendency to resist flowing.

Surface Tension

☆ Give each child an eyedropper, a piece of wax paper, a cup of water, and a cup of soapy water.

☆ Ask the children to drop eyedroppers of water onto a sheet of wax paper and observe the drops.

☆ Then have them drop eyedroppers of soapy water onto the wax paper and observe the drops. *What differences do you observe between the two different drops?*

Sink and Float

☆ Give the children small plastic containers, pebbles, and sand at the water table.

☆ Challenge them to figure out how to make the containers sink and float.

Fingerpaint Experiment

☆ Give the children slick paper and some fingerpaint.

☆ Encourage them to drag craft sticks or tongue depressors through the paint.

☆ After the children have played with the paint for a while, add several drops of water to the paint. *How does this change the paint? Which way do you prefer the paint? Why?*

Solid

Ice Melting Race

☆ Place ice cubes in paper cups.

☆ Let the children place the cups in different spots in the room. Make sure that some put their cups in a sunny spot.

☆ Encourage the children to watch the ice to see which cubes melt more quickly. *What causes ice to melt more quickly?*

☆ Try the experiment again on another day. Place salt on some of the cubes. What happens?

Slipping and Sliding on Ice

☆ Freeze water on a cookie sheet.

☆ Give the children small cars to run across the ice. *How can you keep the cars from skidding? What happens if you sprinkle a little salt or sand on the ice?*

The Instant Curriculum

Evaporation (Gas)

Vanishing Art

☆ Provide paintbrushes and small plastic buckets of water. Let children "paint" with water on easels.

☆ As the water disappears, they will discover the principles of *evaporation.*

☆ Go outside and give the children small plastic buckets of water and large brushes.

☆ Let them "paint" the sidewalk, the side of the building, and the wheeled toys. They will enjoy the "painting" but they will also discover that the water "goes away" (evaporates).

Old-Fashioned Wash Day

☆ On a sunny day, prepare a big pan of soapsuds and two pans of rinse water.

☆ Let children wash doll clothes or other small items on an old-fashioned washboard. (If a washboard is unavailable, show children how to rub fabric against itself to scrub it.)

☆ After rinsing twice, they hang the clothes on a line (or on the fence) to dry.

☆ Bring in the dry clothes a few hours later; discuss the results.

Diffusion

Will This Dissolve?

☆ Fill five clear glasses with water.

☆ Show the children the following items: a rock, salt, a leaf, sugar, and pepper.

☆ Ask them to predict whether or not the items will dissolve in water.

☆ Test each item with the children. Verify predictions.

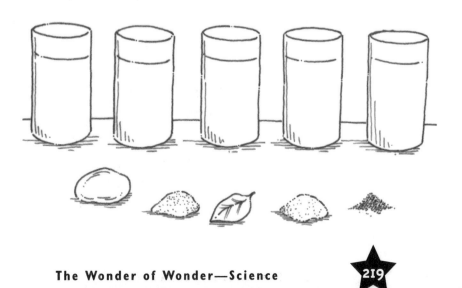

Fingerpaint Finale

☆ After the children have finished fingerpainting, have a tub of water (or water table) ready to receive painted hands.

☆ Children will enjoy watching the color diffuse through the water.

☆ The color will change as more hands and different colors are placed in the water.

Color Bottles

☆ Fill liter-size plastic bottles with water.

☆ Drop a few dots of red food coloring in the bottles. Cap tightly.

☆ Encourage the children to roll the bottles back and forth across a table and watch the color diffuse through the water.

☆ Uncap the bottles and add drops of blue. Repeat the following process to observe the creation of the new color—purple.

☆ Place the bottles in the window for room decoration.

Insoluble Substances

Invisible Names

☆ Invite the children to write their names or draw pictures on butcher paper with cooking oil.

☆ When held up to a light source, names or pictures will become visible.

☆ Challenge the children to wipe their picture off with a damp sponge. *Will it disappear?*

Wave Maker

☆ Demonstrate this activity for the children.

☆ Fill a clear plastic bottle (at least 10" high) three-fourths full, using denatured alcohol.

☆ Add blue food coloring (enough to make it deep blue). Fill the bottle with cooking oil, leaving a small distance at the top. Glue on the top for safety.

☆ The substances will not mix and the water will move like a wave over the oil when moved up and down.

☆ Place the bottle on the table for the children's use, observation, and questions.

Force and Motion

Force and Motion (see the definitions of *force, friction, gravitation,* and *magnetism* on page 210 at the beginning of this chapter)

Force

Wind Wheels

☆ Cut out a large circle from a large plastic lid so that only a rim remains.

☆ Tape strips of newspaper, crepe paper, ribbon, or cloth onto one side of the rim.

☆ Bring the rims outside. The children can clutch the rim easily and run to make the streamers "fly."

☆ Call their attention to the direction of the streamers. *What directs the flight of the streamers?*

Wind Wands

☆ Roll up two sheets of newspaper to make a "wand."

☆ Tape or glue crepe paper streamers to the wand from the mid-point to the top of the wand.

☆ As children run with the wand, the streamers flap in the breeze like a flag.

☆ Discuss the wind as a director of movement. (Objects are blown or moved by the wind and the direction of the wind determines the direction the object moves.) *What causes the streamers to fly in the direction that they do?*

Swing, Pendulum, Swing

☆ Obtain a large funnel with a small exit hole. Punch holes in the sides of the funnel and tie a long string to both sides.

☆ Suspend the funnel over a large flat tray or a plastic shower curtain liner. Or, rest a yardstick across the back of two chairs and hang the funnel from the yardstick.

☆ Fill the funnel with sand and watch it dribble out. *What happens if you swing the funnel? What happens if you change the direction of the swing? What happens if you change the length of the string holding the funnel?*

Bowling

☆ Provide a tennis ball and six to eight empty, clean ½ liter soda bottles to use as bowling pins.

☆ Encourage the children to toss or roll the ball to knock down the pins.

☆ Discuss the relationship between how hard they roll or throw the ball to the outcome and talk about the direction of the throw to the outcome.

Can Race

☆ Give children two coffee cans and several smaller items that can be placed inside the cans, such as a block, crayon, roll of tape, small book, and any other item that will fit.

☆ Encourage the children to put different items into the cans and explore the way the item affects the cans' abilities to roll.

☆ Use masking tape for a finish line and let the children race their cans.

Friction: Resistance to Motion

Erosion

☆ Cut one end out of a shoebox and then tape it back in place.

☆ Fill the shoebox with damp sand and pack it down.

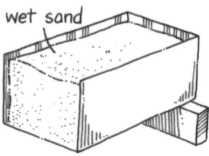

wet sand

☆ Remove the taped end of the shoebox. Prop up the closed end of the shoebox at a slight angle.

☆ Ask the children what they think will happen if you pour water into the box at the high end.

☆ Try it. What happens? Explain that this is the way canyons are formed.

☆ Try this experiment again. Add a few rocks in the sand before pouring the water. What happens?

☆ Talk with the children about the role grass plays in *erosion*. (Erosion is the gradual wearing away of a solid by the force of another solid or a liquid.)

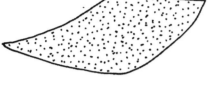

Sanding

☆ Write each child's name on a separate block of wood. Give the children the block with their name on it and a piece of sandpaper.

☆ Show them how to sand the wood. As they sand, ask questions. *What happens to the wood? Does it get warm? Does it feel smooth?*

☆ Children will also discover that sandpapering the block erodes, or wears away, the surface when they see their name disappear. Ask about the sawdust they have created. *What is the dust that is created by the rubbing?* Explain that sawdust is a by-product of friction.

Making Sand

☆ Give each child two rocks to rub together.

☆ Place a sheet of dark paper on the table so that they can see the sand that is produced by the rubbing action.

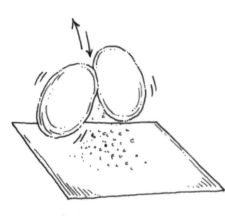

☆ Explain to the children that it is the friction created by rubbing the rocks together that creates the sand.

☆ The children may also notice that the rocks get warm. This is another by-product of friction.

☆ Let the children use a magnifying glass to observe the rock shape of the sand.

Rocks and Shells

Note: Rocks are a by-product of erosion and shells that are worn and smoothed show the effect of being rubbed against the sand on the ocean bottom.

☆ Prepare two small boxes for classifying rocks and shells by placing a rock in the bottom of one box and a shell in the bottom of the other.

☆ Place a quantity of rocks and shells on the table for the children to sort into appropriate boxes.

Hand Warm-Up

☆ Demonstrate rubbing your hands together to make them warm. Tell the children that rubbing creates friction and friction creates heat.

☆ Encourage the children to rub their hands together. Then have them look at their hands. *What do you see on your hands?*

(continued on the next page)

☆ Explain that the small black specks look like dirt but are actually bits of skin that were exfoliated by the rubbing. Friction also causes wear and tear on the surface to which it is applied.

Rough or Smooth

☆ Provide examples of both rough and smooth surfaces, such as a brick and a smooth rock. Rough surfaces provide traction; smooth surfaces allow easy sliding.

☆ Talk to the children about different surfaces. *What are rough surfaces? What are some smooth surfaces?*

☆ Take the children on a walk to look for rough and smooth surfaces.

Shoe Skating

☆ Play a waltz tape or CD and encourage the children to "pretend-skate" across the floor.

☆ After the first tape, let the children sit and discuss the experience: *Was it easier for some to move across the floor?* Ask the children to look at the soles of their shoes; try to arrive at the conclusion that rubber soles are more difficult to slide across the floor than leather soles.

☆ Play another song and let them skate with their shoes off. Compare socks and bare feet, if appropriate.

☆ Have the children skate across a carpet and compare it with a tile floor.

Chalk Experiment

☆ Give the children a piece of chalk and a variety of items with rough and smooth surfaces to write on—sandpaper, a brick, foil, burlap, satin, piece of tile, and different textures of wallpaper.

☆ What differences do children experience when writing on a smooth surface versus a rough surface? Remind the children about friction and its by-products.

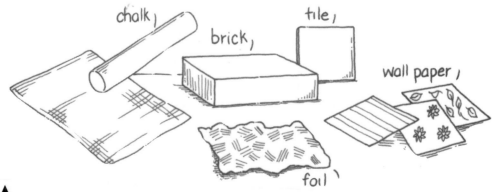

Gravitation: Force That Attracts

Marble Run

☆ Tape an empty paper towel tube to the edge of a table. Then tape another tube to the bottom of the first tube. Continue taping tubes together in this manner to create a running tube to the floor.

☆ When the run is finished, drop a marble into the top of the first tube. *What happens?*

☆ Provide additional tubes and invite the children to see how long they can make the run. Show them how to add interesting curves and slopes to the course.

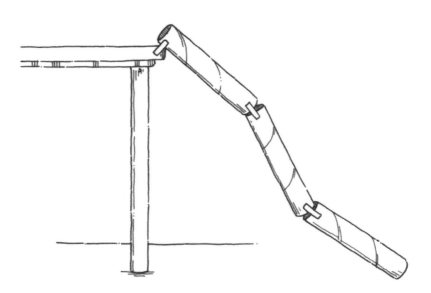

Drop It

☆ Ask the children if they think a tennis ball and a marble will land on the ground at the same time if they are dropped from the same distance at the same time.

☆ Test their predictions by placing a cookie sheet on the ground and dropping a soft ball and a marble from the same distance at the same time. Listen for the sound. *What happens?*

☆ Let the children try this experiment with other objects.

Balloon Bounce

☆ Ask the children to select a partner. Give each pair a balloon. **Safety Warning:** Popped balloons present a possible choking hazard. Make sure you account for all balloons (and pieces of balloons) at all times.

☆ Have pairs of children work together to keep balloons aloft. Discuss the lightness of balloons. Point out that they are filled with air.

Down It Goes

☆ Give the children several objects to drop, such as feathers, marbles, Styrofoam packaging, small blocks, sponges, cotton, and rocks.

☆ After individual experimentation, help the children draw conclusions based upon their observations. *Which items dropped slowly and which items dropped quickly?*

Cardboard Tube Slide

☆ Cut holes in the sides of a large cardboard box and insert long cardboard tubes (from gift wrap, butcher paper, or carpet rolls) into the holes (see illustration).

☆ Place one at a level position. Place one tilted to the right side of the box and one tilted to the left side.

☆ Provide balls small enough to fit through the tubes.

☆ Let the children discover that the balls will roll down the inclined tubes, but not the level tube.

Downhill Racer

☆ Create an inclined plane in the Block Center by stacking two or three small square blocks and placing one end of a long (18" to 24") board on the blocks.

☆ Encourage the children to roll small balls, small cars, or spools down the inclined plane.

☆ Provide additional blocks for further experimentation.

☆ Help the children draw the conclusion that raising the height of the plane increases the speed of the rolling object.

Stringing Up

☆ Hang a string or piece of yarn from the ceiling.

☆ Provide one child with stringing beads or spools.

☆ Ask the child to string the beads and attempt to fill the string all the way to the ceiling.

☆ When the beads fall, ask the child why. Explain that *gravity* is a force that pulls objects to the ground.

Magnetism: Another Kind of Force

Magnetic Attraction

☆ Tie a string to a disk magnet and suspend it from a yardstick that is propped across the back of two chairs.

☆ Give the children a basket of objects with some objects that will attract the magnet and some that will not attract the magnet.

☆ Encourage the children to experiment with the materials to determine which objects will move the magnet.

Metal Hunt

☆ Give the children small magnets and have them test them on objects around the room to find out which objects are metal and which are not.

☆ When the children have finished their hunt have them name as many metal things as they can remember.

Toy Towing

☆ Attach a magnetic strip or disk magnet to the back of a toy car or truck and a metal washer to the front of a lightweight second car.

☆ Let the children use the first car to tow the second.

Home Hunt

☆ Ask the children to look around their homes and identify ways in which magnets are used.

☆ Discuss magnets on the refrigerator, magnets on cabinet doors to keep them shut, and magnetic rims on paper clip holders. *Does anyone have a screwdriver with a magnetic head?*

Magnetic Puppets

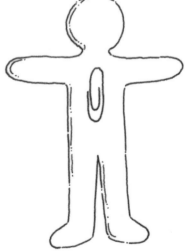

☆ Make simple cardboard puppets (paper dolls). Glue a paper clip on the back of each puppet.

☆ Glue a disk magnet to a tongue depressor.

☆ Create a background for the puppets using poster board.

☆ Demonstrate using the tongue depressor behind the poster board to move the puppets.

☆ Invite the children to put on a show.

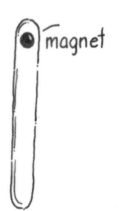

magnet

Dancing Nail

☆ Place a nail in a glass of water.

☆ Give the children a magnet and show them how to move it around the sides of the glass to make the nail "dance."

Magnet Chasers

☆ Stack several disk magnets so they stick together. Remove the first magnet and put it on a table without turning it over. Do the same thing with the second magnet.

☆ Show the children how to put their fingers in the first or second magnet and move it toward the other magnets. *What happens?*

Magnetic Stories

☆ Attach strips of magnetic tape to the back of flannel board characters to create a magnetic story. Provide a large cookie sheet for a background.

☆ Invite the children to retell stories using the magnetic pieces.

Magnetic Designs

☆ Cut out geometric shapes from a sheet of magnetic vinyl (available in craft stores).

☆ Give the children a large cookie sheet and the magnetic shapes and challenge them to create different designs.

Magnet Car Races

☆ Place a metal thumbtack in the bottom of a couple of wooden toy cars or tape a large paper clip to the bottom of the cars.

☆ Draw a racetrack on a sheet of stiff plastic or cardboard.

☆ Attach a disk magnet to a couple of tongue depressors.

☆ Give the children the tongue depressors and show them how to move the magnets to race the cars.

Magnet Painting

☆ Put a sheet of paper in a cookie sheet or pie pan. Squirt a few drops of paint on the paper.

☆ Place a metal object on the paper.

☆ Show the children how to use a magnet to scoot the metal object around in the paint.

Speedy Cleanup

☆ Deliberately spill a box of paper clips.

☆ Provide children with several items for cleaning up the spill, including a broom, masking tape, dust pan, and magnet.

☆ Encourage the children to experiment with each item to determine which item picks up the paper clips most efficiently.

Simple Tools

Pulleys

☆ Hang a pulley from a beam in the ceiling or from a tree outdoors.

☆ Run a rope through the pulley and tie a plastic pail to one end of the rope and tie a knot in the other end of the rope.

☆ Provide soft items for the children to load in the pail and lift. *How does a pulley make work easier?*
Safety Note: Supervise this activity closely. If children let go of the rope, the pail may drop on someone.

Water Transfer

☆ Provide a variety of materials for the water table, such as plastic bottles and jars, plastic measuring spoons, turkey basters, plastic straws, eyedroppers, and funnels for the children to learn how to move water from one place to another.

☆ If possible, provide both short, wide plastic jars and tall, thin plastic bottles. This will help the children understand that the size of the container affects the quantity of liquid and that appearances don't always accurately portray that one container has more water than another.

Filter Catch

☆ Provide a variety of materials, such as Styrofoam chips, gravel of varying sizes, leaves, a plastic colander, tea strainer, and funnels, at the water table for the children to discover how to filter or strain objects from water.

☆ Talk with the children as they play with the materials. *How do strainers make our work easier?*

Kitchen Tools

☆ Bring kitchen tools, such as a manual eggbeater, potato masher, can opener, and funnel into the classroom.

☆ Create opportunities for the children to see how these tools make kitchen work easier. For example, provide soapy water for the children to beat with the egg beater, bananas to mash with the potato masher, and so on.

☆ Discuss other methods they could use for these activities if they did not have the kitchen tools.

Home Connection: Encourage the children to watch family members working in the kitchen at home. *What tools do they use to make their work easier?*

Easy Movers

☆ Show the children some of the ways that make moving an item easier. Following are some possible strategies:

☆ Cut two holes in one end of a shallow box, such as a beverage holder box. Run a rope through the holes to create a handle. Provide materials for the children to load on the "sleigh" and let them explore moving the items from one place to another.

☆ Teach the children how to use a "water line" (pass water down a line to its destination) like firefighters in a water brigade. Have them line up in a row from one part of the room to another. Pass a block or a book from one person to the next until it reaches the end of the line and the other side of the room.

☆ Lay two 12" dowels on the floor and place a box on top of them. Ask the children to load the box with a few blocks and then push it a short distance to a shelf.

☆ Discuss the use of wheels. Use a tricycle as an example. Have the children carry something from one place to another using the tricycle as a means of transportation.

Home Connection: Ask the children to look around their homes to find things that are used to move things. They might find wheelbarrows, wheels on furniture, luggage with wheels, and so on.

Light and Color

Color Shadows

☆ On a sunny day, give each child a 3' sheet of colored cellophane.

☆ Take the children onto the playground and encourage them to make colored shadows with their cellophane sheets.

Playdough Color Mixing

☆ Mix a batch of red and a batch of yellow playdough (see recipes on pages 46-47).

☆ Give each child two playdough balls, one of each color. As they mix the two colors, they will create orange playdough. Talk about how yellow and red make orange.

☆ Try this activity on another day with different colors of playdough.

Color Tubes

☆ Place a cork in one end of a piece of clear plastic tubing, at least ½" in diameter and 30" long. Fill it with water. Add a few drops of blue food coloring to the open end of the tube. Place a cork in that end of the tube.

☆ Remove the cork from the opposite end and add a few drop of yellow color. Replace the cork.

☆ Show the children how to wiggle the tube or turn it end over end to work the color in each end of the tube to the center and mix. *What color is the water in the middle?*

☆ Try this experiment again on another day using different colors. **Safety Note:** Supervise this activity closely so that the children do not remove the corks from the ends of the tube.

Rose-Colored Glasses

☆ Cover eyeglass frames with colored cellophane (same color on each side).

☆ Ask the children to look through the glasses and describe what they see.

☆ Now cover the frames with different colors of cellophane. Put red on one side and green on the other.

☆ Have the children look again. *How does the world look?*

Color Mixer

☆ Make a roller toy from an empty round box, such as an oatmeal or cornmeal box.

☆ Cut a hole in each end of the box and run a long piece of yarn through the holes. Tie the ends of the yarn together.

☆ Encourage the children to help color the box with markers and paints. When the box is dry, have a child pull it across the floor. *What happens to the colors?*

Shadow Puppets

☆ Make a puppet stage by cutting a square out of the bottom of a cardboard box.

☆ Tape a white sheet of paper over the cutout area.

☆ Turn the box on its side so that the square faces the audience.

☆ With a light source behind the box (projector light or strong flashlight), act out stories with stick puppets.

Guess Who?

☆ Hang a white sheet to make a "stage front." Place a light source behind the sheet.

☆ Have the children take turns walking between a light source and the back of the sheet.

☆ Challenge the audience (the remainder of the children) sitting in front of the sheet to try to identify each mystery guest.

Sun Art

☆ Ask the children to cut out a large design from drawing paper and place it on dark construction paper.

☆ Place the paper with the design in direct sunlight.

☆ After a couple of days, ask the children to remove the design and note how the paper has faded, but the design remains on the covered area. *Why?*

Rainbows

☆ Hang a prism in an east- or west-facing window.

☆ When rainbows appear in the room, call attention to the source of the rainbows.

☆ Move the prism so the children can see the direct relationship between sun, prism, and rainbow.

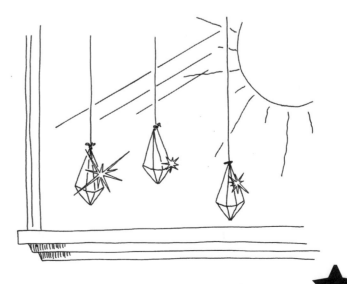

Strobe Light

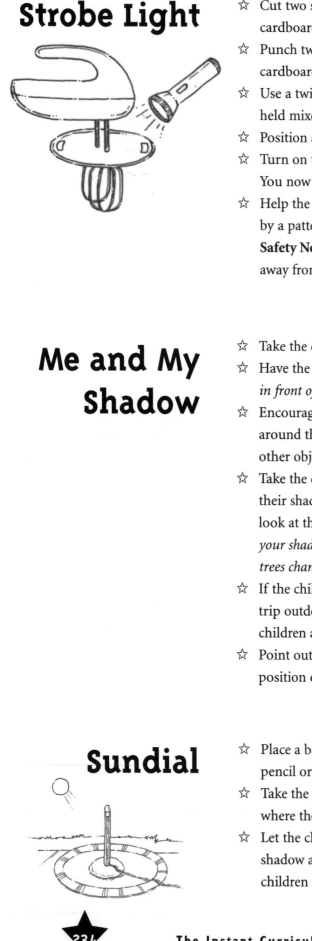

☆ Cut two slots about 1" by 2" opposite each other on small pizza cardboard.

☆ Punch two holes about 2" apart in the center of the pizza cardboard.

☆ Use a twist tie to attach the cardboard to the beaters of a hand-held mixer.

☆ Position a flashlight so that it will shine through one of the slots.

☆ Turn on the flashlight, turn off the lights, and start the mixer. You now have a strobe light.

☆ Help the children determine that the strobe light effect is created by a pattern of light and absence of light.

Safety Note: Supervise this activity closely. Keep children's fingers away from the mixer.

Me and My Shadow

☆ Take the children outdoors early in the morning on a sunny day.

☆ Have the children look at their shadow. *Is it tall or is it short? Is it in front of you or behind you?*

☆ Encourage the children to look at the shadows of the things around them—the trees, buildings, outdoor equipment, and any other objects.

☆ Take the children outdoors again around noon. As they look at their shadows again, ask them the same questions. Have them look at the other things around them. *What is different about your shadow? Is it taller or shorter? How have the shadows of the trees changed?*

☆ If the children are still there in the late afternoon, take another trip outdoors and assess the changes in the shadows of the children and their surroundings.

☆ Point out that the differences in their shadows are caused by the position of the sun as the earth moves.

Sundial

☆ Place a ball of playdough in the center of a paper plate. Stick a pencil or dowel in the playdough.

☆ Take the plate outdoors or to a sunny window. Mark the spot where the shadow falls and write the time beside it.

☆ Let the children check the plate each hour. Help them mark the shadow and write in the hour. At the end of the day, ask the children what they notice about the marks on the plate.

The Instant Curriculum

Scattered Light

☆ Explain to the children that light scatters in all directions off rough surfaces and bounces back off smooth surfaces.

☆ Have children look at a piece of rough sandpaper suing a magnifying glass. Point out that each grain of sand has a surface of its own. When light reflects from the surface of sandpaper, it is actually bouncing off of many surfaces.

☆ Provide several types of surfaces, such as aluminum foil, Mylar, metal mirrors, glass mirrors, glass bowls, eyeglasses, sheets of plastic, and so on for the children to explore.

☆ Have the children sort the items by those that act as a mirror and those that do not.

Mirror Magic

☆ Tape two small, flat mirrors together like a book (mirrored side facing in).

☆ Stand the mirror up for the children and place a small piece of masking tape on the table centered with the fold of the mirrors. **Note:** As the children not to move the mirrors one you have them positioned.

☆ Encourage the children to use the mirrors to examine small objects such as cars, decorative buttons, crayons, and marbles. **Note:** You may want to start with simple objects, such as pattern blocks, before offering items like buttons and cars.

☆ The children will be able to see that both sides of the item are alike. Explain that this is called *symmetry*.

Mirror Drawing

☆ Provide a mirror, drawing paper, and crayons. Encourage the children to experiment with mirror drawing and writing.

☆ Demonstrate how to position the mirror so that they can write or draw using the mirror reflection instead of directly looking at their paper. *What happens?*

Periscopes

☆ Clip a mirror to the end of a ruler or a yardstick to create a simple periscope.

☆ Invite the children to experiment with using the periscope to see around corners.

Lemon Juice Magic

☆ Provide construction paper and a squirt bottle of lemon juice.
☆ Ask the children to squirt lemon juice on the construction paper.
☆ In a short period of time, the lemon juice will fade the color in the paper. Placing the paper in the sun will speed up the process.

Weather and Seasons

"The Weather Song"

☆ Teach the children "The Weather Song" (sung to the tune of "Clementine"). Sing it from time to time, especially when the weather is especially cloudy, sunny, rainy, or foggy.

The Weather Song

Sunny, sunny,
Sunny, sunny,
It is sunny in the sky.
S-u-n-n-y, sunny
It is sunny in the sky.

Cloudy, cloudy,
Cloudy, cloudy,
It is cloudy in the sky.
C-l-o-u-d-y, cloudy
It is cloudy in the sky.

Rainy, rainy,
Rainy, rainy,
It is rainy in the sky.
R-a-i-n-y, rainy.
It is rainy in the sky.

Foggy, foggy,
Foggy, foggy,
It is foggy in the sky.
F-o-g-g-y, foggy.
It is foggy in the sky.

Cloud Watch

☆ On a cloudy day, when the sun is in a location that won't be directly in the children's eyes, take the class outside.
☆ Have everyone lie down on their backs, on a towel or sheet.
☆ Ask the children to look at the clouds and describe the shapes they see (camels, castles, snowmen, and so on).
☆ Suggestions are limited only by children's imaginations.
Home Connection: Suggest that the children play this game with their family members on the way home.

Wind Walk

☆ Take a walk with the children to discover indicators that the wind is moving.

☆ Ask questions to help them see the wind, such as:

★ *Is the flag waving?*

★ *Is trash blowing around?*

★ *Are people leaning into the wind as they walk?*

★ *Do you see people's hair blowing?*

★ *Are the trees and bushes bending?*

★ *Is tall grass moving?*

★ *Do you feel the wind on your face?*

Rain Gauge

☆ Place a tub outside to collect rainwater. Attach a ruler to the inside of the tub to determine how many inches of rain have fallen.

☆ Use the rainwater to water the indoor plants.

Shadow Tracing

☆ Take chalk outdoors on a sunny day.

☆ Let the children choose partners and take turns tracing each other's shadow on the sidewalk.

☆ Ask the children if this activity would work on a cloudy day. Children may be aware that their shadow is not present on cloudy days.

☆ Explain that shadows occur when an object or a person stands between a light source and another surface.

☆ You can demonstrate this in the classroom by turning off the light and having a child stand between the light of a flashlight and a wall.

Season Walks

☆ Take the children out for a walk as the seasons change.

☆ Encourage them to look for signs of the season. When you return to the classroom make a list of the changes they observed, such as falling leaves, leaves changing colors, or flowers blooming.

Seasonal Trees

☆ To develop the concept that some trees change with the seasons, prepare a tree mural at the beginning of each season.

☆ Draw a large tree shape on butcher paper and hang it on the wall. Add a new tree shape before doing each season.

☆ To emphasize seasonal changes, have the children add appropriate collage bits or paint at the beginning of each season.

☆ Examples for each season include:

★ **Fall**—brown, yellow, red, purple, and orange paper bits for leaves

★ **Winter**—bare tree with brown leaves on the ground and a gray painted sky

★ **Spring**—balls of wadded tissue paper and small green paper bits or paint

★ **Summer**—fully covered with green paper or paint

☆ At the end of the year, all four season will be represented on the wall display.

Spotlight on Seasons

☆ Prepare a special place (table or shelf) to spotlight the seasons and seasonal changes.

☆ Arrange a basket of fall leaves and fall vegetables, evergreens with cotton "snow" for winter, a twig with buds (secured in a container of sand) for spring, and a bouquet of greenery and flowers or a potted flowering plant for summer.

☆ As children bring in other items from home, add them to the display.

The Instant Curriculum

Seasonal Observation Bottles

☆ Collect seasonal items and place them in clean empty ½-liter soda bottles. Examples for each season include:
  ★ **Fall**—acorns, colored leaves, apple seeds, pumpkin seeds
  ★ **Winter**—artificial snowflakes, bare branches
  ★ **Spring**—clover, discarded eggshells of hatched birds, flowers
  ★ **Summer**—sand, seashells, seaweed
☆ The children will enjoy looking at the various items collected in the bottles.
Home Connection: Invite the children to bring in a seasonal item from home.

Senses

The Eyes Have It

☆ Fill five glasses with water, four with room temperature water and one with cold water (no ice cubes).
☆ Ask the children to identify the glass containing cold water without touching them.
☆ Children should notice droplets on the outside of the cold glass of water. If unobserved, stimulate thinking by asking children to notice the outside of the glasses.

What's for Snack?

☆ On days when the snack has a specific, identifiable aroma (cinnamon toast or bananas), bring it in on a tray covered by a cloth.
☆ Let the children take turns smelling and whispering their prediction in your ear.
☆ Reveal the snack, verify predictions, and eat.
  ☆ If the classroom is near the kitchen, while the food is cooking, ask the children to predict the lunch menu. Verify predictions when lunch is served.

Sound Makers

☆ Let the children take turns making sounds with a variety of objects and materials. They can crush paper, shake maracas, chew something crunchy, and so on. Record their sounds on a tape recorder. Save the objects used.

☆ The next day, place the objects on a tray, play the tape, and challenge the children to identify the object used to make each particular sound.

Taste Test

☆ Prepare popcorn for snack time.
☆ Divide popcorn into three bowls.
☆ Season one bowl of popcorn with powdered cheese, one with salt, and one with sugar.
☆ Challenge the children to identify the substance on the popcorn in each bowl (after telling them the three choices).

Tactile Temperatures

☆ Prepare a jar of ice water and a jar of warm water.
☆ Ask the children to take turns touching the jars to see which is warm and which is cold.
☆ Children may wish to close their eyes when touching the jars. This helps them concentrate on using one sense.

Hot and Cold

☆ During lunch, discuss the temperature of the food as children eat.
☆ Ask questions. *Which foods taste good both hot and cold? Which foods are only good when they are cold?*

Sounds Abound

☆ Take the children on a "nature walk" in search of sounds.
☆ Before the walk, have the children make a list of the sounds they think they will hear.
☆ Upon return, look at the list with the children. *Which sounds on your list did you hear? What sounds need to be added to the list?*

Puffs of Smell

☆ Douse powder puffs with massage oils or extracts. Create two puffs for each aroma.

☆ Place the puffs in a small box. Let the children smell each puff and then find the two puffs that have the same aroma and place them in pairs.

The Nose Knows

☆ Take the children outdoors just ahead of an oncoming storm or just after a rainfall.

☆ Ask them to describe the smell of the air.

A World of Scents

☆ Take a "nature walk" in search of smells.

☆ Bring a clipboard, paper, and pen and list the items that you find. Bring samples back to the room, if possible, and place them in the Science Center for further exploration.

Scented Bubbles

☆ Add massage oil to bubble mixture (see recipe on page 43) to create scented bubbles.

☆ Encourage the children to blow the bubbles and challenge them to identify the scent.

Sensory Alert

☆ Regularly play a game with the children in which you ask them to name things they saw that were pretty, things they touched that felt good, things they smelled that were pleasing, things they heard that were beautiful, or things they tasted that were good.

Change of State

Stone Soup

☆ Read *Stone Soup* by Marcia Brown.

☆ Ask each child to bring a vegetable from home to contribute to a pot of vegetable soup.

☆ Use bouillon to make a broth.

    ☆ Let the children help prepare the vegetables they brought. Provide plastic knives and let them help wash, peel, and cut the vegetables. Talk with them about the texture of the vegetables. *Are they hard? Rough? Smooth?*

    ☆ As the children eat the cooked soup, discuss the vegetables again. *How have they changed?*

Ice Meltdown

☆ Let each child put an ice cube in a zipper-closure plastic bag.

☆ Discuss how the ice feels hard and cold.

☆ Place the bags on a table until the cubes have melted. Talk about the change that has taken place, using the terms "solid" and "liquid."

☆ Place the bags in a freezer or let the children freeze them at home.

☆ The following day, examine the bags again and discuss the changes that have taken place.

Soda Fizz

☆ Place a teaspoon of baking soda into an empty ½-liter soda bottle and add a teaspoon of vinegar. The two substances create a gas when they are mixed.

☆ Place a balloon over the top of the soda bottle. It will expand from the gas. More of each substance will expand the balloon even more.

☆ After the children have watched you demonstrate, let them mix the two substances. Provide a paper plate, a small cup of vinegar, and a small cup of baking soda.

☆ Let each child use a spoon to put baking soda on his plate and an eyedropper to add the vinegar. The mixture will fizz.

Gelatin Jigglers

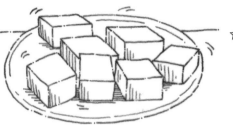

☆ Make gelatin with the class. Call attention to the solid state of the powdered gelatin in the package.

☆ Lead the children to note the change to a liquid when the gelatin is dissolved in water.

☆ The following day, serve the gelatin as a snack, noting the change back to a solid.

☆ If desired, use less water than the recipe requires so it may be cut into cubes and served as finger food. Say the following "Gelatin Jigglers" poem when you serve the gelatin jigglers:

Gelatin Jigglers by Pam Schiller
Gelatin jigglers on my tray.
They make me laugh and want to play.
Wiggle, giggle, smooth and cool.
What a treat to eat at school.

Plants

Nature Bracelets

☆ Give each child a list of labeled pictures of nature items, such as a flower, grass, a seed, a leaf, and so on. Review the list with the children.

☆ Wrap a piece of masking tape, sticky side out, around each child's wrist.

☆ Take the children outside with the list to find the objects. As they find each object, they place it on their masking tape to make a "nature bracelet."

☆ Review the list and findings with the class when all are finished.

Tire Garden

☆ Make a tire garden on the playground by filling a tire(s) with garden soil.

☆ Let children plant flower seeds and take turns pulling weeds and watering.

☆ Enjoy the flowers when they bloom.

☆ Make sure the children understand that using the tire as a planter is recycling. If we don't recycle tires, they end up taking up space in landfills (garbage dumps) and they cannot decompose the way some garbage (organic matter like leaves) does.

Vegetable Garden

☆ Plant carrots and onions in a tire garden on the playground, following directions on the seed packages. Show the children how to water and weed the garden.

☆ When mature, pull up vegetables for children to see and feel.

☆ Cook and eat.

Hairy Larry

☆ Provide potting soil, Styrofoam cups, markers, and rye grass seeds.

☆ Invite the children to draw a face on their Styrofoam cup.

☆ When they have finished, let them fill their cup with potting soil and drop rye grass seeds on top of the soil. Water sparsely.

☆ In a few days, the seeds will sprout and look like hair on the head of the face the children have drawn.

The Instant Curriculum

Grocery Bag Leaves

☆ Provide each child with a large square cut from a brown grocery bag.
☆ Display fall leaves and discuss the variety of colors.
☆ Help the children sprinkle red, yellow, brown, green, and orange dry tempera paint on their paper squares.
☆ Encourage them to mix the colors by painting with water and a brush.
☆ When dry, show the children how to place a leaf pattern on the painted paper and cut it out.

Leaves—All Sizes, All Shapes

☆ Display baskets or boxes of different kinds of leaves, such as oak leaves, magnolia leaves, pine needles, and willow leaves.
☆ Encourage the children to note differences in the sizes and shapes of leaves. Discuss the attributes of the leaves, and help them expand their vocabulary.
Home Connection: Ask the children to bring in a leaf from outside their home. Pass those leaves around for comparison.

Leaf Rubbings

☆ To help the children notice the veins in leaves and the different shapes, provide a variety of leaves for them to place (underside up) under a piece of light-colored construction paper.
☆ Remove paper from old crayons. Demonstrate how to make rubbings of the leaves by rubbing the sides of the crayons over the paper.

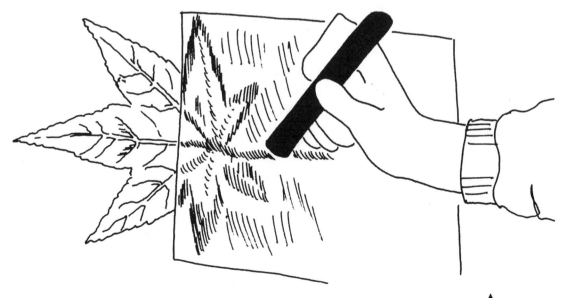

Treasure Hunt

☆ Give each child a sack for collecting leaves.

☆ Go on a leaf "treasure hunt" in the playground or park. Point out trees that can be identified by their distinctive leaves.

☆ Place the collected leaves in a large box on a table.

☆ Create sorting mats by placing a different type leaf on each piece of construction paper.

☆ Encourage the children to choose a leaf from the remaining leaves in the large box and match it to the leaves glued on the mats.

Window Garden

☆ Have the children plant small plants in empty milk cartons, cups, or clay pots.

☆ Discuss placement of the plants in sunny vs. shady areas of the room. *Why is it better to place plants in a sunny area?*
Note: Experiment with the placement of plants in different parts of the room, but don't let a plant die. Move it back to a lighted area after talking with the children about what happened to the plant.

☆ Keep eyedroppers and a bowl of water nearby so that the children can water their own plant every day.
Note: Have the children use eyedroppers to prevent over-watering the plants.

Egg Carton Planters

☆ Remove the top from a Styrofoam egg carton. Poke small holes in the cups of the bottom half.

☆ Place the top of the egg carton under the bottom of the carton to use as a saucer.

☆ Put potting soil in each cup and plant seeds. Water the seeds from the bottom by adding water to the saucer, which allows the soil to soak up the moisture.

☆ Cover the top of the planter with plastic wrap until seedlings appear. After germination, remove the plastic wrap and watch the plants grow.

☆ The children can measure the growth of their plants by marking the height on a craft stick stuck into the soil behind their plant.

Mini-Terrariums

☆ Place potting soil in a large bucket and pour a little bit of water on the soil to moisten it.

☆ Let each child scoop enough soil from the bucket to fill a large plastic cup half full.

☆ Invite the children to sprinkle radish or grass seeds lightly on top of the soil. Help them invert a second clear plastic cup over the top of the seeded cup and tape the seams with clear plastic tape.

☆ Place the cups in a warm, sunny spot and wait for the seeds to sprout. The moisture from the soil is trapped inside the container and recycles itself constantly as it evaporates and dribbles back down the sides of the "terrarium."

☆ Encourage the children to keep a journal to record the growth of the seeds.

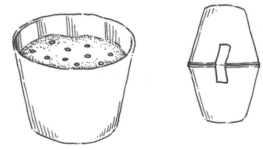

Little Sprouts

☆ Provide baby food jars, paper towels, and lima bean seeds.

☆ Show the children how to place a dampened paper towel inside the baby food jar and nestle the lima bean between the folds of the paper towel.

☆ Place the top on the jar, but don't screw on too tightly.

☆ The children will be able to observe the bean sprouting.

☆ When sprouted, let the children plant the sprouts in cup or garden.

Sweet Potato Vines

☆ To help the children see the growth of roots and leaves, "plant" a sweet potato in a jar of water.

☆ First, insert toothpicks in spoke fashion around the middle of the potato.

☆ Place the bottom half of the potato in a jar of water, resting the toothpicks on top of the jar. The top half of the potato will be above water

☆ Place in a lighted area and watch the vine and roots grow.

What's a Nut?

☆ Start a display of nuts by bringing in a coconut and a pecan.

☆ Ask the children to bring in additional nuts (walnuts, hazelnuts, and so on) to add to the display throughout the week. (Peanuts are not really nuts but are from the legume family.)

☆ Provide time for them to share and talk about the nuts they bring from home.

☆ Extend this activity by showing products produced from nuts, such as coconut oil and almond butter.

Natural Dyes

☆ Boil beets, broccoli, blackberries, coffee, and tea in separate pots. Reserve the liquid from each item to create dye.

☆ Allow the liquid from each item to cool. Show the class which item produces which color.

☆ Invite the children to dip strips of cloth into the different liquids to reinforce dye concepts.

Animals

Feed the Birds

☆ To encourage children's interest in birds and to attract birds to the playground, let the children take turns being responsible for throwing crumbs out for the birds.

☆ In addition to crumbs, save seeds from fruit and place them on top of fence posts.

Bird Bath

☆ Obtain a shallow plastic pan or clean garbage can lid.

☆ Place it in a safe but observable location in or near the playground.

☆ Pour water in the pan or lid to make a bird bath.

☆ Encourage the children to observe birds taking a "bath." Remind them to observe quietly so they won't scare the birds away.

Pinecone Bird Feeders

☆ Spread wax paper on the table.

☆ Place a thin layer of smooth peanut butter on the wax paper.

☆ Invite the children to roll a pinecone in the peanut butter and then in birdseed.

☆ Attach a string to the pinecone and hang it in a tree.

Safety Note: Check for allergies to peanut butter before doing this activity.

Looking Loops

☆ Tie the ends of several pieces of cord or heavy string to make several loops.

☆ Place the loops at various locations around the playground.

☆ Assign a couple of children to each loop and ask them to look inside the circle and see how many insects they can find.

☆ If possible, give the children a magnifying glass to assist in the observation process.

☆ Extend this activity to include looking for rocks and plants, if desired.

Ant Watch

☆ After a picnic, leave chicken bones on the picnic table to attract ants. Watch from a distance. Everyone will be fascinated with the speed that ants arrive and start working to clean the bones.

☆ When the ants are gone, remove the bones to avoid harm to dogs.

☆ See "The Little Ants" (page 201) for a movement extension activity.

Ant Helpers

☆ Invite the children to help bury freshly collected seashells in the ground.
Note: If you live close to the seashore, collect seashells. If you do not live close to the seashore, collect shells from seafood stores or restaurants.

☆ Explain that ants will clean off any remaining parts of the sea creatures that used to live in the shell, which will remove the odor.

☆ After a few days, dig up the shells, wash them, and place them on a table for display.

Bug Bottles

☆ To observe live insects, make a "bug bottle" from a clean plastic bottle.

☆ Cut large circles in the sides of the bottle so the insects can breathe. Then place the bottle in a stocking.

☆ Collect insects in the bottle and tie the stocking closed at the top.

☆ Release the insects at the end of the day so the children will learn to respect the insects' freedom and lives.

Animal Habitats

☆ Divide a large wall chart into three sections. Draw or glue a picture of a meadow (or flat, grassy area) in the first section, a picture of a tree in the second section, and a picture of water in the third section. Explain that these are animal *habitats*.

☆ Distribute pictures of animals, such as cows, sheep, birds, squirrels, fish, crabs, and so on to the children and ask them where each animal usually lives.

☆ Invite them to place the pictures of the animals in the appropriate sections on the chart.

Who Lives Where?

☆ Open a manila folder to make a poster. Draw waves on one side and a landscape on the other.

☆ Provide the children with a variety of pictures of things that live on land (squirrels, dogs, people) and things that live in the sea (whale, starfish, crab).

☆ Invite the children to place the pictures on the correct side of the folder.

Feathers, Fur, Scales, and Shells

☆ Provide photos of a variety of animals with an assortment of skin coverings.

☆ Talk with the children about the covering on the animals. Birds have feathers, dogs have fur, turtles have shells, fish have scales, and so on.

☆ Encourage the children to look at each animal and classify it according to its skin covering.

Animal Homes

☆ Take the children on a nature walk to look for animal homes.

☆ Look for earthworm casings, bird nests, spider webs, and squirrel nests. Talk about the different homes.

Mothers and Babies

☆ Provide pictures of mother and baby animals.

☆ Invite the children to match the mother animals with the correct baby animals.

Insect Body Parts

☆ Show the children photos of insects.

☆ Discuss the body parts of the insects: head, thorax, abdomen, legs, antennae, and wings.

☆ Count the legs, the antennae, and the wings. Explain that insects always have six legs and two antennae. The number of legs and the antennae are hallmarks that separate insects from other bugs like spiders and centipedes.

☆ Sing "The Insect Song" to the tune of "Head, Shoulders, Knees, and Toes."

The Insect Song
Head, thorax, abdomen,
Abdomen.
Head, thorax, abdomen,
Abdomen.
Six legs, four wings, antennae two.
Head, thorax, abdomen,
Abdomen.

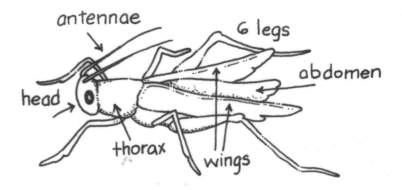

The Instant Curriculum

Everyone's a Piece of the Puzzle— Social Studies

Overview

Social studies in the preschool begins with the child's understanding of herself and then expands to include her family and friends. Eventually, social studies will include the larger community and the broader world.

Children's understanding of self is at the heart of healthy social development. As children become confident in their motor skills and thinking abilities they build an internal sense of self. Self-awareness is critical to children's ability to understand others. Self-confidence grows as children begin to understand how the world works and as they come to feel confident in their abilities to solve "child-sized" problems.

As children learn to establish and maintain positive relationships in the classroom, they are building a foundation for the many relationships they will encounter throughout their lives. The classroom is a "mini society" that provides meaningful experiences that will help children develop their social and emotional intelligence. Children will learn not only to follow rules but also how to help make the rules. They will learn to respect the rights of others as they learn to navigate group experiences. They learn when to compromise and how to negotiate.

Becoming sensitive to ecological and environmental issues is another aspect of the preschool social studies curriculum. If children form good habits related to conservation and recycling in the early years, they will develop lifelong behaviors.

Although social studies lessons occur everywhere in the classroom, the Dramatic Play Center and the playground are particularly fertile areas for learning opportunities. Prop boxes can help children explore the work of community helpers in dramatic play. The playground provides space for large-group participation in games and cooperative activities.

Brain Fast Facts

☆ Social-emotional intelligence is wired between birth and 4 years.
☆ Problem-solving skills and self-esteem go hand in hand.
☆ The habits children develop between birth and puberty will become lifelong habits.

This chapter offers activities and experiences to help children develop a sense of self. It provides support for the concepts of sharing and cooperating. It provides activities and experiences to encourage sharing and cooperating and to develop tolerance, health and safety habits, and environmental awareness.

Through planned activities children will become more knowledgeable about their families, friends, and the community. The teacher is key in children's development of appropriate social behaviors and healthy habits. He or she is both role model and guide.

Feeling Good About Me

I Am Special

☆ To help children know they are valued as individuals, begin each day and continue throughout the day with activities that focus on the individual child—greet children at the door each morning, always speak to them at their eye level, listen carefully when they speak, respond with caring comments, and so on.

My Name Means a Lot

☆ Label each child's cubby and place on the carpet.
☆ Sing songs that use children's names. Following are two examples:

This Is Quinn (Tune: "Here We Go 'Round the Mulberry Bush")
Here is our friend, his name is Quinn,
His name is Quinn, his name is Quinn.
Here is our friend, we're glad he's here.
Say hello to our friend, Quinn.

Did You Ever See My Tiffany?
(Tune: "Did You Ever See a Lassie?")
Did you ever see my Tiffany,
My Tiffany, my Tiffany?
Did you ever see my Tiffany,
My Tiffany, my friend?

☆ See also "Hicky Picky Bumblebee" on page 94.

Home Connection: Suggest that children ask their parents how they selected their child's name. *Are you named after a relative? Is your name a favorite name for someone?*

Accentuate the Positive

☆ Find opportunities to praise each child in an honest and positive manner.

☆ Avoid using comments that label a child or compare one child's abilities to another's.

☆ Following are some examples of positive statements that focus on individual children and their specific situation.

★ *"Richele, I like the way you added the blue to your picture."*

★ *"You really put a lot of time into your building, David."*

★ *"Blair, you put back every block exactly where it belongs."*

★ *"Cara, that was nice of you to pick up the paper scraps."*

V.I.P. Treasure Chest

☆ Decorate a box to be a "V.I.P. Treasure Chest."

☆ Draw a number of happy faces on construction paper and cut them out.

☆ At periodic intervals throughout the year, select a child to be the "V.I.P. for the day," making sure each child has a turn.

☆ During circle time, ask the children to take turns telling the V.I.P. what they like about her.

☆ Write each dictated phrase on the back of construction paper happy faces.

☆ Place the happy face phrases in the treasure chest and let the V.I.P. take it home for the night to share with her family.

☆ Have the child return the treasure chest the following day.

Artist of the Week

☆ If you put every child's artwork up each week, it doesn't seem special, and it can also make the classroom environment over-stimulating.

☆ Select a few children each week to be the featured artists.

☆ By selecting only a few pieces of artwork to display, everyone will notice the artwork.

Responsibility Roster

☆ Develop a Responsibility Roster. Glue picture hanger hooks in rows on a poster board.

☆ Write a classroom chore above each hook, for example, wipe tables, put away toys, and straighten bookshelves.

☆ To help children understand the directions, glue or draw a small picture next to each chore. Or use a pocket chart and index cards with pictures to represent chores.

☆ Write each child's name on a 3" x 5" index card. Punch two holes in each card and tie a piece of yarn through the holes to create a hanger. Or, if using a pocket chart, place the child's name card in each pocket.

☆ Hang the children's names underneath the chores they are responsible for each week.

Responsibility Straws

☆ Cover juice cans with paper. Label each with a classroom chore, such as wipe tables, straighten books, pick up trash in play yard, and sweep sand off sidewalk.

☆ Place the cans in box labeled "Chore Box."

☆ Cut paper into small strips about 1" x 3". Print each child's name on a strip.

☆ Attach the strips to straws to make "flag straws" and place them in the box.

☆ When the children come in each Monday, have them choose a chore for the week by placing the straw with their name on it in the can of choice.

☆ Be sure to provide time for children to accomplish their chores and make sure to acknowledge them.

Understanding and Controlling Emotions

My Feelings

☆ Cut out circles from construction paper. Draw a happy face on half of them and a sad face on the rest. Make a happy and sad face for every child in the room.

☆ Glue the faces back to back on a Popsicle stick so that one side has a happy face and the other side has a sad face. Give one to each child.

☆ Each morning, ask the children to show the face that illustrates how they feel.

☆ Randomly choose a few children to tell the group why they feel the way they do.

Happy and Sad

☆ Give each child two paper plates. If children have the skills, ask them to draw a happy face on one plate and a sad face on the other.

☆ An alternative would be to use a digital camera to take two pictures of each child, one smiling and one frowning. Print the pictures and let the children glue one to each of their plates.

☆ Play music that exemplifies different moods (light-hearted, happy melodies and somber, sad songs).

☆ Ask the children to hold up the paper plate that they think most fits the music.

☆ Discuss how the music makes them feel.

Home Connection: Suggest children talk with their family members about what type of music they enjoy the most.

Feeling

☆ Tell the children the following story:

Lee got a brand new puppy for his birthday. He loved the puppy very much, but the puppy was very naughty. The first day he chewed up Daddy's slipper. The second day he chewed up the garbage sack and spilled garbage all over the kitchen floor. The third day he woke up everyone by barking at the cat on the windowsill. That day, his mother said, "No more puppy in the house."

☆ Ask the children questions about how Lee might feel, how his daddy might feel, how his mother might feel, and how the puppy might feel.

Face to Face

☆ Cut out ten circles from durable paper (tagboard, wallpaper, or poster board).

☆ Draw five sets of matching facial expressions on the circles.

☆ Encourage the children to find the matching pairs of faces.

☆ To increase difficulty, increase the number of face pairs.

My Family

Family Portrait

☆ Encourage the children to draw all the members of their families in a family portrait.

☆ Label each family member as he or she is described by the child.

☆ Ask the children questions about their roles in their families. *Are you the oldest child? Youngest? What do you do to help your family? Do you help clean up? Do you help fix dinner?*

☆ Extend this activity by inviting the children to tell their classmates about their family.

Home Connection: Ask the children to work with their families to write a short story about their family on the back of their portraits.

Family Tree

☆ Ask the children to bring in pictures of grandparents, family members, and themselves.

☆ Place family groupings in chronological order as the children talk about their lineage.

☆ If pictures are unavailable, use magazine pictures to categorize age groups.

Home Connection: Ask families to create a family tree with their children.

Names for Relatives

☆ Talk with the children about special names they have for their grandparents and other special relatives.

☆ Tell them the special names you use for special people in your life.

☆ Make a list of all the special names. Point out to the children how many different names there are on the list.

Home Connection: Suggest that children ask their family members what special names they used for their grandparents.

Classroom "Concerts"

☆ Send out a family questionnaire that includes a question on talent.

☆ If there is a family member who plays an instrument, ask him or her to demonstrate the instrument to the class.

☆ If performers are not available, ask if any family members could show an instrument they have, and if possible, let the children touch it and hold it.

☆ Follow up with music that makes individual instruments distinguishable. *Do you hear the trumpet? Do you hear the violin?*

Sharing and Cooperating

Tips for Taking Turns

☆ Invite the children to sign up for time on the tricycle.

☆ Ask the children to draw a number for their place on the "turn" list.

☆ Use an egg timer or hourglass to time each child's turn.

☆ When one child's turn is over, call the next name on the list.

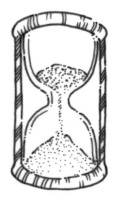

Pass It Along

☆ Have a hall or sidewalk "garage sale" to pass on outgrown clothes and small household items. Ask families for contributions and to participate in the sale.

☆ Price the items at two, five, ten, twenty-five cents, and a dollar so that the children can experience working with money as they sell and make change for the items.

☆ Let the children select a new classroom toy from a catalog with the proceeds.

Tips for Sharing

☆ When a child brings an item to school to share, write her name on a piece of masking tape and stick it on the item.

☆ Children will be much more content to share when they are sure that everyone knows to whom the item belongs.

Participating and Contributing

Classroom Quilt

☆ Give each child the same size piece of art paper and ask her to draw a picture on it.

☆ When they have finished, arrange the pictures as quilt squares in a quilt.

☆ When the desired pattern is arranged, turn the pictures over and tape together.

☆ Hang the "quilt" on the wall.

Trash Truck

☆ To help develop experience in sharing responsibilities, prepare a "trash truck" by punching two holes in the front of a box and tying a small rope through to make a handle.

☆ Paint the box. After it dries, paint the words "Trash Truck" on the side.

☆ Let the children take turns pulling the box around the play yard (or classroom after snack). The classmates place trash in the truck and the "driver" empties it into a trashcan.

Litter Brigade

☆ Punch a hole in each side of a cereal box and tie a cord through. Make one for each child.

☆ Help the children hang the boxes over their shoulders to make "litter collectors."

☆ Go for a walk and ask the children to put any trash they find in their litter collectors.

Safety Note: Make sure children do not pick up any sharp or dangerous items, and that they wash their hands when they get back to the classroom.

Sidewalk Art Sale

☆ Save children's artwork for a period of time. Frame the artwork with mats cut from construction paper or wallpaper scraps, giving each piece of artwork a finished look.

☆ Use clothespins to attach artwork to a fence or place on the hall walls.

☆ Put price tags ranging from five to twenty-five cents on each piece.

☆ Invite families and friends to the "art sale." Place proceeds in the class funds.

☆ After the event, let the children decide on a charity to donate their revenue to.

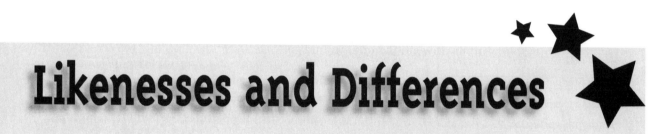

Likenesses and Differences

International Feast

☆ Plan an International Feast Day with a variety of foods for children to sample, for example, Japanese tea, Polynesian poi, Mexican enchiladas, African yams, Chinese egg rolls, Italian pasta, and Polish sausage. Involve families and appropriate staff members.

☆ Explain to children that some of the members of certain cultures eat these foods, and some do not. Make it clear that these foods originate from certain cultures but not every person of these cultures eats this food (for example, not every person of Italian descent eats pasta).

☆ An alternative could be to have a family-involved international "pot-luck" dinner, with each family bringing an item of food.

Home, Sweet Home

☆ Take a field trip to view various homes (an apartment, a two-story home, a one-story home, a mobile home, and so on).

☆ Discuss what is unique about each one.

☆ Provide magazines and encourage the children to cut out pictures of different kinds of houses.

☆ Discuss homes with children. Conclude that families live in many types of homes.

The Instant Curriculum

There Is More Than One Way

☆ To create interest in an understanding of people of differing cultures, prepare a series of pictures of people involved in interesting but different activities (for example, eating with chopsticks, dressing in a sari, carrying a baby on a cradleboard, and so on).

☆ Glue the pictures on manila folders in a vertical position. Cut off the tabs of the folders to make them even.

☆ Hinge the folders together with tape. When all the folders are opened, one long line of pictures will be displayed in accordion fashion.

☆ Discuss the pictures with the children. In what ways do the pictures display a different approach to activities that the children are familiar with?

☆ To create additional interest, place the "string" of folders on the floor in a semi-circle. Children can lie on the floor and look at the pictures.

See, Touch, and Hear

☆ At various times during the year, create interest centers based upon a particular culture.

☆ For example, for an Asian culture, you might display pictures, a bonsai plant, fans, teapot and teacups, tatami mats, chopsticks, and so on.

☆ Plan a related activity, such as painting on construction paper and folding it into a fan.

☆ Read a children's book about the featured country or culture.

☆ Repeat periodically, featuring another culture.

Everyone's a Piece of the Puzzle—Social Studies

Goodbye, Adios, and Sayonara

☆ Since children are particularly sensitive to auditory sounds during the first five years of life, use this opportunity to expose them to several words of a second language.

☆ Ask families, friends, or children in the classroom if they speak another language, and ask them to help you learn simple, everyday words in other languages.

☆ Many teachable moments arise throughout the day when a second language can be used in meaningful context, for example, to count children in line, answer a yes/no question, and say "hello" and "goodbye."

Community Workers and Friends

Career Prop Boxes

☆ Develop a variety of prop boxes for various careers and professions. Place dramatic play equipment for specific jobs in each prop box (medical careers, administrative assistants, teachers, bus drivers, and so on).

☆ Bring each box into the Dramatic Play Center for a week or two at a time so that children can develop their own play. (See pages 64-65 for prop box suggestions.)

Baker's box

The Instant Curriculum

Job Fair

☆ Invite family members (or individuals from the community) to visit the class and describe what they do at their job.

☆ Encourage speakers to bring something tangible for each child to take home, or touch and see that is related to their work (for example, pharmacists—an empty pill bottle, banker—blank checks, pilot—pictures of a plane, computer programmer—mouse).

Home Connection: Ask children to talk with their families about the work they do. Encourage them to discuss their family member's job during morning circle.

Small Mall

☆ Bring in assorted items from garage sales for children to sell (keys, old scarves, baseball caps, and so on).

☆ Let the children take turns playing "shopkeepers," "shoppers," and "bankers."

☆ Shopkeepers can place previously prepared price tags, ranging from one to ten cents, on items. Shoppers get pennies from bankers to pay for items, which they take home if it is okay with families.

☆ The shopkeeper returns the pennies to the banker at end of the day to be reused the next day. Continue for a week or until items run out.

☆ After sales, invite the children to trade if they wish, so they can learn the concept of bartering.

Senior Citizens' Day

☆ Invite grandparents or residents from a local retirement center to visit the classroom and, if appropriate, have lunch with the children.

☆ Encourage the children to talk with individual seniors. Suggest that they tell the visitors about what they do at school.

☆ Invite seniors to tell the children about what they did when they were children.

Note: Enhance this activity by asking the seniors to share their childhood pictures.

Concepts of Time

Yesterday, Today, and Tomorrow

☆ On occasion and when appropriate, start the day using sentences that describe the events that were experienced yesterday, events that will happen today, and events that are planned for tomorrow.

☆ Help the children use the terms "yesterday," "tomorrow," and "today" in their descriptions of information.

Tomorrow Box

☆ Provide a "Tomorrow Box" in the Art Center for unfinished projects. Children can place unfinished artwork in the box to finish the next day.

☆ Provide a "Tomorrow Shelf" for unfinished books that children are "reading."

Growing Up

☆ Ask each child to bring a picture of herself as a baby, a toddler, and at present age (representative magazine pictures can be used, if necessary).

☆ Challenge the children to think about things they can do now but could not do when they were smaller. Discuss clothing differences, food differences, and toy differences.

☆ Sequence the pictures chronologically on a chart.

Bygones

☆ Have the children ask family members or neighbors to help them locate items that were used in the past (such as a flat iron, butter churn, hand fan, manual juice squeezer, washboard, lantern, or button hook), but have been replaced or are no longer needed in modern society.

☆ Ask the children to bring the items to class to share with classmates.

Morning, Noon, and Night

☆ Provide pictures of activities typically done in the morning—getting out of bed, brushing teeth, eating breakfast, and so on.

☆ Collect pictures of activities that are more likely to occur in the middle of the day, and activities that occur during the night.

☆ Discuss the activities with the children. Be sure to address those activities that may show up in more than one part of the day (brushing teeth, for example).

☆ Invite the children to sort the pictures into the appropriate categories.

Environmental Awareness

Use and Reuse

☆ To help children understand that some items can be reused, send a grocery bag and a note home with each child asking family members to help children collect items that can be reused—plastic butter tubs, clean bottles, egg cartons, corks, soap bits, old stockings, and so on.

☆ When the children are done bringing in items, sort the items into categories related to use.

☆ Use the items for many activities described in other chapters, as well as for the activities in this chapter.

Recycled Products

☆ Involve families in saving the following items for school use:
  ★ greeting cards (cut them into puzzles)
  ★ stickers (use them for memory games and art projects)
  ★ envelopes (to hold individual collections of leaves, alphabet letters, or pictures)
  ★ meat trays (use for art activities such as crayon drawing trays)
  ★ discarded paper (use as art paper)
  ★ file folders (individual art folders)

Clothes Corner

☆ Establish a "clothes corner" where children can regularly bring out-grown clothing to pass on to other children.

Pen Pals

☆ Save dried-out felt-tip pens and markers.
☆ Place them at the art easel for the children to use as brushes.

Crayon Conservation

☆ Collect crayons that are too broken and too small to use.
☆ Place the pieces in muffin tins and melt on a warming tray or a microwave-safe dish if using the microwave
☆ Remove from heat when the crayons reach soft stage (not liquid).
☆ The children can use the cooled crayons from the muffin tin cups as multi-colored crayons.

Safety Note: Closely supervise this activity.

Sandbox Tools

☆ Collect clean bleach bottles or similar types of bottles to make buckets, sand scoops, and funnels.
☆ Use one bottle to make a bucket and a scoop. Cut the bottle in half and use the bottom half for a bucket and the top half with the handle (and screwed-on cap) to make a scoop.
☆ To make a funnel, remove the cap from the top half of the bottle.

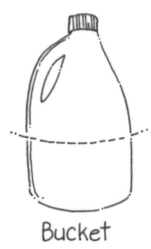

Bucket

funnel

scoop

Re-Bow

☆ Use old gift wrapping bows to make flower leis.
☆ Cut a cord or ribbon into necklace length; string bows on the cord.

The Instant Curriculum

Recycled Soap

☆ Encourage the children to bring old soap bits to school instead of throwing them away.

☆ Place the old soap bits in a clean, sheer stocking.

☆ Tie the stocking to the handle of the sink for use as hand-washing soap. This also keeps soap off the floor.

☆ If desired, use a plastic tub instead of a stocking.

Bits and Pieces

☆ To help children learn how to save materials, keep a container on the art shelf for bits of paper that are left over from cutting activities.

☆ Establish a practice with the children of tearing these scraps into little bits and saving them in the container for future collage activities. A clear plastic container makes the project more interesting for children because they can watch the "bit" pile grow.

Rainwater Recycle

☆ Place containers on the playground to collect rainwater.

☆ Let the children use the collected water to water plants in the room or on the playground.

☆ Use a permanent marker to draw inch markings inside the container to show how much rainwater has been collected.

Rainbow Bottles

☆ Use empty ½ liter soda bottles to create a "rainbow of color" on the windowsill.

☆ Put a couple of drops of food coloring (one color to a bottle) in bottles filled with water. Glue on the cap for safety.

☆ Invite the children to roll the bottles across the table to diffuse the color.

☆ Place the bottles in a window for decoration and as a resource for color identification.

A Tree From Me

☆ Obtain a number of small trees (5" to 10" in height) from friends, family members, your own yard, or your county agricultural extension service. Usable types include acorns that have sprouted, small tallow trees that have "volunteer" saplings under them, or small pine seedlings.

☆ Bring the small trees to the classroom and help the children plant them in milk cartons (with tops cut off).

☆ Let the children take care of the trees by watering them and keeping them in the sun.

☆ After a period of growth, the trees will need to be replanted. Let each child take a tree home to plant. If yards are not available to children, plant on school grounds or in the yards of "friends of the school."

☆ Discuss with children that years from now, other children will enjoy the trees, animals will makes homes in them, and so on. Remind them that they are making a contribution to the future. Thank them for their thoughtfulness.

Health and Safety

Safety Rituals

☆ Safety and well-being are the first concerns of all of us. Our brains can't focus on anything else until our safety is ensured.

☆ Have a morning ritual that encourages children to leave any fears or concerns they may have at the door.

☆ One suggestion is to have each child place her name, photo, or special trinket inside of a locked box (the box represents the classroom and is symbolic for a safe place).

☆ Gather the children together and tell them, "In our classroom we are all safe. We take care of each other at all times."

☆ Look for more suggestions in *I Love You Rituals* by Becky Bailey.

The Instant Curriculum

A Healthy Song

☆ When children are learning about healthy food to eat, reinforce the concept with this song. Sing to the tune of "She'll Be Coming 'Round the Mountain":

We'll be coming to the table very soon.
We'll be coming to the table very soon.
We'll be coming to the table,
We'll be coming to the table,
We'll be coming to the table very soon.

We'll be eating celery and carrots very soon.
We'll be eating celery and carrots very soon.
We'll be eating celery and carrots,
We'll be eating celery and carrots,
We'll be eating celery and carrots very soon.

☆ Encourage the children to make up more verses with different food pairs, such as apples and bananas, strawberries and milk, and broccoli and peas.

Cross-Lateral Brain Energizers

☆ Teach the children about the value of cross-lateral movements. Explain that these movements energize our brains and help us think more clearly.

☆ Explain that cross-lateral movements are those that require taking the limbs on one side of the body and passing them across your midline (the section of your body that goes from your nose to your navel).

☆ Challenge the children to think of some cross-lateral movements they can do every day, several times a day, such as giving yourself a hug or changing the hand movements to a familiar song. For example, when you sing "If You're Happy and You Know It" and you clap to your left and then to your right, you have changed the traditional movements to cross-lateral movements.

Breathe Deeply

☆ The human brain needs oxygen in order to stay alert. Teach the children about the role oxygen plays in keeping their brains alert.

☆ Help the children brainstorm a list of ways to increase their oxygen level, for example, exercise, running, deep breathing, singing, and so on. Discuss their ideas.

☆ Try some of their suggestions and see if they feel more alert.

Thirsty Brains Can't Think

☆ Explain to the children that water keeps the brain alert. (Brain research tells us that if you drink water throughout the day, you will be able to think more quickly and more clearly.)

☆ Challenge the children to brainstorm a list of ideas for increasing the amount of water they drink each day. Discuss their ideas. Try some of the suggestions.

Home Connection: Suggest that children talk with their families about the importance of water in their diet.

Homemade Toothpaste

☆ Invite the children to help make toothpaste.

☆ Mix baking soda and water to make a paste. Add a couple of drops of peppermint extract.

☆ Invite the children to brush their teeth with the homemade toothpaste.

Note: Ask families to send a toothbrush to school that will remain at school.

☆ Teach the children proper brushing techniques. Sing the following song to the tune of "Here We Go 'Round the Mulberry Bush":

This Is the Way We Brush Our Teeth
This is the way we brush our teeth,
Brush our teeth, brush our teeth.
This is the way we brush our teeth,
Every morning and evening.

We move the brush up and down…

Squeaky Clean

☆ Talk with the children about cleanliness. Discuss washing their hands, face, and hair.

☆ Sing the following song to the tune of "Here We Go 'Round the Mulberry Bush" to help teach children about washing their faces.

This Is the Way We Wash Our Face
This is the way we wash our face,
Scrub our cheeks, scrub our ears.
This is the way we wash our face,
Until we're squeaky clean.

Food Group Pyramid

☆ Gather five medium-size boxes (about the size of a copy paper box). Use one box to represent each of the five food categories in the food pyramid: milk and dairy products; meats, fish, poultry, eggs, and nuts; fruits; vegetables; and breads and grains.

☆ Cut out photos of different foods from magazines and glue them to the appropriate box.

☆ Use the boxes to define each food group for the children. Introduce the groups one at a time. Stack the boxes as each group is introduced so that after introducing all five groups, you will have a food pyramid.

Paper Plate Food Collage

☆ Gather cardboard boxes. Write the name of a food group on each box (meat, fruit, vegetables, and so on).

☆ Invite the children to cut out magazine pictures of food. For younger children, you may want to do the cutting ahead of time.

☆ Help the children place the pictures in the boxes.

☆ Give each child a paper plate. Invite the children to select a picture from each food group box to paste on their paper plates to create a balanced meal.

Home Connection: Ask the children to pay special attention to their dinner. *Which food groups are on your dinner plate?* Tell the children that the next day they will discuss the food groups they have eaten.

Heartbeats

☆ Ask the children to put their hands on their chests to feel their heartbeat or use a cardboard tube (such as a paper towel or toilet paper tube) to listen to a friend's heart. If you have access to a stethoscope, let the children use it to listen to their heartbeats and the heartbeats of their friends.

Note: The cardboard tube helps isolate the sound of the heartbeat and block out other sounds.

☆ Play some lively music and ask the group to do some exercises. Then ask them to recheck their heartbeats in the same manner.

☆ Children will notice that after exercise, their hearts beat faster and they breathe faster. Point out that exercise is good for a person's health because increasing one's heartbeat and breathing pumps blood through the body and gets oxygen to all the right places in the body.

☆ Ask the children to check their heartbeats when they wake up from a nap, before getting up. Point out the value of rest for their hearts. Hearts are muscles, and they need rest too.

Traffic Lights

☆ Cut out green, yellow, and red circles from construction paper.

☆ Discuss what each color means (green: go, yellow: slow down, and red: stop).

☆ Let the children paste the circles in a shoebox lid in the order of a real traffic signal: red, yellow, and then green.

☆ Discuss crossing the street by watching the traffic light.

Home Connection: Suggest that children watch traffic lights on the way home from school. Encourage them to watch people crossing the street. *Do they cross when the light says it is safe?*

Stop Signs

☆ Draw a stop sign shape (octagon) on construction paper. Make one for each child.

☆ Help the children write the word "STOP" using a black crayon inside the drawing.

☆ Encourage them to use a sponge or brush to paint the sign.

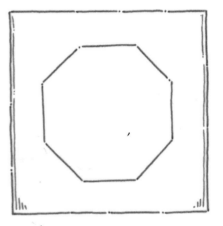

☆ When the paint is dry, children can cut out the sign.

☆ The children can use the sign as a prop with tricycle traffic.

Home Connection: Suggest children count stop signs on their way home from school.

Stop, Look, and Listen

☆ Teach the children the "Stop, Look, and Listen" rule for crossing the street. When you get to an intersection or a street that you want to cross, first stop, then look and listen in both directions for traffic that is coming. When it is safe (no traffic coming), proceed across the street.

☆ After practicing in the classroom, take the children on a walk around the neighborhood to practice the rule.

Home Connection: Suggest the children ask a family member to walk across the street in front of their house with them so they can demonstrate the rule for crossing the street safely.

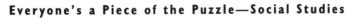

Stop, Drop, and Roll

☆ Teach the children the "Stop, Drop, and Roll" rule for putting out a fire that has spread to their clothing or hair. (Stopping reduces the opportunity for the air to fuel the fire. Dropping and rolling on the ground will smother the fire.) Sing the following to the tune of "Hot Cross Buns."

☆ If possible, invite a firefighter to come to class to demonstrate.

Stop, Drop, and Roll
Stop, drop, and roll.
Stop, drop, and roll.
If ever your clothes catch on fire,
Stop, drop, and roll.

Remember this rule,
This golden safety rule.
If ever your clothes catch on fire,
Stop, drop, and roll.

Preparing for the Future—Critical Thinking and Problem Solving

Overview

Children are born curious and capable of generating solutions to problems. Everyone has seen a young child, intent on reaching a toy, try various strategies until he gets what he wants. Every parent has experienced the endless maneuvers of a child trying to secure adult attention.

If the natural curiosity of children is supported by the adults they encounter, they will continue to use creativity and imagination in their approach to daily experiences. If it is stifled, they will become dependent on adult approval and less likely to have enough confidence to forge ahead alone. The critical steps involved in trial and error learning begin to be extinguished.

It is important for adults to model creativity and imagination in both their thinking and in their strategies to solve problems. Children need to be encouraged to think independently and creatively. Questions should be presented in an open-ended fashion so that children are free to express their divergent perspective on activities and events. "How" and "why" questions are hallmarks of the critical thinking supportive classroom.

The alert teacher will set a tone for critical thinking by valuing alternate answers to these questions, by refraining from offering ready solutions, and by encouraging children to feel free to express their ideas (see Questioning Strategies on page 117).

Activities in this chapter are designed to stimulate children's natural ability to think critically and creatively. They are intended to encourage the teacher to follow processes that enhance this development. Following are some specific steps used in problem solving that are easy to employ with young children.

Step 1: Help children identify the problem (for example, a ball is in a large puddle of water on the playground and is impossible to retrieve without getting shoes wet).

Brain Fast Facts

☆ The brain "feeds" on problems and constantly searches for patterns.
☆ Problem solving and self-esteem go hand in hand.
☆ Thinking skills are wired between birth and age four and are reinforced from age five to puberty.

Step 2: Assist the children in generating several possible solutions to the problem. For example, using a stick to move the ball, throwing another ball at the ball to move it, riding a tricycle into the puddle to get the ball, and taking their shoes off and wading in the puddle to get the ball.

Step 3: Let the children select a solution to test (for example, using the stick to get the ball). You may need to help the children clarify their thinking. *Why do you think that will work, Georgia?* Verbalizing thoughts can be helpful in determining the best choice of solutions.

Step 4: Allow the children to test safe solutions, such as trying to use a stick to reach the ball.

Step 5: Help the children evaluate the results. *Did it work? Was it the best solution? Is the problem solved permanently or just temporarily?*

These steps may seem second nature to adults, but they must be practiced by children for them to internalize them. There will be many opportunities each day with and without formal activities to practice these steps. Use teachable moments—someone spills juice, Adam and Matthew both want a turn on the tricycle, and so on.

In the area of critical thinking, the goal is to help children move beyond the naming and labeling stages of critical thinking and verbalization and into application, analysis, and evaluation. As they do this, their self-confidence and self-esteem will flourish. The preschool child who generates five solutions for getting a ball out of a puddle today may be the scientist of tomorrow who discovers alternate forms of energy, or the diplomat who successfully arbitrates peace between two conflicting factions.

Critical Thinking and Problem Solving

Arm Stretchers

☆ Place a book on a high shelf or on top of a cabinet or locker out of the reach of children.
☆ Ask the children to think of possible safe ways to reach the book.
☆ Pick a solution and try it.
☆ Evaluate the results.
☆ Follow the problem-solving steps described in the overview of this chapter.

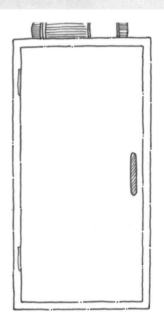

Two Parts, Three People!

☆ Propose the following situation to the children:

Madison and Gabrielle have just made a peanut butter sandwich. They have used the last two pieces of bread. They cut the sandwich in half and are just getting ready for their first bite when into the room comes Juan. Juan would like some of the sandwich. What can Madison and Gabrielle do?

☆ Use the problem-solving steps described in the overview of this chapter. Let the children propose solutions, test their solution, and evaluate the results.

How Many People in Your Family?

☆ After introducing children to one-to-one matching, give each child a baggie with six to eight pebbles inside.

☆ Ask the children to take the bags home and match the pebbles to their family members using one-to-one correspondence.

☆ Instruct the children to discard extra pebbles.

☆ When the children return to school, invite them to show how many pebbles are left in their bags.

☆ Make comparisons. *Who has the most people in their family? Who has the fewest? How many children have the same number of family members?*

What Can You Do With This?

☆ Gather the children in a circle. Give each child a piece of paper.

☆ Ask the children to think of something they can do with their paper, without moving from the circle.

☆ Give them time to think, and then close your eyes while the children do something with their paper—tear it in half, crumple into a ball, put it under their foot, sit on it, and so on.

☆ Repeat this activity at other times as children become more comfortable with trying original ideas. Try other shapes and other types of paper. Foil can be interesting.

What Will Go in This?

☆ Obtain three to four different size boxes; put a classroom item in each box.

☆ Hold up each box and ask the children to name some things that could fit in the box. For example, a small box might hold a toy car, a bracelet, or a ribbon. Repeat with each box.

☆ Reveal the contents after each guessing session.

Home Connection: Extend the activity by giving each child a box to fill with something from home and bring back the next day. On the following day, give each child a turn having the class guess what's in his box.

Water Brigade

☆ Pose this question to children: *How many different ways could we take water from the water fountain to the water table?* Explain that they can use anything in the room to transfer the water.

☆ Let each child demonstrate a different method of his own creation—cup, spoon, baster, funnel with finger on spout, and so on. The rules for this game are: no one can repeat a process previously used, and no one can offer suggestions.

☆ Encourage children to think of more ideas. *Is there anything under or around the sink that you could use?* Additional ideas might include soaking a paper towel or washcloth and squeezing it out at the water table, carrying water in a soap dish, and so on.

☆ Ask the children to think again. *Is there any way you could use your body to transfer water?* They might carry it in cupped hands.

Follow the Arrows

☆ Make a number of cardboard arrows—some straight, some right-angled, and some left-angled.

☆ Hide a "treasure" or "treat" somewhere in the room or on the playground.

☆ Create a path with the arrows that will lead children to the hiding spot. Be sure to place arrows far enough apart to be challenging.

Ping-Pong Races

☆ Place two long strips of masking tape on the floor, approximately 5' apart.

☆ Ask the children how they could move a ping-pong ball from one taped line to the other without touching it.

☆ Make several suggestions and supply several possible tools. Possibilities include blowing with your mouth, fanning with a book, blowing with a straw, and blowing through a paper towel tube.

☆ Invite the children to try suggestions.

☆ Extend thinking by asking them to determine which method accomplished the task the fastest.

☆ Turn this activity into a game by having one child on each side of a line moving the ball back and forth, or inviting a pair of children to have a ping-pong ball race.

Where's the Birdie?

☆ Cut out some bird tracks and cat tracks from black construction paper.

☆ Tape the footprints on the floor with the bird prints (about three pairs) going vertically and the cat prints going horizontally, so that the two sets of prints meet at a right angle and then only the cat prints continue. Ask the children what they think happened.

☆ Children will guess many things—the bird flew away, the cat ate the bird, the bird jumped on the cat's back, and so on.

☆ Ask the children if there is any way they can know for sure what happened. Talk about clues.

Wacky Wednesday

☆ Read the story *Wacky Wednesday* by Theo LeSieg to the children on a Tuesday.

☆ This book is a "what's wrong here?" type of story where everything is different from the way it should be.

☆ Explain to the children that when they come to school the next day, it's going to be "Wacky Wednesday." If they want to participate, they may do so by dressing in a way that is unusual, such as wearing a shirt inside out.

☆ On Wednesday, do several things to the classroom that are obviously unusual. For example, turn a table upside down, reverse the characters on a bulletin board, or move items from one center to another area of the room. Dress in an unusual way, such as wearing a pair of skates. Use your imagination: the wackier, the better!

☆ Challenge the children to find all the things that are "wacky."

Home Connection: Invite families to join the fun. The story begins with a little boy waking up and seeing a shoe on his wall. Suggest families find a way to place a shoe on the wall or in another unusual place.

The Instant Curriculum

Is This Cup Full?

☆ Fill a glass almost all the way with pebbles. Ask the children if the glass is full. If they don't think so, have them add pebbles until everyone agrees that the glass is full. Then ask if they think anything else will fit in the glass. The children will probably say no.

☆ Pour either salt or sand into the glass. The children will be surprised to see the glass can hold more. Call their attention to how the salt or sand fills in the spaces left between the pebbles. Now ask again if the glass is full. The children will say probably say yes.

☆ Now pour water into the same glass. The children will again be surprised. Ask if anybody knows why the glass could hold the water.

☆ Ask the children if the process could work in reverse, starting with a full glass of water and adding salt and rocks. Try their suggestions.

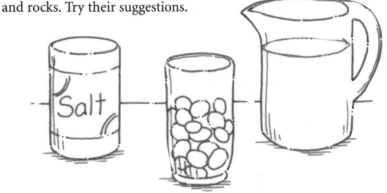

Separating Solids

☆ Mix one cup of pebbles, one cup of sand, and one cup of birdseed together in a bowl.

☆ Provide the children with a strainer and a colander and ask them to separate the items in the bowl into three separate bowls—one with pebbles, one with sand, and one with birdseed.

☆ After the children are successful, ask them if they can think of another way to accomplish the task.

☆ When you are finished with this activity, feed the birdseed to the birds.

Spill Cleanup

☆ When a spill occurs, ask the children to think of as many ways as they can to clean it up.

☆ Help them become aware of the steps they use to solve the problem:

  ★ **Problem:** How can I clean up the spill? Possible solutions include paper towels, mop, or sponge.

  ★ **Select a method:** Use a paper towel to clean up the spill.

  ★ **Test the method:** Try using a paper towel.

  ★ **Evaluate:** Did it work? Was it efficient?

☆ Think of other problems and have the children go through the above process to solve them.

From Many to One

☆ Give the children a set of nesting bowls.

☆ Ask the children how they could pack the bowls in a small box.

Puzzle Challenge

☆ Turn a puzzle over and ask the children to put it together with the backside up.

☆ Increase the difficulty by increasing the number of pieces in the puzzle.

Funnel Race

☆ Roll sheets of paper into funnels with various sizes of openings at the bottom.

☆ Tape the funnels so that they retain their shape.

☆ Let the children explore the speed at which sand travels through the different-sized funnels.

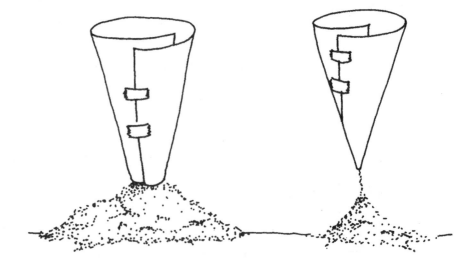

Greeting Card Cut-Ups

☆ Cut old greeting cards into puzzle-like shapes.
☆ Give each child a cut-up card (puzzle) and a piece of background paper and encourage them to fit the pieces back together to form a card.

Pass the Purse

☆ Place three to five purse-related items (such as a lipstick, emery board, bobby pin, and comb) in each of several purses or paper bags.
☆ Have the children sit in a circle. Pass a purse while music is playing.
☆ When the music stops, the child holding the purse attempts to identify the object inside by touch only, without looking.
☆ The child sitting next to the purse- or bag-holder verifies the contents by looking.
☆ Continue music and passing other purses or bags.

Bubbles Aloft

☆ Provide bubble solution (see page 43 for recipe) for children to blow bubbles.
☆ Challenge the children to keep the bubbles aloft as long as possible.

Rollers and Clunkers

☆ Provide a box of assorted items—some that roll and some that don't (a small wheel, paper plate, block, book, and so on).
☆ Let the children experiment with each item to see if it will roll or not. Challenge them to sort the objects into the two categories.

Back Together Again

☆ Cut large magazine pictures into three or four vertical strips.
☆ Invite the children to glue the pictures back together on a piece of construction paper.

Go-Togethers

☆ Gather a group of items that includes pairs of items that go together, such as a shoe and a sock, a pencil and paper, a comb and brush, soap and a washcloth, or a flower and a vase.

☆ Mix up the items.

☆ Challenge the children to take turns matching items that go together.

Adapting to Change— Transitions

Overview

Moving children from activity to activity throughout the day is not easy. Moving any group of people from activity to activity is always challenging, but when the members of the group are all less than five years old, the challenge can be overwhelming.

Transitions make the changing of activities a much smoother event in the preschool classroom. Transitions should be fun as well as functional. Asking children to move in an imaginative way from one place to another helps them focus on getting to the next activity instead of on a request for change.

Special songs and musical cues, such as the ringing of a bell or beating of a drum, can be used for transitions that are part of the daily routine, for example, cleanup and getting ready for lunch. With non-verbal directives, children are more likely to "tune-in" to what they are being asked to do and view the transition as a playful experience.

The activities that follow are a few examples of ways to reduce the stress of changing from one activity to another.

Brain Fast Facts

☆ Transitions allow the brain time to adjust from one environment to another or from one activity to another. It generally takes the brain a full five minutes to make adjustments to change.

Transitions

Pretend Places

☆ As children are completing cleanup tasks and gathering for circle time, ask them to pretend they are in the library.

☆ Other environments they can pretend to be in for quiet waiting periods include sitting at the lake fishing, in the nursery rocking a baby, and sitting at a computer typing.

Who Am I?

☆ As children leave circle and go outside for play, invite some to move like tightrope walkers, some as horseback riders, and still others as clowns, basketball players, and toddlers.

Musical Cues

☆ Use specific songs on CDs or tapes as cues to direct children to a specific activity.

☆ Good choices for cleanup time include "Dance of the Sugar Plum Fairies" (Tchaikovsky) or "Time to Pick Up the Toys" (sung to the tune of "Here We Go 'Round the Mulberry Bush").

Time to Pick Up the Toys
Now it's time to pick up toys,
Pick up the toys, pick up toys.
Now it's time to pick up toys
For all the girls and boys.

☆ A good song to signal map time is "Lullaby" (Brahms).

☆ Use rhythm band instruments to direct activities. For circle time, tap on a triangle.

The Instant Curriculum

Cues From Classics

☆ Select well-known classics, such as Tchaikovsky's "Nutcracker," Beethoven's "Fifth Symphony," or Mozart's "Minuets." Introduce songs at circle time and play regularly during quiet times, pointing out correct titles and composers' names.

☆ Playing classical music is a great way to help children calm down after active play outdoors or participating in a vigorous indoor music and movement activity.

☆ When the children are familiar with a few classics, ask which they would like you to play, again using the correct names of composers and titles.

☆ At naptime, tune in to a classical radio station as an alternative. Be sure to turn music off after five or ten minutes so that children can sleep more soundly.

Groovy Moves

☆ As children move from a large group activity to an individual activity, invite them to demonstrate a way to move other than on their feet—crawl on hands and knees, scoot on seat, roll or wiggle like a worm, and so on.

Weather Walks

☆ As children move as a group, or individually, encourage them to demonstrate how they would walk in a strong wind, on a hot day, in a snowstorm, or in a flood.

Butterfly Flutter

☆ As children move from the classroom down the halls, have them pretend to be butterflies.

☆ Before beginning, ask the children if a butterfly makes any noise. Ask several children to demonstrate their interpretation of how a butterfly moves before the group starts.

☆ Other suggested animal movements are elephants, cats, mice, and spiders.

Wacky Walks

☆ As children move from a group activity to individual activities, have them demonstrate how they would walk on any of the following surfaces: caramel candy, ice, hot tin roof, mud, rocks, tall field of grass, or a mattress.

The Instant Curriculum

Roll Call

☆ Prepare a name card for each child in the class.

☆ Use the name cards to direct children for transitional activities or for playing games. For example, "This boy (show name) may go to the snack table." "This girl (show name) can take a bow."

Rhyming Roll Call

☆ At opportune times during the day when it's necessary to call a child's name, use as a teachable moment for children to learn rhyming sounds.

☆ Ask, "Would the child whose name rhymes with *ham* get in line?" Pam or Sam or any other person with a name that rhymes responds to the request.

The Instant Curriculum

Keeping Connected— Families as Partners

Overview

Helping children develop to their fullest potential is a full-time, 24-hour-a-day job in which teachers and family members must work together. It requires communication, alignment of goals, staying abreast of the newest information regarding early development, and both parties monitoring development and progress.

Research on family involvement in children's schooling indicates that there is a positive correlation between the degree of involvement and cognitive development, self-esteem, motivation, and academic performance.

Part of our job as early childhood professionals is keeping families involved and helping them stay abreast of the latest information regarding early development. This can be done by sharing information in newsletters, putting notes next to the area where family members sign in, seminars, family conferences, open houses, and in a number of other creative ways.

Throughout this book there have been numerous references to involving immediate and extended family members in actual classroom participation and in extended classroom activities (Home Connections). This chapter provides additional ideas to strengthen the bond between home and school.

Brain Fast Facts

☆ A three-year-old's brain is twice as active as an adult's brain. Much of the wiring for life-long learning has already been done by the time a child is three.

☆ Children learn best when they are able to take knowledge gained in the classroom into their home environment. It makes learning practical and meaningful and, therefore, provides the optimum opportunity for learning to become long term.

Families as Partners

Printed Labels

☆ Print short phrases that describe what children learn during an activity (the lesson objective) on computer labels. For example, if the children glued scoops of ice cream to ice cream cones during a lesson on one-to-one correspondence, the label might read, "Math: one-to-one correspondence."

☆ Attach the labels to children's work. This makes it quick and easy to send information home with all the children.

What We Did This Week

☆ Encourage the children to dictate a list of activities they have participated in during the week.

☆ Copy the list and send it home with the children.

Second Time Around

☆ Create a list of recyclable items to use in the classroom, such as old greeting cards, clean meat trays, egg cartons, small jars, buttons, stickers, clothing (for dramatic play), dried-up felt tip pens, folders, and old jewelry.

☆ Send the list home to families or post it in the area where families sign in children each day.

☆ You may want to include information about how you will be using these items in the classroom.

Special Guest Day

☆ Invite grandparents, special friends, and family members to bring their lunch to school and eat with the children.

The Instant Curriculum

Family Networking

☆ Encourage the development of a family networking group.

☆ You may want to have this group serve as an advisory group—a committee that acts as a liaison between families and teaching staff.

☆ You might also assign them the task of fundraising. Suggest they organize a garage sale, bake sale, yard cleanup, and so on.

Calendars

☆ Send calendars home with important happenings at school marked, such as picture day, water play day, field trips, "bring your pet to school" day, and so on.

☆ Calendars help disseminate a lot of information at one time and also provide a quick easy-to-read reference.

Communication Notes

☆ Make standardized weekly or daily note sheets where you only have to fill in the blanks.

Newsletters

☆ Develop a monthly newsletter. Title it something like "Preschool Times" or "Small Talk."

☆ Include information on child development (such as building self-esteem), a calendar of events, news happening in the school (such as a donation for new playground equipment), news happening among families (such as Lee has a new baby brother), and so on.

The Instant Curriculum

Appendix

Skills	Activities	Theme Connections
Drawings	Drawing Tools (page 22)	Artists
		Things That Go Together
	Drawing Surfaces (page 22)	Opposites
	Crayon Melt (page 22)	Colors
		Shapes
		Sizes
	Doodli-Do (page 22)	Imagination
		Let's Pretend
	Good Graffiti (page 23)	Artists
	Meat Tray Art (page 23)	Textures
	Buttermilk Drawing (page 23)	Opposites
		Textures
	Scented Markers (page 23)	Senses
	Seurat Dots (page 24)	Artists
	Wet Sand Drawings (page 24)	Body Parts
		Colors
		Ocean
		Shapes
		Sizes
Painting	Scratch-and-Sniff Paint (page 25)	Senses
	Fingerpaint and Fingerpaint Relief (page 25)	Body Parts
		Colors
		Opposites
	Splatter Painting (page 25)	Colors
	Cotton Swab Painting (page 26)	Tools
	Textured Painting (page 26)	Opposites
	Bubble Painting (page 26)	Shapes
	Deodorant Bottle Painting (page 26)	Colors
	Spray Painting (page 26)	Colors
	Roller Painting (page 27)	Colors
	Squirt Bottle Painting (page 27)	Colors
	Gadget Painting (page 27)	Tools
	Sponge Painting (page 27)	Textures
	Feather Painting (page 28)	Birds
	Epsom Salt Paint (page 28)	Colors
		Weather
	Icing Paint (page 28)	Colors
		Water
		Weather
	Puff Paint (page 28)	Opposites
	Salt Paint (page 28)	Opposites
Designs	Fingerpaint Baggies (page 29)	Shapes
		Textures
	Marble Prints (page 29)	Cause and Effect
		Shapes
	Car Tracks (page 29)	Transportation/Travel
	Glue Drop Designs (page 30)	Shapes
		Textures
		Weather
	Shaker Art (page 30)	Shapes

Skills	Activities	Theme Connections
	Absorption Designs (page 30)	Water
	Mobiles (page 31)	Nature
	Rubbings (page 31)	Shapes
		Textures
	Sand Designs I (page 31)	Senses
	Sand Designs II (page 32)	Senses
	Mondrian Masterpieces (page 32)	Artists
		Colors
		Shapes
	Template Designs (page 33)	Shapes
	Stained Glass Windows (page 33)	Colors
		Light and Dark
	More Stained Glass Windows (page 33)	Colors
		Light and Dark
	Rock Salt Designs (page 33)	Textures
Prints	Cookie Cutter Prints (page 34)	Use theme-related items
	Gadget Printing (page 34)	Tools
	Bubble Prints I (page 34)	Shapes
	Bubble Prints II (page 34)	Shapes
	Sponge Prints (page 35)	Absorption
		Textures
		Use theme-related sponge shapes
	Blotto Prints I and II (page 35)	Imagination
		Use theme-related items
	Hand Mural (page 36)	All About Me
		Body Parts
	Hand Wreaths (page 36)	All About Me
		Body Parts
	Fingerprint Creations (page 36)	All About Me
		Body Parts
	Footprints (page 36)	All About Me
		Body Parts
Collages	Torn Paper Collages (page 37)	Imagination
	Torn Paper Silhouettes (page 37)	Imagination
	Tissue Paper Collages (page 37)	Colors
	Nature Collages (page 38)	Growing Things
	Confetti Art (page 38)	Celebrations
		Colors
		Shapes
	Humpty Dumpty Reconstruction (page 38)	Nursery Rhymes
	Happy Face Montage (page 38)	All About Me
	Monochromatic Masterpieces (page 39)	Colors
	Shapes on Shapes (page 39)	Shapes
	Textured Collages (page 39)	Senses
Sculpting and Molding	Papier-Mâché (page 40)	Textures
	Goop and Gak (page 40)	Opposites
		Senses
	Cloud Dough (page 40)	Day and Night
		Weather
	Playdough Sculpting (page 41)	Use theme-related ideas for sculptures

Skills	Activities	Theme Connections
Art and Crafts Recipes	Wood Sculpting (page 41)	Imagination
	Box Sculpting (page 41)	Imagination
	Stabiles (page 42)	Use theme-related ideas for sculptures
	Sandcastles (page 42)	Ocean
		Summer
	Mud Pies (page 42)	Imagination
		Weather
	Soap Suds Clay (page 42)	Textures
	Foil Sculptures (page 42)	Imagination
	Cloud Dough (page 43)	Weather
	Colored Glue (page 43)	Colors
	Colored Rock Salt (page 43)	Colors
		Textures
	Epsom Salt Solution (page 43)	Weather
	Gak (page 45)	Senses
		Textures
	Goop (page 45)	Senses
		Textures
	Icing Paint (page 45)	Textures
	Paints (page 46)	Imagination
		Textures
	Papier-Mâché Paste (page 46)	Senses
	Paste (page 46)	Senses
	Playdough Recipe #1 (page 46)	Imagination
		Senses
	Playdough Recipe #2 (page 46)	Imagination
		Senses
	Playdough Recipe #3 (page 47)	Imagination
		Senses
	Puff Paint (page 47)	Imagination
		Textures
	Salt Paint (page 47)	Senses
	Scented Playdough (page 47)	Senses
	Scratch-and-Sniff Paint (page 47)	Senses
	Soap Paint (page 47)	Colors
	Soapsuds Clay (page 47)	Textures
No-Cook Recipes	Milkanilla (page 51)	Animals
		Farms
		Food/Nutrition
	Purple Cow Shakes (page 51)	Animals
		Farms
	Baggie Ice Cream (page 52)	Farms
		Food/Nutrition
		Opposites
	Can Ice Cream (page 52)	Food/Nutrition
		Opposites
	Butter (page 52)	Farms
	Sun Salad (page 52)	Day and Night
	Peanut Butter (page 53)	Growing Things
	Peanut Butter Balls (page 53)	Celebration
		Shapes

Skills	Activities	Theme Connections
	Friendship Mixes (page 54)	Friends
	Banana Pudding (page 54)	Food/Nutrition
	Shake-a-Puddin' (page 54)	Textures
	Banana Wheels (page 54)	Transportation/Travel
	Candy Mints (page 55)	Colors
		Shapes
	Glittery Sugar Mallows (page 55)	Colors
	Tooty Fruity (page 56)	Senses
	Apple and Carrot Salad (page 56)	Food/Nutrition
		Growing Things
	Fruit Sticks (page 56)	Food/Nutrition
	Sandwich Animals (page 56)	Animals
	Sandwich Fillings (page 57)	Food/Nutrition
	Toast Tidbits (page 57)	Imagination
Toaster Oven/Oven Recipes	Pizza Faces (page 58)	All About Me
		Body Parts
	Bear Claws (page 58)	Animals
		Traditional Tales
	Pigs in a Blanket (page 58)	Animals
		Food/Nutrition
		Traditional Tales
	Marizipan (page 59)	Celebrations
Refrigerator/Freezer Recipes	Gelatin Jigglers (page 59)	Colors
		Shapes
		Sizes
	One-Cup Salad (page 59)	Food/Nutrition
	Party Pops (page 59)	Seasons
	Shooting Stars (page 60)	Day and Night
Hot Plate/Electric Skillet/Popper Recipes	Chili Popcorn (page 60)	Senses
	Skillet Cookies (page 60)	Celebrations
		Food/Nutrition
	Donuts (page 61)	Shapes
	Grilled Cheese Delights (page 62)	Food/Nutrition
	Prop Boxes--Office (page 66)	Our Community
Imaginative Play	Prop Boxes--Beauty Salon (page 67)	Our Community
	Prop Boxes--Circus (page 67)	Our Community
	Prop Boxes--Hat (page 67)	Our Community
	Car Wash (page 68)	Transportation/Travel
	Gas Station (page 68)	Transportation/Travel
	Tent Town (page 68)	Camping
	Drive-Throughs (page 69)	Our Community
	Dinner Is Served (page 69)	Families
	Baby Bathtime (page 70)	Families
	The Nursery (page 70)	Families
	Box Hideaway (page 71)	Families
		Friends
	Pantry Match (page 71)	Families
		Food/Nutrition
		Matching

Chapter 2—Cooking

Chapter 3—Dramatic Play

Skills	Activities	Theme Connections
Creative Play	What's in the Trunk? (page 72)	Families Our Community Seasons
	Floral Arrangements (page 72)	Our Community
	My Hat (page 72)	Let's Pretend
	Mad Hatters (page 73)	Let's Pretend
	Bakery Goods (page 73)	Food/Nutrition
	Little Designers (page 73)	Let's Pretend Our Community
	Baubles, Beads, Bangles and Belts (page 74)	Let's Pretend
	What Is It? (page 74)	Imagination
	Stocking Snakes (page 74)	Animals
	Soft Blocks (page 75)	Imagination
	Let's Pretend (page 75)	Let's Pretend
Listening	"Go-fers" (page 80)	Body Parts Senses
	Listening Walk (page 80)	Nature Senses
	Sound Canisters (page 80)	Senses
	Where's the Sound? (page 81)	Senses Sounds
	Follow the Sound (page 81)	Senses
	Mystery Sounds (page 81)	Senses Sounds
	Musical Hot and Cold (page 81)	Opposites
	Gossip (page 82)	Body Parts
	Ears Up (page 82)	Body Parts Senses
	Which Instrument Do You Hear? (page 82)	Music Senses
	Do You Hear What I Hear? (page 82)	Senses
	The Sound of Silence (page 83)	Senses
	I've Got Rhythm (page 83)	Music
	Sound Makers (page 83)	Body Parts Celebrations
	Taped Directions (page 84)	Colors
	I Spy (page 84)	Body Parts
	Listening Stories (page 84)	Use theme-related stories
	Simon Says (page 84)	Body Parts Movement
	Twin Tunes (page 85)	Senses
	Listening Tunes (page 85)	Senses
	Clapping Names (page 85)	All About Me Numbers
Oral Language	The Long and the Short of It (page 86)	Sizes
	Reading Vocabulary (page 86)	Use theme-related books
	Singing Vocabulary (page 86)	Use theme-related songs
	Word of the Day (page 86)	Use theme-related words
	A Picture's Worth a Thousand Words (page 87)	Use theme-related photos

Skills	Activities	Theme Connections
	Baggie Book Photo Albums (page 87)	All About Me Families
	Vocabulary Fun (page 88)	Use theme-related vocabulary
	Shopping Fun (page 88)	Our Community
	Sequencing Concrete Objects (page 88)	All About Me
	In the Bag (page 89)	Use theme-related objects
	Positional Words (page 89)	Spatial Concepts
	Opposites (page 89)	Opposites
	Opposites Hunt (page 90)	Opposites
	Sign Language Vocabulary (page 90)	Senses
	Show-and-Tell (page 90)	Families
	Ticklers (page 90)	Friends
	Deluxe Show-and-Tell (page 91)	Families Our Community
	String a Story (page 91)	Imagination
	Nursery Rhyme Pantomimes (page 91)	Nursery Rhymes
	Magic Mirror (page 91)	Make-Believe
	Magic Pebble (page 92)	Make-Believe
	Magic Wand (page 92)	Make-Believe
	Sally Sad and Harry Happy (page 92)	All About Me
	Puppet Party (page 92)	Imagination
	What Do You Know About This? (page 93)	Imagination
	Posing Questions (page 93)	Ask theme-related questions
	Recipe Dictation (page 93)	Food/Nutrition
	Flannel Board Stories (page 93)	Use theme-related stories
	Expanding Story Concepts (page 93)	Use theme-related stories
	Word Police (page 94)	Our Community
Phonological Awareness	Hicky Picky Bumblebee (page 94)	All About Me
	Clapping Words (page 94)	Use theme-related objects
	Silly Sentences (page 95)	Imagination
	Tongue Twisters (page 95)	Senses
	Alliteration Fun (page 95)	Imagination
	Alliterative Songs (page 95)	Sing theme-related songs
	The Sounds of Rain (page 96)	Weather
	Onomatopoeia Songs (page 96)	Sing theme-related songs
	Name Game (page 96)	All About Me
	Pick-a- Pair (page 96)	Use theme-related pairs
	Rime Time (page 97)	Senses
	Rhyme or Reason (page 97)	Senses
	Rhyming Game (page 97)	Senses
	Fill-In Nursery Rhymes (page 98)	Nursery Rhymes
	Rhythmic Nursery Rhymes I (page 98)	Nursery Rhymes
	Rhythmic Nursery Rhymes II (page 98)	Nursery Rhymes
	Whispered Rhymes (page 98)	Sounds
	Rhyme in a Can (page 98)	Imagination
	Say and Touch (page 99)	Body Parts
Letter Knowledge and Recognition	What's Missing? (page 99)	Use theme-related items
	Whoops! (page 100)	Senses
	What's the Order? (page 100)	Use theme-related items
	Can You Remember? (page 100)	Colors

Skills	Activities	Theme Connections
	Wallpaper Lotto (page 101)	Patterns
	Alphabetical Order (page 101)	Imagination
	Which Letter Is Missing? (page 102)	Use theme-related letters
	Gel Bags (page 102)	Senses
	Playdough Letters (page 102)	All About Me
	Pretzel Letters (page 102)	All About Me
	Thumbprint Letters (page 103)	All About Me
		Body Parts
	Freckle Names (page 103)	All About Me
	Letter Tracing (page 103)	Use theme-related words
	Letter Matching (page 103)	Use theme-related letters
		Matching
	Pair, Think, and Share (page 104)	Friends
	Circle the Letter (page 104)	Use theme-related letters
	Letter Tic Tac Toe (page 104)	Use theme-related letters
	Sand Writing (page 104)	Senses
	Sand Letters (page 104)	Senses
	Finger Writing (page 104)	Body Parts
	Tactile Letters (page 105)	Senses
	Tablecloth Lotto (page105)	Use theme-related letters
	Lucky Letters (page 105)	Use theme-related letters
	Bingo (page 106)	Animals
		Farms
	Scrabble Letters (page 106)	Spell theme-related words
	E-I-E-I-O (page 106)	Farms
	Mail Call (page 106)	Friends
	Manual ABC's (page 107)	Body Parts
		Music
Print Awareness	Top, Middle, and Bottom (page 107)	Friends
	More Top, Middle, and Bottom (page 107)	Body Parts
	Left to Right (page 108)	Patterns
	Cozy Comics (page 108)	Imagination
	"Reader's Wiggle" (page 109)	Body Parts
	Name Puzzles (page 110)	All About Me
	Letter Puzzles (page 110)	All About Me
	String a Letter (page 110)	Shapes
	Cereal Box Puzzles (page 110)	Food/Nutrition
	Nametags (page 111)	All About Me
	Grocery Put Away (page 111)	Our Community
	Funny Funny Papers (page 112)	Imagination
	Story Dictation (page 112)	Select theme-related topics
	Experience Charts (page 112)	All About Me
	Classroom Pen Pals (page 113)	Friends
	Rebus Charts (page 113)	Use theme-related examples
	Rebus Treasure Hunt (page 113)	Problem Solving
	Rebus Recipes (page 114)	Food/Nutrition
	Nursery Rhyme Fill-Ins (page 114)	Nursery Rhymes
	Writing Rhymes (page 114)	Nursery Rhymes
	Story Starters (page 114)	Imagination
	Wordless Books (page 114)	Imagination

Skills	Activities	Theme Connections
	Baggie Books (page 115)	Use theme-related pictures
	Lists (page 115)	Make theme-related lists
	Journal Writing (page 116)	Days of the Week
	Pen Pal Buddies (page 116)	Friends
	News Events (page 116)	Families
Comprehension	Story Detectives (page 117)	Use theme-related stories
	True/Not True (page 117)	Opposites
	Questioning Strategies (page 117)	Problem Solving
	Story Maps (page 118)	Use theme-related stories
	Word Webs (page 119)	Use theme-related topics
	Story Re-Enactments (page 119)	Let's Pretend
		Traditional Tales
	Story Pantomime (page 120)	Let's Pretend
		Traditional Tales
	Action Stories (page 120)	Movement
Free Exploration	Junk Boxes (page 123)	Families
		Tools
	Naming Attributes (page 124)	All About Me
	I Spy (page 124)	Problem Solving
	Can You Find It? (page 124)	Hide theme-related items
	Tree Tag I (page 124)	Nature
	Tree Tag II (page 125)	Colors
	Hand Match-Up (page 125)	Friends
		Matching
		Size
	Descriptive Vocabulary (page 125)	Opposites
	More Vocabulary (page 125)	Use theme-related vocabulary
Spatial Relationships	Top, Middle, and Bottom (page 126)	All About Me
	Little Box Surprises (page 126)	Spatial Concepts
	Inside Outside (page 126)	Spatial Concepts
	Over and Under (page 127)	Body Parts
	Where's the Button? (page 127)	Problem Solving
	"Going on a Bear Hunt" (page 127)	Animals
	Circle Commands (page 129)	Shapes
	Twister (page 129)	Colors
Classification	Classmate Classifications (page 130)	All About Me
	Classification Books (page 130)	Make theme-related books
	Button Match (page 130)	Colors
		Matching
	Shoes, Shoes, Shoes (page 131)	All About Me
	Eyes Open, Eyes Shut (page 131)	All About Me
		Body Parts
		Day and Night
	Classifying Snacks (page 131)	Foods/Nutrition
Classifying by Color	Stringing Bead Sort (page 132)	Colors
	Fabric Sort (page 132)	Colors
	Eyes of All Colors (page 132)	Body Parts
Classifying by Shape	Shape Match (page 132)	Matching
		Shapes
	Block Cleanup (page 133)	Sizes

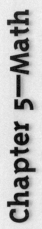

Skills	Activities	Theme Connections
Classifying by Size	Cracker Snackers (page 133)	Celebrations Food/Nutrition
	Shape Step (page 133)	Music
	Big and Little (page 133)	Opposites
	Short and Tall (page 134)	Opposites
	Long and Short (page 134)	Opposites
Classifying Using Senses Other Than Sight	Hard and Soft (page 135)	Opposites
	Loud and Soft (page 135)	Opposites Sound
	Sweet/Not Sweet (page 135)	Food/Nutrition Opposites
	Nice Smell? (page 136)	Senses
Open-Ended Classification	Things That Are…/Things That Are Not… (page 136)	Opposites Nature
	Book Classification (page 137)	Problem Solving
Classification Applications	Questions (page 137)	Use theme-related questions
	Real Life Uses (page 137)	Families Our Community
Patterning	People Patterns (page 138)	Movement
	Object Patterns (page 138)	Use theme-related objects
	Paper Patterns (page 138)	Shapes
	Crayon Patterns (page 138)	Colors
	Paper Chains (page 139)	Colors
	Set Patterns (page 139)	Use theme-related items
	Block Patterns (page 139)	Shapes
	Fruit Kabobs (page 139)	Food/Nutrition
Vertical Patterns	Up and Down (page 140)	Opposites
	Tube Bands (page 140)	Sizes
	Balls in a Tube (page 140)	Colors
	Stacking Cans (page 140)	Under Construction
Circular Patterns	Around We Go (page 141)	Colors
	Stringing Beads (page 141)	Colors
	Paper Clip Chains (page 141)	Colors
Wrap-Around Patterns	Around the End and Back Again (page 141)	Colors
	Pegboard Patterns (page 142)	Colors
	Footprint Patterns (page 142)	Body Parts
Movement Patterns	Jumping Jack Patterns (page 142)	Movement
	Head, Shoulders, Knees and Toes (page 142)	Body Parts Movement
Musical and Sound Patterns	Sound Patterns (page 143)	Senses
	Clapping Patterns (page 143)	Numbers
	Predictable Language Patterns (page 143)	Use theme-related books
Cultural Patterns	Days of the Week (page 143)	Use theme-related books
	Months of the Year (page 144)	Seasons
	Seasons (page 144)	Seasons
Environmental Patterns	Pattern Hunt (page 144)	Nature
	Pattern Rubbings (page 145)	Nature
	Clothing Patterns (page 145)	All About Me
One-to-One Correspondence	Partner Match (page 145)	Friends Matching

Skills	Activities	Theme Connections
Equal Sets	One Pebble for Every Child (page 145)	All About Me
	On With the Show (page 146)	Let's Pretend
	Ice Cream Cones (page 146)	Matching
	Penny Match (page 147)	Matching
	Rings and Fingers (page 147)	All About Me
	Pompoms to Suction Cups (page 147)	Matching
Unequal Sets	One Left (page 148)	Problem Solving
	Musical Chairs (page 148)	Music
	More or Less (page 148)	Friends
	Who Has the Most? (page 148)	Celebrations
Ordering		
Ordering by Height	Friends in a Row (page 149)	Friends
	Books on a Shelf (page 149)	Use theme-related books
	Tube Towers (page 149)	Under Construction
Ordering by Length	Caterpillar Line-Up (page 150)	Animals
	Go Fishing (page 150)	Let's Pretend
		Ocean
Ordering by Weight	Egg Weigh (page 151)	Problem Solving
	Bell Envelopes (page 151)	Sounds
Ordering by Liquid Measurement	Water Play (page 151)	Problem Solving
	Most to Least (page 152)	Problem Solving
	Tone Bottles (page 152)	Sound
Ordering by Position and Size	First, Next, Last (page 152)	Movement
	Top, Middle, Bottom (page 152)	Food/Nutrition
		Under Construction
	Tree Surprise (page 153)	Shapes
	Block Pyramids (page 153)	Under Construction
	Concentric Circles (page 153)	Shapes
Ordering by Comparing Sets	Least to Most (page 153)	Celebrations
	Dot Order (page 154)	Numbers
Numeration	Math Number Bags (page 154)	Problem Solving
	Beanbag Throw (page 155)	Movement
	Number Cards (page 155)	Families
	The Shape of Things (page 156)	Problem Solving
	Number Clips (page 156)	Problem Solving
	Counting Patterns (page 156)	Numbers
	Pasting Sets (page 157)	Colors
		Shapes
	Plates and Clips (page 157)	Problem Solving
	Mix It Myself Snack (page 157)	Food/Nutrition
	Piggy Banks (page 158)	Problem Solving
	Card Match (page 158)	Matching
	Musical Numbers (page 158)	Music
	Circle 'Round the Zero (page 159)	Movement
	Number Bingo (page 159)	Numbers
	My Number Book (page 159)	Numbers
	Golf Tee Combinations (page 160)	Colors
		Problem Solving
	Living Sets (page 160)	Friends
	Washer Drop (page 160)	Colors

Chapter 5—Math

Skills	Activities	Theme Connections
	Candy Sets (page 161)	Celebrations
	Crunchy Sets (page 161)	Food/Nutrition
	Mud Cakes (page 161)	Let's Pretend
	And One More (page 161)	Problem Solving
	Egg Carton Shake (page 162)	Numbers
	Target Practice (page 162)	Movement
	Subtraction Action (page 162)	Movement
		Music
	In the Bag (page 162)	Problem Solving
Shapes	Cookie Cutter Shapes (page 163)	Food/Nutrition
	Shape Construction (page 163)	Shapes
	Playdough Shapes (page 163)	Shapes
	Shape Hunt (page 163)	Shapes
	Musical Shapes (page 164)	Music
		Shapes
	Squares and Rectangles (page 164)	Colors
		Shapes
	Triangles and Rectangles (page 164)	Colors
		Shapes
Measurement *Linear Measurement*	Hand Match (page 165)	Body Parts
		Friends
		Matching
	Four Hands High (page 165)	Body Parts
		Sizes
	Who Is the Tallest? (page 165)	Friends
		Sizes
	Chain Links (page 165)	Sizes
	A Yard Long (page 166)	Sizes
	Two-Feet Long (page 166)	Body Parts
	Inch by Inch (page 166)	Numbers
	Foot Lengths (page 166)	Body Parts
	Big Steps, Small Steps (page 166)	Body Parts
		Numbers
Weight Measurement	How Much Do I Weigh? (page 166)	All About Me
	Using Scales (page 166)	Problem Solving
Capacity Measurement	How Many Children Can Sit in a Dinosaur's Footprint? (page 167)	Animals
		Sizes
	How Many? (page 167)	Numbers
Temperature Measurement	Coolest to Warmest (page 167)	Weather
	Temperature Experiment (page 167)	Weather
	Temperature Indicators (page 167)	Weather
Time Measurement	Morning and Night (page 168)	Day and Night
	Daily Schedule (page 168)	Colors
		School
		Time
	Yesterday and Tomorrow (page 168)	School
		Time
	Into the Future (page 169)	School
		Time
Graphs	Brothers and Sisters (page 169)	Families
	My Favorite Juice (page 169)	Food/Nutrition

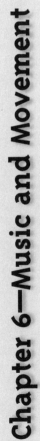

Skills	Activities	Theme Connections
	Color of the Day (page 169)	Colors
	Popular Pets (page 170)	Animals Pets
	More Popular Pets (page 170)	Animals Pets
	From Pictorial to Symbolic (page 170)	Food/Nutrition Numbers
	How Do I Get to School? (page 171)	Transportation/Travel School
	My Favorite Fruit (page 171)	Food/Nutrition
	Let's Vote (page 171)	Our Community
Fractions	The Same Amount for Everyone (page 172)	Celebrations Friends
	What Is a Half? (page 172)	Problem Solving
Songs	Happy Birthday (page 174)	All About Me Celebrations
	Variations of Old-Time Favorites (page 174)	Sing theme-related songs
	Different Voices (page 174)	All About Me
	Sing and Listen (page 175)	Sounds
	Crescendo (page 175)	Music
	Do As I Do (page 175)	Movement
	Circle Songs (page 175)	Movement
	Roofs and Windows (page 176)	Friends
	Hummin' (page 177)	Sounds
	"If You're Happy and You Know It" Variations (page 177)	All About Me Feelings
	"Itsy Bitsy Spider" Variations (page 177)	Insects
	"Tinkle, Twinkle, Little Star" Variations (page 177)	Day and Night
	Singing Discussions (page 178)	Sounds
Chants	Who Took the Cookies? (page 178)	Food/Nutrition
	Giant Stomp (page 179)	Traditional Tales
	"The Flight of the Fairies" (page 179)	Make-Believe
	"Oni Woni" (page 180)	Body Parts
Creative Movement	Giants and Elves (page 180)	Let's Pretend Opposites Traditional Tales
	Olympic Streamers (page 180)	Movement
	Preschool Fitness (page 181)	Movement
	Around the Chairs (page 181)	Music
	Butterfly Wings (page 181)	Insects
	Cool Music (page 181)	Music
	Circles to Music (page 182)	Imagination
	Friendship Circles (page 182)	Friends
	Pompoms (page 182)	Movement
	Freckles and Stripes (page 182)	Sounds
	Hi-Low (page 183)	Opposites
	Ball Roll (page 183)	Movement
	"Hey! My Name Is Joe" (page 183)	Body Parts
	"Tooty-Ta" (page 184)	Body Parts

Skills	Activities	Theme Connections
Moving Freely	"Metamorphosis" (page 184)	Insects
	Deejay for the Day (page 185)	Let's Pretend
	On Stage (page 185)	Let's Pretend
Music Makers	Tabletop Band (page 185)	Sounds
	Leader of the Band (page 186)	Let's Pretend
	Bottle Maracas (page 186)	Sounds
	Drum and Sticks (page 186)	Sounds
	Body Rhythms (page 186)	Body Parts
		Sounds
	Bottle Band (page 186)	Sounds
	Homemade Music Makers (page 187)	Sounds
Dances	Scarf Dancing (page 187)	All About Me
	Paper Plate Flying (page 187)	Let's Pretend
	Shadow Dancing (page 188)	Let's Pretend
	Preschool Limbo (page 188)	Body Parts
	Pick Your Partner (page 189)	Friends
	Dance, Thumbkin, Dance (page 189)	Body Parts
Games	Pass the Beanbag (page 190)	Opposites
	Freeze (page 190)	Weather
	Who's That Traipsing on My Bridge? (page 191)	Let's Pretend
		Traditional Tales
	Cooperative Musical Chairs (page 191)	Shapes
	Snack Pass (page 191)	Food/Nutrition
		Shapes
	Hopscotch (page 192)	Shapes
	Paper Chase (page 192)	Body Parts
	Inchworm Race (page 192)	Friends
		Insects
Gross Motor	Obstacle Course (page 195)	Body Parts
	Big Steps, Giant Steps (page 195)	Opposites
		Traditional Tales
	Hula Hoop Toss (page 195)	Shapes
	Musical Cues (page 196)	Movement
		Music
	Mirror Reflections (page 196)	All About Me
		Friends
	Amazing Mazes (page 196)	Movement
	Blanket Toss (page 197)	Friends
	Homemade Balls (page 197)	Movement
	Basket Balance (page 198)	Movement
	Walk a Crooked Line (page 198)	Movement
	Duck Waddles (page 198)	Animals
	Spider Walk (page 198)	Insects
	Back-to-Back Lifts (page 199)	Friends
	Tunnels (page 199)	Travel
	Broad Jumps (page 199)	Movement
	Ring That Bell (page 200)	Sounds
	Indoor Croquet (page 200)	Numbers
	"The Little Ants" (page 201)	Insects
Fine Motor	Bubbles in My Hand (page 202)	Body Parts

Skills	Activities	Theme Connections
	Balls and Cups (page 202)	Matching
	Liquid Movers (page 202)	Numbers
	Wire Creations (page 202)	Shapes
	Easy Cutouts (page 203)	Shapes
	Nut Sorting (page 203)	Food/Nutrition
	Colorful Confetti (page 203)	Colors
	Tracing Lids (page 204)	Shapes
	Cookie Cutter Tracing (page 205)	Colors
	Cups of Color (page 205)	Colors
	Little Ships (page 205)	Transportation/Travel
	Greeting Card Puzzles (page 205)	Use theme-related cards
	Torn Paper Creations (page 206)	Imagination
	Grass Tug of War (page 206)	Friends
	Weaving Variations (page 207)	Nature
	Shadow Puppets (page 207)	Body Parts
	Finger Puppets (page 207)	Body Parts
	Me Puzzles (page 207)	All About Me
	Paper Cutting (page 208)	Shapes
	Playdough Fun (page 208)	Imagination
Air	Sacks of Air (page 211)	Sounds
	Air Pushers (page 211)	Problem Solving
	Air Pusher Experiment (page 212)	Cause and Effect
	Circle Kites (page 212)	Shapes
		Weather
	Bubble Machines (page 213)	Opposites
	Floaters and Droppers (page 213)	Opposites
	When the Wind Blows (page 213)	Nature
		Weather
	Air Conditioning Hoops (page 214)	Opposites
		Weather
	Helicopters (page 214)	Transportation/Travel
Sound: What We Hear When Air Moves	Megaphones (page 215)	Sounds
	Who's Coming? (page 216)	Animals
		Cowboys and Cowgirls
	Sound Vibrations (page 216)	Sounds
	Kazoos (page 217)	Music
	Tuning Fork Exploration (page 217)	Music
		Sounds
Water		
Liquid	All Liquids Flow (page 217)	Opposites
	Sink and Float (page 218)	Opposites
		Transportation/Travel
	Fingerpaint Experiment (page 218)	Opposites
Solid	Ice Melting Race (page 218)	Cause and Effect
		Seasons
		Weather
	Slipping and Sliding on Ice (page 218)	Seasons
		Weather
Evaporation (Gas)	Vanishing Art (page 219)	Opposites
	Old-Fashioned Wash Day (page 219)	Families
		Opposites
Diffusion	Will This Dissolve? (page 219)	Problem Solving

Chapter 8—Science

Skills	Activities	Theme Connections
Insoluble Substances	Fingerpaint Finale (page 220)	Colors
	Color Bottles (page 220)	Colors
	Invisible Names (page 220)	All About Me Cause and Effect
	Wave Maker (page 220)	Ocean
Force and Motion *Force*	Wind Wheels (page 221)	Weather
	Wind Wands (page 221)	Seasons
	Swing, Pendulum, Swing (page 221)	Motion
	Can Race (page 222)	Transportation/Travel
Friction: Resistance to Motion	Sanding (page 223)	Under Construction
	Making Sand (page 223)	Earth
	Rocks and Shells (page 223)	Earth
	Hand Warm-Up (page 223)	Weather Seasons
	Rough or Smooth (page 224)	Opposites
Gravitation: Force That Attracts	Marble Run (page 225)	Cause and Effect Shapes
	Drop It (page 225)	Problem Solving Sounds
	Balloon Bounce (page 225)	Friends
	Down It Goes (page 226)	Problem Solving
	Downhill Racer (page 226)	Problem Solving
	Stringing Up (page 226)	Cause and Effect
Magnetism: Another Kind of Force	Magnetic Attraction (page 227)	Opposites
	Metal Hunt (page 227)	Opposites
	Toy Towing (page 227)	Transportation/Travel
	Home Hunt (page 227)	Families
	Magnetic Puppets (page 227)	Let's Pretend
	Magnet Chasers (page 228)	Cause and Effect
	Magnetic Stories (page 228)	Traditional Tales
	Magnetic Designs (page 228)	Shapes
	Magnet Car Races (page 228)	Transportation/Travel
	Magnet Painting (page 228)	Colors
	Speedy Cleanup (page 229)	Problem Solving
Simple Tools	Pulleys (page 229)	Tools
	Water Transfer (page 229)	Tools
	Filter Catch (page 230)	Problem Solving
	Kitchen Tools (page 230)	Tools
	Easy Movers (page 230)	Problem Solving
Light and Color	Color Shadows (page 231)	Colors Day and Night
	Playdough Color Mixing (page 231)	Colors
	Color Tubes (page 231)	Colors
	Rose-Colored Glasses (page 232)	Colors
	Color Mixer (page 232)	Cause and Effect
	Shadow Puppets (page 232)	Let's Pretend
	Guess Who? (page 233)	Let's Pretend
	Sun Art (page 233)	Day and Night Opposites

The Instant Curriculum

Skills	Activities	Theme Connections
	Rainbows (page 233)	Colors
	Strobe Light (page 234)	Opposites
	Me and My Shadow (page 234)	Day and Night
		Opposites
	Sundial (page 234)	Day and Night
		Time
	Scattered Light (page 235)	Cause and Effect
	Mirror Drawings (page 235)	Colors
	Lemon Juice Magic (page 236)	Cause and Effect
Weather and Seasons	Cloud Watch (page 236)	Imagination
	Wind Walk (page 237)	Weather
	Rain Gauge (page 237)	Numbers
	Shadow Tracing (page 237)	Friends
		Opposites
	Season Walks (page 237)	Nature
	Seasonal Trees (page 238)	Nature
Senses	The Eyes Have It (page 239)	Cause and Effect
	What's for Snack? (page 239)	Food/Nutrition
	Sound Makers (page 240)	Sounds
	Taste Test (page 240)	Food/Nutrition
	Tactile Temperatures (page 240)	Opposites
	Hot and Cold (page 240)	Opposites
	Sounds Abound (page 240)	Nature
		Sounds
	Puffs of Smell (page 241)	Matching
	The Nose Knows (page 241)	Weather
	A World of Scents (page 241)	Nature
Change of State	Stone Soup (page 242)	Food/Nutrition
	Ice Meltdown (page 242)	Opposites
		Senses
	Soda Fizz (page 242)	Cause and Effect
	Gelatin Jigglers (page 243)	Cause and Effect
		Shapes
		Textures
Plants	Nature Bracelets (page 243)	Nature
		Seasons
	Tire Garden (page 244)	Growing Things
	Vegetable Garden (page 244)	Food/Nutrition
		Growing Things
	Hairy Larry (page 244)	Growing Things
	Grocery Bag Leaves (page 245)	Colors
		Seasons
	Leaves—All Sizes, All Shapes (page 245)	Seasons
		Sizes
	Leaf Rubbings (page 245)	Colors
		Seasons
	Treasure Hunt (page 246)	Nature
	Window Garden (page 246)	Growing Things
	Egg Carton Planters (page 246)	Growing Things
	Mini-Terrariums (page 247)	Growing Things

Skills	Activities	Theme Connections
	Little Sprouts (page 247)	Growing Things
	Sweet Potato Vines (page 248)	Growing Things
	What's a Nut? (page 248)	Food/Nutrition
		Seasons
	Natural Dyes (page 248)	Colors
		Food/Nutrition
		Growing Things
Animals	Feed the Birds (page 249)	Birds
	Bird Bath (page 249)	Birds
	Pinecone Bird Feeders (page 249)	Nature
	Looking Loops (page 250)	Insects
	Ant Watch (page 250)	Insects
	Ant Helpers (page 250)	Insects
	Bug Bottles (page 251)	Insects
	Animal Habitats (page 251)	Houses/Homes
	Who Lives Where? (page 252)	Houses/Homes
	Animal Homes (page 252)	Houses/Homes
	Mothers and Babies (page 252)	Matching
		Sizes
	Insect Body Parts (page 253)	Insects
		Numbers
Feeling Good About Me	I Am Special (page 256)	All About Me
	My Names Means a Lot (page 256)	All About Me
	Accentuate the Positive (page 257)	All About Me
	V.I.P. Treasure Chest (page 257)	Families
		Friends
	Artist of the Week (page 258)	Artists
Understanding and Controlling Emotions	My Feelings (page 259)	All About Me
	Happy and Sad (page 260)	All About Me
	Feeling (page 260)	All About Me
		Animals
		Pets
	Face to Face (page 260)	All About Me
		Shapes
My Family	Family Portraits (page 261)	Families
	Family Tree (page 261)	Families
	Names for Relatives (page 261)	Families
	Classroom Concerts (page 262)	Families
		Music
Sharing and Cooperating	Tips for Taking Turns (page 262)	Friends
		Time
	Pass It Along (page 262)	Friends
		Numbers
	Tips for Sharing (page 262)	Friends
Participating and Contributing	Classroom Quilt (page 263)	Friends
	Trash Truck (page 263)	Nature
	Litter Brigade (page 263)	Nature
	Sidewalk Art Sale (page 264)	Artists
Likenesses and Differences	International Feast (page 264)	Food/Nutrition
	Home, Sweet Home (page 264)	Houses/Homes

Skills	Activities	Theme Connections
	There Is More Than One Way (page 265)	Families
	See, Touch, and Hear (page 265)	Senses
	Goodbye, Adios, and Sayonara (page 266)	Families Friends Sounds
Community Workers and Friends	Career Prop Boxes (page 266)	Our Community
	Job Fair (page 267)	Families Our Community
	Small Mall (page 267)	Numbers Our Community
	Senior Citizens' Day (page 267)	Families Friends
Concepts of Time	Yesterday, Today, and Tomorrow (page 268)	Time
	Tomorrow Box (page 268)	Time
	Growing Up (page 268)	All About Me
	Bygones (page 268)	Families
	Morning, Noon, and Night (page 269)	Day and Night Opposites
Environmental Awareness	Use and Reuse (page 269)	Families Nature
	Recycled Products (page 269)	Families Nature
	Clothes Corner (page 270)	Families
	Crayon Conservation (page 270)	Colors
	Sandbox Tools (page 270)	Tools
	Re-Bow (page 270)	Colors
	Rainwater Recycle (page 271)	Growing Things Weather
	Rainbow Bottles (page 271)	Colors
	A Tree From Me (page 272)	Growing Things Nature
Health and Safety	Safety Rituals (page 272)	All About Me Friends
	A Healthy Song (page 273)	All About Me Food/Nutrition
	Cross-Lateral Brain Energizers (page 274)	All About Me Movement
	Thirsty Brains Can't Think (page 274)	All About Me Food/Nutrition
	Homemade Toothpaste (page 274)	All About Me Families
	Squeaky Clean (page 275)	All About Me
	Food Group Pyramid (page 275)	Food/Nutrition
	Paper Plate Food Collage (page 275)	Food/Nutrition
	Heartbeats (page 276)	All About Me
	Traffic Lights (page 277)	Transportation/Travel
	Stop Signs (page 277)	Transportation/Travel
	Stop, Look, and Listen (page 277)	All About Me Transportation/Travel
	Stop, Drop, and Roll (page 278)	All About Me

Skills	Activities	Theme Connections
Critical Thinking and Problem Solving	Arm Stretchers (page 281)	All About Me
	Two Parts, Three People! (page 281)	Friends
	How Many People in Your Family? (page 282)	Families
		Numbers
	What Can You Do With This? (page 282)	Imagination
	What Will Go in This? (page 282)	Imagination
	Water Brigade (page 283)	Friends
	Follow the Arrows (page 283)	Spatial Concepts
	Where's the Birdie? (page 284)	Birds
	Wacky Wednesday (page 284)	Opposites
	Separating Solids (page 285)	Animals
	Greeting Card Cut-Ups (page 287)	Shapes
	Bubbles Aloft (page 287)	Movement
	Rollers and Clunkers (page 287)	Opposites
		Shapes
	Go-Togethers (page 288)	Matching
Transitions	Pretend Places (page 290)	Let's Pretend
	Who Am I? (page 290)	Let's Pretend
	Musical Cues (page 290)	Music
	Cues From Classics (page 291)	Music
	Groovy Moves (page 291)	Movement
	Weather Walks (page 291)	Weather
	Butterfly Flutter (page 292)	Insects
		Movement
	Wacky Walks (page 292)	Movement
	Roll Call (page 293)	All About Me
	Rhyming Roll Call (page 293)	All About Me
Familes as Partners	Printed Labels (page 296)	Familes
	What We Did This Week (page 296)	All About Me
	Second Time Around (page 296)	Families
	Special Guest Day (page 296)	Families
		Our Community
	Family Networking (page 296)	Our Community
	Calendars (page 297)	Seasons
		Numbers
	Communication Notes (page 297)	Families
	Newsletters (page 297)	All About Me

The Instant Curriculum

Songs, Chants, and Fingerplays

Alphabet Song
(Tune: Twinkle, Twinkle, Litte Star)

A - B - C - D - E - F - G

H - I - J - K - L - M - N - O - P

Q - R - S - T - U and V,

W - X - Y and Z.

Now I know my A - B - C's

Next time won't you sing with me?

The Ants Go Marching
(Tune: When Johnny Comes Marching Home)

The ants go marching one by one,

Hurrah, hurrah.

The ants go marching one by one,

Hurrah, hurrah.

The ants go marching one by one,

The little one stops to look at the sun.

And they all go marching down,

To the ground,

To get out,

Of the rain.

BOOM! BOOM! BOOM! BOOM!

Additional verses:

…two…tie her shoe…

…three…climb a tree…

…four…shut the door…

…five…take a dive…

…six…pick up sticks…

…seven…pray to heaven…

…eight…shut the gate…

…nine…check the time…

…ten…say "The End!"

Apples and Bananas

I like to eat eat eat apples and bananas.
I like to eat eat eat apples and bananas.

I like to ate ate ate ay-ples and bay-nay-nays.
I like to ate ate ate ay-ples and bay-nay-nays.

I like to eet eet eet ee-ples and bee-nee-nees.
I like to eet eet eet ee-ples and bee-nee-nees.

I like to ite, ite, ite, i-ples and by-by-nys
I like to ite, ite, ite, i-ples and by-by-nys

I like to ote ote ote oh-ples and bo-no-nos.
I like to ote ote ote oh-ples and bo-no-nos.

I like to ute ute ute upples and bununus.
I like to ute ute ute upples and bununus.

Now we're through, through, through, through,
Now we're through with the apples and bananas,
Now we're through, through, through, through,
With A, E, I, O, and U.

Are You Sleeping?

Are you sleeping, are you sleeping?
Brother John? Brother John?
Morning bells are ringing.
Morning bells are ringing.
Ding, ding, dong.
Ding, ding, dong.

Autumn Leaves

Autumn leaves are falling, falling, falling.
   (move from standing position to squatting)
Autumn leaves are spinning, spinning, spinning.
(stand and turn)
Autumn leaves are floating, floating, floating.
   (sway side to side)
Autumn leaves are turning, turning, turning.
   (turn slowly)

Autumn leaves are dancing, dancing, dancing.
(stand on toes, sway forward and back)
Autumn leaves are blowing, blowing, blowing.
(take several steps forward)
Autumn leaves are falling, falling, falling. *(squat)*
Autumn leaves are sleeping, sleeping, sleeping.
(place hands together on side of face)

Baby Bumblebee

I caught myself a baby bumblebee.
Won't my mommy be so proud of me?
I caught myself a baby bumblebee,
Ouch! He stung me!

I'm talking to my baby bumblebee.
Won't my mommy be so proud of me?
I'm talking to my baby bumblebee,
"Oh," he said, "I'm sorry."

I'm letting go my baby bumblebee.
Won't my mommy be so proud of me?
I'm letting go my baby bumblebee,
Look he's happy to be free!

Bingo

There was a farmer had a dog,
And Bingo was his name-o.
B-I-N-G-O!
B-I-N-G-O!
B-I-N-G-O!
And Bingo was his name-o!
There was a farmer had a dog,
And Bingo was his name-o.
(Clap)-I-N-G-O!
(Clap)-I-N-G-O!
(Clap)-I-N-G-O!
And Bingo was his name-o!

There was a farmer had a dog,
And Bingo was his name-o.
(Clap, clap)-N-G-O!

(Clap, clap)-N-G-O!
(Clap, clap)-N-G-O!
And Bingo was his name-o!

There was a farmer had a dog,
And Bingo was his name-o.
(Clap, clap, clap)-G-O!
(Clap, clap, clap)-G-O!
(Clap, clap, clap)-G-O!
And Bingo was his name-o!

There was a farmer had a dog,
And Bingo was his name-o.
(Clap, clap, clap, clap)-O!
(Clap, clap, clap, clap)-O!
(Clap, clap, clap, clap)-O!
And Bingo was his name-o!

There was a farmer had a dog,
And Bingo was his name-o.
(Clap, clap, clap, clap, clap)
(Clap, clap, clap, clap, clap)
(Clap, clap, clap, clap, clap)

And Bingo was his name-o!

Do Your Ears Hang Low?

Do your ears hang low?
Do they wobble to and fro?
Can you tie them in a knot?
Can you tie them in a bow?
Can you throw them o'er your shoulder,
Like a Continental Soldier?
Do your ears hang low?

Five in the Bed

There were five in the bed, *(hold up five fingers)*
And the little one said,
"Roll over! Roll over!"
So they all rolled over and one fell out.

Additional verses:

There were four in the bed. . .

There were three in the bed. . .

There were two in the bed. . .

There was one in the bed,

And the little one said,

"GOOD NIGHT!"

Five Little Monkeys

Five little monkeys, jumping on the bed. *(hold up five fingers)*

One fell off and bumped her head. *(rub head)*

Mamma called the doctor and the doctor said,

> *(pretend to make telephone call)*

"No more monkeys jumping on the bed!" *(scolding motion)*

Additional verses:

Four little monkeys. . .

Three little monkeys. . .

Two little monkeys. . .

One little monkey. . .

Five Little Monkeys *(teasing Mr. Crocodile)*

Five little monkeys sitting in a tree, *(hold up five fingers)*

Teasing Mr. Crocodile.

"You can't catch me! You can't catch me!"

Along came Mr. Crocodile, quiet as can be.

Snap! *(put elbows together and clap hands together,*
making the motion of a crocodile's jaws snapping shut)

Additional verses:

Four little monkeys…

Three little monkeys…

Two little monkeys…

One little monkey…

Five Little Speckled Frogs

> *(Five children sit in a row and the other childrensit in a circle*
> *around them. All children act out the words to the song.)*

Five little speckled frogs *(hold up five fingers)*

Sitting on a speckled log

Eating some most delicious bugs. *(pretend to eat bugs)*

Yum! Yum!

One jumped into the pool, *(one child from center jumps back into the circle)*

Where it was nice and cool. *(cross arms over chest and shiver)*

Now there are four little speckled frogs.

Burr-ump!

(Repeat, counting down until there are no little speckled frogs.)

Going on a Bear Hunt

We're going on a bear hunt.

Want to come along?

Well, come on then.

Let's go! *(walk in place)*

Look! There's a river.

Can't go over it.

Can't go under it.

Can't go around it.

We'll have to go through it. *(pretend to walk into river, swim through the water and walk up other bank; then resume walking in place)*

Look! There's a tree.

Can't go under it.

Can't go through it.

We'll have to go over it. *(pretend to climb up and over tree; then resume walking in place)*

Look! There's a wheat field.

Can't go over it.

Can't go under it.

Can't go around it.

We'll have to go through it. *(pretend to walk through field, make swishing sounds with hands against thighs; then resume walking in place)*

(Add verses with actions to make the story as long as you like.)

Look! There's a cave.

Want to go inside?

Ooh, it's dark in here. *(look around, squinting)*

I see two eyes.

Wonder what it is. *(reach hands to touch)*

The Instant Curriculum

It's soft and furry.

It's big.

It's a bear! Let's run! *(retrace steps, running in place, through wheat field, in place, over tree, in place, across river, in place, then stop)*

Home safe.

Whew!

Good Morning to You

Good morning to you.

Good morning to you.

We're all in our places

With bright, shiny faces.

Oh, this is the way

To start a great day.

Gray Squirrel

Gray squirrel, gray squirrel, *(stand with hands on bent knees)*

Swish your bushy tail. *(wiggle your behind)*

Gray squirrel, gray squirrel, *(stand with hands on bent knees)*

Swish your bushy tail. *(wiggle your behind)*

Wrinkle up your funny nose, *(wrinkle nose)*

Hold an acorn in your toes. *(pinch index and thumb fingers together)*

Gray squirrel, gray squirrel, *(stand with hands on bent knees)*

Swish your bushy tail. *(wiggle your behind)*

Hey, Diddle Diddle

Hey, diddle diddle,

The cat and the fiddle,

The cow jumped over the moon.

The little dog laughed to see such a sight,

And the dish ran away with the spoon.

Hickory, Dickory, Dock

Hickory, dickory, dock, *(stand, swing arm like pendulum)*

The mouse ran up the clock. *(bend over; run hand up body)*

The clock struck one, *(clap hands over head once)*

The mouse ran down, *(run hand down to feet)*

Hickory, dickory, dock. *(stand; swing arm like pendulum)*

Humpty Dumpty

Humpty Dumpty sat on a wall.

Humpty Dumpty had a great fall.

All the king's horses and all the king's men

Couldn't put Humpty Dumpty together again.

If You're Happy and You Know It

(act out motions that words indicate)

If you're happy and you know it,

Clap your hands.

If you're happy and you know it,

Clap your hands.

If you're happy and you know it,

Then your face will surely show it.

If you're happy and you know it,

Clap your hands.

If you're happy and you know it,

Stomp your feet…

Pat your head…

Say hello…

It's Raining, It's Pouring

It's raining, it's pouring,

The old man is snoring.

He went to bed with a pain in his head

And didn't get up until morning.

The Itsy, Bitsy Spider

The itsy, bitsy spider climbed up the water spout. *(put the tip of the forefinger of each hand to the tip of the thumb of the other hand, creating an oblong diamond; then release the forefinger and thumb that are on the bottom and swing them up to the top of the diamond. Do this repeatedly.)*

Down came the rain and washed the spider out. *(wiggle fingers while streaming down)*

Out came the sun and dried up all the rain. *(create the arch of the sun with hands)*

And the itsy, bitsy spider climbed up the spout again. *(repeat first movement with forefingers and thumbs)*

Jack and Jill

Jack and Jill
Went up the hill
To fetch a pail of water.
Jack fell down
And broke his crown,
And Jill came tumbling after.

Up Jack got
And home did trot
As fast as he could caper.
Went to bed
And plastered his head
With vinegar and brown paper.

Jack Be Nimble

Jack be nimble,
Jack be quick;
Jack jump over
The candlestick.

Johnny Works With One Hammer

Johnny works with one hammer, *(make hammering motion with
    right hand)*
One hammer, one hammer.
Johnny works with one hammer,
Then he works with two.

Johnny works with two hammers… *(make hammering motion with
    left and right hands)*
Johnny works with three hammers… *(motion with both hands and
    right foot)*
Johnny works with four hammers… *(motion with both hands and
    both feet)*
Johnny works with five hammers… *(motion with both hands and feet
    and with head)*
Then he goes to bed.

*(A variation of this song uses the name "Peter" instead of "Johnny" and
ends each verse with the words, "all day long.")*

Little Bo Peep

Little Bo Peep has lost her sheep,
And can't tell where to find them;
Leave them alone, and they'll come home,
Wagging their tails behind them.

Then she took her little crook,
Determined for to find them;
What a joy to behold them nigh,
Wagging their tails behind them.

Little Boy Blue

Little Boy Blue, come blow your horn.
The sheep are in the meadow, the cow's in the corn.
But where is the boy who looks after the sheep?
He's under a haystack, fast asleep.

Mary Had a Little Lamb

Mary had a little lamb,
Little lamb, little lamb,
Mary had a little lamb,
Its fleece was white as snow.

And everywhere that Mary went ,
Mary went, Mary went,
Everywhere that Mary went,
The lamb was sure to go.

It followed her to school one day,
School one day, school one day,
It followed her to school one day,
Which was against the rules.

It made the children laugh and play,
Laugh and play, laugh and play,
It made the children laugh and play,
To see a lamb at school.

And so the teacher turned it out,
Turned it out, turned it out,
And so the teacher turned it out,
But still it lingered near.

It waited patiently about,
patiently about, patiently about,
It waited patiently about,
'Til Mary did appear.

"What makes the lamb love Mary so,
Mary so, Mary so"?"
"What makes the lamb love Mary so?"
the eager children cried.
"Why, Mary loves the lamb, you know,
Lamb you know, lamb you know."
"Why, Mary loves the lamb, you know,"
The teacher did reply.

Miss Mary Mack

Miss Mary Mack, Mack, Mack
All dressed in black, black, black,
With silver buttons, buttons, buttons
All down her back, back, back.
She asked her mother, mother, mother
For fifteen cents, cents, cents
To see the elephants, elephants, elephants
Jump over the fence, fence, fence.
They jumped so high, high, high,
They touched the sky, sky, sky,
And they didn't come back, back, back
'Til the Fourth of July, ly, ly
And they never came down, down, down,
'Til the Fourth of July.

The More We Get Together

The more we get together, together, together,
The more we get together, the happier we'll be.
For your friends are my friends,
And my friends are your friends.
The more we get together, the happier we'll be.

Mr. Sun

Oh Mr. Sun, Sun, Mr. Golden Sun,
Please shine down on me.
Oh Mr. Sun, Sun, Mr. Golden Sun,
Hiding behind a tree,
These little children are asking you
To please come out so we can play with you.
Oh Mr. Sun, Sun, Mr. Golden Sun,
Please shine down on me!

The Muffin Man

Oh, do you know the muffin man,
The muffin man, the muffin man?
Oh, do you know the muffin man
Who lives on Drury Lane?

Oh, yes, we know the muffin man,
The muffin man, the muffin man.
Oh, yes, we know the muffin man
Who lives on Drury Lane.

The Mulberry Bush

Here we go round the mulberry bush, *(hold hands, walk in circle, and
    act out the motions)*
The mulberry bush, the mulberry bush.
Here we go round the mulberry bush,
So early in the morning.

This is the way we wash our clothes,
Wash our clothes, wash our clothes.
This is the way we wash our clothes,
So early Monday morning.

This is the way we iron our clothes....Tuesday morning.
This is the way we scrub the floors...Wednesday morning.
This is the way we mend our clothes...Thursday morning.
This is the way we sweep the house...Friday morning.
This is the way we bake our bread. . .Saturday morning.
This is the way we go to church...Sunday morning.

The Instant Curriculum

The North Wind Doth Blow

The north wind doth blow

And we shall have some snow.

And what will the robin do then, poor thing?

He will sit in the barn and keep himself warm,

With his little head tucked under his wing, poor thing!

Old MacDonald Had a Farm

Old MacDonald had a farm. E-I-E-I-O.

And on that farm, he had some chicks. E-I-E-I-O.

With a chick, chick here,

And a chick, chick there.

Here a chick,

There a chick,

Everywhere a chick, chick.

Old MacDonald had a farm. E-I-E-I-O.

Other verses:

Ducks—quack

Horses—neigh

Cows—moo

Pigs—oink

Donkeys—heehaw

Open, Shut Them

(perform the hand motions described)

Open, shut them.

Open, shut them.

Give a little clap.

Open, shut them.

Open, shut them.

Put them in your lap.

Walk them, walk them, *(walk fingers up chest to chin)*

Walk them, walk them.

Way up to your chin.

Walk them, walk them, *(walk fingers around face, but not into mouth)*

Walk them, walk them,

But don't let them walk in.

Pease Porridge Hot

(Have children clap hands together with a friend. Challenge older or more skilled children to alternate hands when clapping.)

Pease porridge hot.
Pease porridge cold.
Pease porridge in the pot
Nine days old.

Some like it hot.
Some like it cold.
Some like it in the pot
Nine days old.

Rain on the Green Grass

Rain on the green grass
And rain on the tree.
Rain on the housetop
But not on me.

Rain, Rain, Go Away

Rain, rain, go away.
Come again another day.

Rain, rain, go away.
Little Johnny wants to play.

Row, Row, Row Your Boat

Row, row, row your boat
Gently down the stream.
Merrily, merrily, merrily, merrily,
Life is but a dream.

She'll Be Comin' Round the Mountain

She'll be comin' round the mountain when she comes,
Toot, toot! *(make motion as if pulling a train's whistle)*
She'll be comin' round the mountain when she comes,
Toot, toot! *(make motion as if pulling a train's whistle)*
She'll be comin' round the mountain,
She'll be comin' round the mountain,
She'll be comin' round the mountain, when she comes,
Toot, toot! *(make motion as if pulling a train's whistle)*

She'll be ridin' six white horses, when she comes,
Whoa back!… *(make motion as if pulling back the horses' reins)*

She'll be wearin' pink pajamas, when she comes,
Scratch, scratch!… *(scratch)*

O, we'll all go out to meet her, when she comes,
"Hi, babe!"… *(wave "hello")*

O, we'll kill the old, red rooster when she comes,
Hack, hack!… *(make motion as if hacking with a knife)*

O, we'll all have chicken and dumplings, when she comes,
Yum, yum!… *(rub stomach in contentment)*

O, she'll have to sleep with grandpa, when she comes,
Snore, snore!… *(put palms of hands together and lay head on back of hands as if sleeping)*

Shoo, Fly, Don't Bother Me

Shoo, fly, don't bother me.
Shoo, fly, don't bother me.
Shoo, fly, don't bother me,
For I belong to somebody.

I feel, I feel, I feel like a morning star.
I feel, I feel, I feel life a morning star.
I feel, I feel, I feel like a morning star.
I feel, I feel, I feel like a morning star.

Shoo, fly, don't bother me.
Shoo, fly, don't bother me.
Shoo, fly, don't bother me,
For I belong to somebody.

Skip to My Lou

Lost my partner, what'll I do?
Lost my partner, what'll I do?
Lost my partner, what'll I do?
Skip to my Lou, my darling.
Lou, Lou, skip to my Lou,

Lou, Lou, skip to my Lou,
Lou, Lou, skip to my Lou,
Skip to my Lou, my darling.

I'll get another one prettier than you…
Little red wagon painted blue…
Flies in the buttermilk, two by two…
Cow's in the barnyard, moo, moo, moo…
Flies in the sugar, shoo, fly, shoo!…
Going to Texas, two by two…
Cat's in the cream jar, what'll I do?…

Teddy Bear, Teddy Bear

Teddy Bear, Teddy Bear, turn around.
Teddy Bear, Teddy Bear, touch the ground.
Teddy Bear, Teddy Bear, read the news.
Teddy Bear, Teddy Bear, shine your shoes.
Teddy Bear, Teddy Bear, go upstairs.
Teddy Bear, Teddy Bear, say your prayers.
Teddy Bear, Teddy Bear, turn out the light.
Teddy Bear, Teddy Bear, say GOOD NIGHT!

This Little Piggy

This little piggy went to market,
This little piggy stayed home,
This little piggy had roast beef,
This little piggy had none.
And this little piggy cried,
"Wee, wee, wee, wee," all the way home.

This Old Man

This old man, he played one,
He played knick-knack on my thumb.
With a knick-knack paddy-whack,
    give your dog a bone.
This old man came rolling home.

This old man, he played two,
He played knick-knack on my shoe…

Additional verses:

…three…on my knee…

…four…on my door…

…five…on my hive…

…six…on my sticks…

…seven…up in heaven…

…eight…on my gate…

…nine…on my spine…

…ten…once again…

Twinkle, Twinkle, Little Star

Twinkle, twinkle, little star,

How I wonder what you are.

Up above the world so high,

Like a diamond in the sky.

Twinkle, twinkle, little star,

How I wonder what you are.

Two Little Ducks

Two little ducks that I once knew, *(hold up two fingers)*

Fat ones, skinny ones, there were two, *(spread hands out and bring hands closer together)*

But the one little duck with the feathers on his back, *(hold up one finger and shake it)*

He led the others with a quack, quack, quack. *(bring hands together and clap)*

Down to the river they would go,

Wibble, wobble, wibble, wobble, to and fro. *(swing hips back and forth)*

But the one little duck with the feathers on his back, *(hold up one finger and shake it)*

He led the others with a quack, quack, quack. *(bring hands together and clap)*

He led the others with a quack, quack, quack. *(bring hands together and clap)*

Wee Willie Winkie

Wee Willie Winkie runs through the town,
Upstairs and downstairs in his nightgown.
Rapping at the window, crying through the lock,
"Are the children in their beds?
For it's past eight o'clock!"

Wheels on the Bus

The wheels on the bus go round and round. *(move hands in circular motion)*
Round and round, round and round.
The wheels on the bus go round and round,
All around the town. *(extend arms up and out)*

The windshield wipers go swish, swish, swish. *(sway hands back and forth)*
The baby on the bus goes, "Wah, wah, wah." *(rub eyes)*
People on the bus go up and down *(stand up, sit down)*
The horn on the bus goes beep, beep, beep. *(pretend to beep horn)*
The money on the bus goes clink, clink, clink. *(drop change in)*
The driver on the bus says, "Move on back." *(hitchhiking movement)*

Where Is Thumbkin?

Where is thumbkin? *(hands behind back)*
Where is thumbkin?
Here I am. Here I am. *(bring out right thumb, then left)*
How are you today, sir? *(bend right thumb)*
Very well, I thank you. *(bend left thumb)*
Run away. *(put right thumb behind back)*
Run away. *(put left thumb behind back)*

Other verses: *(use similar motions, changing fingers as the words indicate)*
Where is pointer?
Where is middle one?
Where is ring finger?
Where is pinky?
Where are all of them?

Who Stole the Cookie From the Cookie Jar?

(Say this chant as you pat your thighs and snap in a rhythmic motion. Continue until everyone has been "accused" at least once.)

Who stole the cookie from the cookie jar?

(Name) stole the cookie from the cookie jar.

Who, me?

Yes, you.

Couldn't be.

Then who? *(Name different child, chosen by the first child accused)*
stole the cookie from the cookie jar.

Who, me?

Yes, you.

Couldn't be.

Then who?

Games

Cooperative Musical Chairs

This game is a variation of Musical Chairs. Make 3' masking tape circles on the floor. *(Start with 4 circles and 8 children.)* Play a piece of music. Encourage the children to walk around the circles until the music stops. When the music stops everyone sits in a circle. Circles can be shared so no one should be left out. The idea is to get everyone in a circle so everyone wins. Remove a circle and go again. The game becomes more amusing as more and more children try to fit into fewer and fewer circles. Continue playing for as long as the children are interested.

Duck, Duck, Goose

For this game everyone but one child who is IT sits in a circle facing the center. The child who is IT walks around the outside of the circle, tapping each child's head as she passes; every time she taps a head she says "duck." *(She can say "duck" as few or as many times as she wants.)* When she taps a child's head and says "goose," the goose has to get up and chase her around the circle. The first child tries to run around the circle and sit in the goose's spot without being tagged. If she is tagged, then she has to sit in the "stew pot" in the center of the circle until another comes to replace her. If she is not tagged, she joins the circle in the goose's empty space. In both cases, the child who was chasing becomes the new one to walk around the circle tapping heads and saying, "duck, duck, goose!"

Drop the Handkerchief

Choose one child to be IT while the other children sit in a circle facing the center. The child who is It skips or walks around the outside of the circle and casually drops the handkerchief behind one of the children sitting in the circle. This child picks up the handkerchief and chases IT around the circle. It tries to run around the circle and sit in the second child's spot without being tagged. If IT is not tagged, then she sits in her new spot in the circle and the child with the handkerchief is now IT. If IT is tagged, then she is IT or another round.

The Instant Curriculum

Variations: Use a heart and play Drop the Heart, or a specific color of handkerchief for color recognition.

The Farmer in the Dell

The children all stand in a circle facing the center, except for one child who stands in the middle and is the "farmer." The children in the circle join hands and walk or skip in a circle around the farmer while singing the song below. The "farmer" chooses a "wife" from the children in the circle to join him in the middle; the "wife" chooses a "child," etc. The child chosen to be the "cheese" stands alone *(the "farmer," his "wife," etc. all rejoin the circle)* and becomes the "farmer" in the next round of "The Farmer in the Dell."

> *The farmer in the dell,*
> *The farmer in the dell,*
> *High-ho the derry-o,*
> *The farmer in the dell.*
>
> *The farmer takes a wife...*
> *The wife takes a child...*
> *The child takes a nurse...*
> *The nurse takes a dog...*
> *The dog takes a cat...*
> *The cat takes a rat...*
> *The rat takes the cheese...*
> *The cheese stands alone...*

Freeze Tag

One child is chosen to be IT. He chases the other children trying to tag them. When he tags a child, she must freeze. She may run again when another child touches her to unfreeze her. The object of the game is for the child who is IT to freeze all of the other players. Then the player who was frozen first is IT in the next game of "Freeze Tag."

Hot and Cold

Two or more children can play this game. All of the children who are not IT must leave the room. The child who is IT hides a small object somewhere in the room. This object, such as a button or an acorn, must be seen by everyone before they leave the room. When everyone returns to the room they begin to hunt for the object. The child who is IT gives hints as to the object's hiding place by saying, "hot," "cold" and "warm." If no one is near the object he says, "cold"; if someone gets closer he says, "warmer"; and if someone is very close, he says "hot!" The child who finds the object is the one to hide it in the next game of "Hot and Cold."

Hot Potato

The children stand in a circle and, while music is played, they pass a "hot potato" (a ball or a beanbag) around the circle as quickly as they can without dropping it. When the music stops, the child holding the potato must sit down. The last child holding the potato wins.

I Spy

One child is chosen to be IT. This child chooses something in the room and says, "I spy with my little eye something that is... (give a characteristic of the object chosen, e.g., "something that is round or red or smooth or hot"). The other children raise their hands and when chosen guess at different objects. When the object is guessed correctly, the first child sits down and the child who guessed correctly becomes the next one to "spy with his little eye..." and choose the object.

In and Out the Windows

This game must have at least seven players. All but one of the children stand in a circle facing the center, holding hands and raising them high to create arched "windows." One child is chosen to be the "dancer," and she stands in the middle. As the song indicates, on the first verse, the "dancer" skips around the circle going in and out of the windows. On the second verse, she stands and faces a child in the circle. On the third verse, she follows her new partner in and out of the windows. And on the final verse they go to the center of the circle together and curtsey/bow to each other. The child who was chosen to be the partner then becomes the next one to go "In and Out the Windows."

> Go in and out the windows,
> Go in and out the windows,
> Go in and out the windows,
> As we have done before.

Additional verses:

Now stand and face your partner...
Now follow her (him) *to London...*
Bow before you leave her (him)...

Leap Frog

As few as two children can play this game. One child crouches down on the ground like a frog (knees bent and hands on the ground between and a little in front of his feet). The next child crouches down as well and then leaps and puts her legs on either side of the first child and her hands on the first child's back. Then she leaps onto the ground in front of the first child. The first child is now behind the second child and he leaps over her in the same way. If you are playing with many children, they can line up so that one child can leap over several "frogs" in one turn, landing on the ground between each frog.

London Bridge Is Falling Down

London Bridge is falling down,
Falling down, falling down.
London Bridge is falling down,
My fair lady.

Take the key and lock her up,
Lock her up, lock her up.
Take the key and lock her up,
My fair lady.

Repeat first verse

Two children stand facing each other, holding hands up over their heads to make an arch (bridge). The rest of the children form a line and go under the bridge and then around and back under the bridge again as the class sings the song, "London Bridge Is Falling Down." When the children sing the words, "my fair lady," the children who are making the bridge bring their arms down to catch the child who is passing under the bridge at that moment. As the children continue to sing the song, have the two bridge makers gently swing their arms back and forth to rock the captive. At the end of the song, the captive takes the place of one of the bridge makers and the game starts again.

One Elephant

Children sit in a circle. One child places one arm out in front of herself to make a trunk, then walks around the circle while the group sings the song. When the group sings "called for another elephant to come," the first child chooses another to join her and become an "elephant." The first "elephant" extends her other hand between her legs to make a tail. The second "elephant" extends one arm out in front to make a trunk and grabs hold of the first "elephant's" tail. The two walk trunk to tail as the song continues and more elephants join.

One elephant went out to play.
Out on a spider's web one day.
He had such enormous fun,
He called for another elephant to come.

Ring Around the Rosie

(Children hold hands and walk in a circle. Everyone falls down on the words "all fall down.")

Ring around the rosie
Pocket full of posies,
Ashes, ashes,
All fall down.

Shoo Fly

Shoo fly don't bother me,
    (walk in a circle to the left)
Shoo fly don't bother me,
    (walk in a circle to the right)
Shoo fly don't bother me,
    (walk in a circle to the left)
For I don't want to play.
    (place hands on hips and shake head no)

Flies in the buttermilk
    (walk around shooing flies)
Shoo fly, shoo.
Flies in the buttermilk
Shoo fly, shoo.
Flies in the buttermilk

Shoo fly, shoo.
Please just go away.
> (place hands on hips and shake head no)

Shoo fly don't bother me,
> (walk to the left in a circle)
Shoo fly don't bother me.
> (walk to the right in a circle)
Shoo fly don't bother me,
> (walk to the left in a circle)
Come back another day.
> (wave good-bye)

Simon Says

Choose one child to be "Simon." All the other children stand side by side in a line facing Simon. The child playing Simon gives the other children orders that they have to carry out, but only when the orders follow the phrase "Simon says..." (e.g., "Simon says touch your nose"). If a child follows an order that Simon did not say (e.g., "Touch your nose"), then he is out and must sit down. The last child standing becomes the new Simon for the next game of "Simon Says."

Statues

Everyone dances around the room to music. When the music stops, everyone must freeze and hold that position, usually becoming a very funny looking "statue." If a child moves, he must sit down. When the music starts again, those who are still standing start to dance again. The last one standing wins. (In another variation of this game, a dancer must become a "statue" when she is tapped on the head by the leader, usually an adult; she may start to dance again when she is tapped on the head again. The music does not stop in this version.)

Telephone

Have children sit in a circle facing the center. One child is chosen to "start the telephone conversation." This child thinks of a word or short phrase and whispers it in the ear of the child next to him. The second child whispers what she heard in the ear of the child next to her. And so the word or phrase continues around the circle. If a child was not able to hear what was whispered in his hear, he may say "operator" and the word can be whispered in his ear again. (Note: a child may only say "operator" if he has not been able to hear the whispered word, not if he did not understand the whispered word. Not understanding the words is half the fun of the game!). When the word is finally whispered in the ear of the last child in the circle, she then announces the word out loud. Then the child who "started the telephone conversation" repeats the original phrase so all can compare and see how it changed. Choose a new child to "start the telephone conversation" and play again.

Who Has the Button?

Have children sit in a circle. Choose a child to be IT. Give IT a button. Have the children close their eyes. Help IT choose a friend to which he will give the button. Invite the children to open their eyes and chant, "Button, button, who has the button?" The children try to guess who has the button. The child who guesses correctly becomes the next IT.

The Instant Curriculum

Indexes

Theme Index

All about me, 36, 38, 58, 85, 87, 88, 92, 94, 96, 102, 103, 110, 111, 112, 124, 126, 130, 131, 145, 147, 166, 174, 177, 187, 196, 207, 220, 256, 257, 259, 260, 268, 272, 274, 275, 276, 277, 278, 281, 293, 296, 297

Animals, 51, 56, 58, 74, 106, 127, 150, 167, 170, 198, 216, 260, 285,

Artists, 23, 24, 258, 264,

Birds, 28, 249, 284

Body parts, 24, 25, 36, 58, 80, 82, 83, 84, 99, 103, 104, 107, 109, 127, 131, 132, 142, 165, 166, 180, 183, 184, 186, 188, 189, 192, 195, 202, 207,

Cause and effect, 29, 212, 218, 220, 225, 226, 228, 232, 235, 237, 239, 242, 243

Celebrations, 38, 53, 59, 60, 83, 133, 148, 153, 172, 174

Colors, 22, 24, 25, 26, 27, 28, 32, 33, 37, 38, 39, 43, 47, 55, 59, 84, 100, 125, 129, 130, 132, 138, 139, 140, 141, 142, 157, 160, 164, 168, 169, 203, 205, 220, 228, 231, 232, 233, 236, 245, 248, 270, 271

Day and night, 40, 52, 60, 131, 168, 177, 231, 234, 269

Families, 69, 70, 71, 72, 87, 90, 91, 116, 123, 137, 155, 169, 219, 227, 257, 261, 262, 265, 266, 267, 268, 269, 270, 274, 282, 296, 297

Farms, 51, 52, 106

Food/nutrition, 51, 52, 56, 57, 58, 59, 60, 62, 73, 93, 110, 114, 131, 133, 135, 139, 152, 157, 161, 163, 170, 171, 178, 191, 203, 239, 240, 242, 244, 248, 264, 273, 274, 275

Friends, 71, 90, 104, 106, 107, 113, 116, 125, 145, 148, 149, 160, 165, 172, 176, 182, 189, 192, 196, 197, 199, 206, 225, 237, 257, 262, 263, 273, 281, 283

Growing things, 38, 53, 56, 245, 244, 246, 247, 248, 271, 272

Houses/homes, 251, 252, 264

Imagination, 22, 35, 37, 41, 42, 46, 47, 57, 74, 75, 91, 92, 93, 95, 98, 101, 112, 114, 182, 206, 208, 236, 282, 282

Insects, 177, 181, 184, 192, 198, 201, 250, 251, 253, 292

Let's pretend, 22, 72, 73, 74, 75, 119, 120, 146, 150, 161, 180, 185, 186, 187, 188, 191, 227, 232, 233, 290

Make-believe, 91, 92, 179

Matching, 103, 125, 130, 132, 145, 146, 147, 158, 202, 241, 252, 288

Movement, 84, 120, 138, 152, 155, 159, 162, 175, 180, 181, 182, 183, 196, 197, 198, 199, 222, 274, 287, 291, 292

Music, 82, 83, 107, 133, 148, 158, 162, 164, 175, 181, 196, 217, 262, 290, 291

Nature, 31, 80, 124, 136, 142, 144, 145, 207, 213, 237, 238, 240, 241, 243, 246, 249, 263, 269, 272

Numbers, 85, 143, 154, 156, 159, 162, 166, 167, 170, 200, 202, 237, 252, 262, 282, 297

Nursery rhymes, 38, 91, 98, 114

Ocean, 24, 42, 150, 220

Opposites, 22, 23, 25, 26, 28, 40, 52, 89, 90, 117, 125, 133, 134, 135, 136, 140, 180, 183, 190, 195, 213, 214, 217, 218, 219, 224, 227, 233, 234, 237, 240, 242, 269, 284, 287

Our community, 66, 67, 69, 72, 73, 88, 91, 94, 111, 137, 171, 266, 267, 296

Patterns, 101, 108

Pets, 170, 260

The Instant Curriculum

Problem solving, 117, 124, 127, 137, 148, 151, 152, 154, 156, 157, 158, 160, 161, 162, 166, 172, 211, 219, 225, 226, 229, 230

School, 168, 171

Seasons, 59, 72, 144, 218, 221, 223, 243, 245, 248, 297

Senses, 23, 25, 31, 32, 39, 40, 45, 46, 47, 56, 60, 80, 81, 82, 83, 85, 90, 95, 97, 98, 100, 102, 104, 105, 136, 143, 242, 265

Shapes, 22, 24, 26, 29, 30, 31, 32, 33, 34, 38, 39, 53, 55, 59, 61, 110, 129, 132, 138, 139, 153, 157, 163, 164, 191, 192, 195, 202, 203, 204, 208, 212, 225, 228, 243, 260, 287

Sizes, 22, 24, 59, 86, 125, 140, 165, 166, 167, 245, 252

Sounds, 81, 98, 135, 151, 152, 175, 177, 182, 185, 186, 187, 200, 211, 215, 216, 217, 225, 240, 266

Spatial concepts, 89, 126, 283

Textures, 23, 27, 29, 30, 31, 33, 35, 40, 42, 43, 45, 47, 243

Time, 168, 169, 234, 262, 268

Tools, 26, 27, 34, 123, 229, 230, 270

Traditional tales, 58, 119, 120, 179, 180, 191, 195, 228

Transportation/travel, 29, 68, 171, 199, 205, 214, 218, 222, 227, 228, 277

Under construction, 140, 149, 152, 153, 223

Water, 28, 30

Weather, 167, 190, 212, 213, 214, 218, 221, 223, 237, 241, 271, 291

Index

A

Abbreviations, 86

Absorption, 30

Acorns, 239, 272

Acrylic paint, 40

Action stories, 120, 127–128

Addition, 160

> defined, 123

Air, 211–217

Alarm clocks, 81

Alcohol, 43, 46, 220

Alliteration, 77–78, 95

> defined, 79

Almonds, 203

Alphabet wall cards, 65

Aluminum foil, 42, 235

Animals, 249–253

> plastic, 170

> stuffed, 67, 93

Apple–carrot salad recipe, 56

Apples, 53, 56, 172

> seeds, 203, 239

Appliance boxes, 69, 71, 199, 226

Appointment books, 65, 67

Aprons, 64–65

Art activities, 21–47, 91–92, 145

> collages, 37–39

> designs, 29–33

> displaying, 258

> drawing, 22–24

> overview, 21

> painting, 25–28

> print-making, 34–36

> recipes, 43–47

> sculpting/molding, 40–42

Art paper, 23, 26–27, 30, 36–37, 263

Artist prop box, 64

Attributes, 124–126, 136, 245

> defined, 122

Auditory discrimination, 240, 266

> defined, 79

Auditory memory defined, 79

Auto repair/garage prop box, 64

B

Baby food jars, 23, 32, 51–52, 247

Backpacks, 64

Baggie ice cream recipe, 52

Bags, 106, 89, 125, 145

> grocery, 39, 64, 75, 111, 212, 245

> lunch, 162, 211

> plastic, 41

> zippered plastic, 29, 45–46, 52, 54–55, 87, 102, 115, 136, 154, 159, 242, 282

Baker's hats, 64

Bakery, 73

> prop box, 64

Baking soda, 242, 274

Balance scales, 166

Balancing, 198

Ballet shoes, 64, 67

Balloons, 225, 242

Balls, 40, 67, 133, 183, 197, 226

> cotton, 135–136

> golf, 29

> homemade, 195, 197

> stocking, 195

Banana pudding, 152

> recipe, 54

Banana wheels recipe, 54

Bananas, 54, 57, 59, 152, 230, 239

Bark, 38, 145

Baseball caps, 67, 267

Baskets, 72–73, 94, 96, 135, 146, 155, 170, 198, 213, 227, 238

    laundry, 207

    shopping, 64

Basters, 202, 229, 283

Bath mats, 147, 202

Bathing suits, 42

Beads, 72–74, 96, 132, 140–141, 208, 226

Beanbags, 81, 126, 148, 190, 192, 195, 200

Bear claws recipe, 58

Bells, 81

    jingle, 80, 151

    service, 81, 200

Belts, 73

    buckles, 74

Berets, 67

Bingo cards, 106

Birdbaths, 249

Birds, 249

Birdseed, 249, 285

Birthdays, 174

Biscuits, 58, 61

Blankets, 197

Bleach bottles, 270

Blenders, 53

Blocks, 25, 68, 89–89, 94, 99–100, 133, 135, 139, 149, 153, 191, 196, 200, 222, 226, 230, 287

    pattern, 235

    soft, 75

Bloom, Benjamin, 117

Boards, 226

Boas, 72

Bobby pins, 287

Body paint recipe, 44

Bolts, 123

Bonsai plants, 265

Books, 65, 86, 99–100, 133, 147, 149, 195, 222, 230, 287

    Abiyoyo by Pete Seeger, 179

    appointment, 65, 67

    Brown Bear, Brown Bear, What Do You See? by Bill Martin, Jr., 115

    Chicken Soup With Rice by Maurice Sendak, 144

    classification, 130, 137

    coloring, 93, 204, 207

    David's Father by Robert Munsch, 93, 179

    Good Dog, Carl by Alexandra Day, 114

    homemade, 87, 115, 130, 159

    I Love You Rituals by Becky Bailey, 272

    If You Give a Mouse a Cookie by Laura Joffe Numeroff, 141

    Imogene's Antlers by David Small, 93

    It Looked Like Spilt Milk by Charles Green Shaw, 206

    Jennie's Hat by Ezra Jack Keats, 73

    number, 159

    Pancakes for Breakfast by Tomie dePaola, 114

    The Snowman by Raymond Briggs, 114

    The Snowy Day by Ezra Jack Keats, 120

    Stone Soup by Marcia Brown, 242

    The Tortilla Factory by Gary Paulsen, 144

    Tuesday by David Wiesner, 143

    The Very Hungry Caterpillar by Eric Carle, 143

    Wacky Wednesday by Theo LeSieg, 284

    Why the Chicken Crossed the Road by David Macaulay, 141

    wordless, 114

    work, 65

Boots, 64

Borax, 45

Bottle brushes, 27

Bottle caps, 33, 61, 123

Bottles, 152, 269

    ½-liter, 186, 222, 239, 242, 271

1-liter, 167, 220

2-liter, 65

bleach, 270

conditioner, 65, 67

detergent, 186

glue, 99

hair spray, 65, 67

plastic, 229, 251

shampoo, 65, 67, 186

soda, 220, 251, 269

spray, 26, 96

squeeze, 43, 211

squirt, 27, 212, 236

Bowls, 34, 43–47, 54–55, 64, 102, 119, 157, 205–206, 208, 213, 240, 246, 285

nesting, 286

Bows, 72, 270

Boxes, 40–41, 64, 66, 72, 93–94, 99, 125–126, 132–133, 155, 195, 223, 230, 232, 241, 246, 257, 259, 263, 272, 276, 282, 286–287

appliance, 69, 71, 199, 226

cereal, 71, 110, 187, 263

copy paper, 275

cornmeal, 232

jewelry, 41, 126

junk, 123

large, 71, 199, 226

medium, 71, 199, 275

oatmeal, 200, 232

pizza, 64

prop, 64–67, 266

rice, 71

round, 200, 232

shallow, 29

shoeboxes, 41, 156, 222

small, 126, 199

tomorrow, 268

Bracelets, 282

Branches, 31, 35, 207, 239

Bread, 56–57, 62, 239

Bricks, 145, 224

Briefcases, 66, 73, 89

Brooms, 229

wisp, 27

Broomsticks, 188

Brushes, 65, 288

Bubble soap, 26, 34, 202, 213, 287

recipes, 43, 84

scented, 241

Bubble wands, 26, 213

Bubble wrap, 34

Buckets, 35, 68, 161, 200, 219, 229, 237

homemade, 270

Bulletin boards, 36, 153

Burlap, 105, 224

Butcher paper, 26, 36, 39, 60, 105, 136, 142, 182, 191, 220, 238

tubes, 226

Butter, 56, 60, 62

churns, 268

recipe, 52

Butterflies, 93

Button hooks, 268

Buttons, 25, 80, 106, 108, 123, 126–127, 130, 135, 139, 148, 159, 162, 206, 208, 213, 235, 296

C

Cabinets, 281

Cake pans, 64, 104, 142

Calendars, 67, 168–169, 297

Cameras, 260

Camping prop box, 64

Can ice cream

recipe, 52

Can openers, 230

Candies, 148, 153, 161

Cans, 98, 111

    1-gallon, 186

    coffee, 52, 83, 187, 200, 222

    film, 80

    food, 71

    juice, 259

    potato chip, 80, 83, 187

    soup, 71

    tennis ball, 140

    tuna, 71

    vegetable, 140

    watering, 240

Capes, 72

Caps, 69, 73

Car wash, 68

Cardboard, 22, 31, 33, 38, 45, 69, 96, 100, 150, 159, 166, 215, 227–228, 283

    corrugated, 105

    tubes, 74, 91, 140, 149, 180, 186–187, 200, 212, 216, 225–226, 276

Cards, 64

    alphabet, 65

    bingo, 106

    flash, 65

    greeting, 42, 205, 269, 287, 296

    index, 102–106, 110, 147, 155–158, 162, 258

    letter, 104

    name, 293

    number, 155–156

    playing, 158

    word, 104

Cardstock, 207

Carpet rolls, 226

Carrots, 56

    seeds, 244

Cars, 29, 68, 226–227, 235, 282

    wooden, 228

Cash registers, 64–65

Cassette tapes, 83–84, 175, 177, 240

    covers, 171

Catalogs, 64

Cats, 96

Cause and effect, 210

CD players, 64, 92, 105, 133, 148, 158, 164, 180–182, 185, 187–188, 190, 192, 196–197, 224, 276, 287, 290

CDs, 64, 92, 105, 133, 148, 158, 164, 180–182, 185, 187–188, 190, 192, 196–197, 224, 276, 287, 290

    covers, 171

Cellophane, 71, 231, 232

Cereal, 54, 191

    boxes, 71, 110, 187, 263

Chairs, 66–67, 119, 148, 165, 181, 188, 195–196, 221, 227

    outdoor, 64

Chalk, 22–23, 31–32, 64–65, 136, 224

Chalkboards, 65

Change of state, 242–243

Chants, 178–180

    "The Flight of the Fairies," 179

    "Giant Stomp," 179

    "Hey! My Name Is Joe," 183

    "Metamorphosis," 184

    "Oni Woni," 180

    "Tooty Ta," 184

    "Who Took the Cookie From the Cookie Jar?" 178, 337

Chart paper, 83, 86, 103, 112, 114, 119

Charts, 65, 157, 251

Cheese, 56, 58, 62, 152

    cheddar, 52

    cream, 57

    powdered, 240

Chili popcorn recipe, 60

Chocolate, 135

    bars, 172

Chopsticks, 265

Cinnamon, 57, 60, 239

Circle time, 91

Circus prop box, 67

Classification, 121, 130–137, 161, 203, 223, 246, 251–252

    applications, 137

    by color, 132

    by shape, 132–133

    by size, 133–134

    defined, 79, 122

    open-ended, 136–137

    using other senses, 135–136

Classroom quilts, 263

Classroom visitors, 267, 296

Clay, 72

    modeling, 42, 202, 204

    potter's, 72

    pots, 246

Cleanup tasks, 290

Clipboards, 66, 80, 241

Clocks, 168

    alarm, 82

    sundials, 234

    ticking, 81

Clotheslines, 219

Clothespins, 27, 68, 136, 264

Clothing, 145, 270, 296

Cloud dough, 40

    recipe, 43

Clouds, 236

Clown costumes, 67

Coasters, 33

Coat hangers, 31

    tubes, 186

Coconuts, 248

    dried, 59

    oil, 248

Coffee, 248

    cans, 52, 83, 187, 200, 222

    filters, 30

Colanders, 230, 285

Cold cream, 44

Collages, 37–39, 276

    materials, 271

Color tiles, 140

Colored glue recipe, 43

Colored pencils, 22

Colored rock salt, 43

Colored tape, 87, 115

Coloring books, 93, 204, 207

Colors, 22, 49, 125, 132–133, 169, 205, 220, 231–236, 245, 248, 271, 277

Combs, 24, 65, 67, 166, 287–288

Comic strips, 108, 112

Community workers, 266–267

Comprehension, 78, 117–120

    defined, 79

Computer keyboards, 66

Computer labels, 296

Computer monitors, 66

Condensation, 239

Conditioner bottles, 65, 67

Conductor's hats, 67

Construction paper, 35–36, 39, 87, 103, 110, 116, 130–131, 141, 146, 153, 156, 169, 198, 203, 206, 214, 233, 236, 238, 245–246, 257, 259, 264, 277, 284, 287

Contact paper, 129, 156, 164

Containers, 30, 33, 151, 160, 167, 238, 271
    covered, 41, 45, 46–47
    food, 64, 71, 111
    plastic, 158, 218
Cookie cutters, 34, 56, 59, 64, 133, 163, 204–205, 208
Cookie sheets, 29, 64, 73, 96, 135, 218, 225, 228
Cookies, 54, 147, 152
Cooking activities, 49–62
    hotplate/popper recipes, 60–62
    no-cook recipes, 51–57
    overview, 49–50
    refrigerator/freezer recipes, 59
    toaster oven/oven recipes, 57–58
Cooking oil, 43, 46–47, 53, 61, 220
Coordination, 129, 198–199, 201
Copy paper boxes, 275
Cords, 250, 270
Corks, 123, 231, 269
Cornmeal boxes, 232
Cornstarch, 44–45
Correction fluid, 112
Corrugated cardboard, 105
Cotton, 226, 238
    balls, 135–136
    swabs, 22, 26, 38
Counters, 139
Counting, 149, 169, 262
    defined, 122
    patterns, 156
Coupons, 64
Cowboy hats, 67
Crackers, 52–53, 133, 152, 161, 191
Craft paper, 218
Craft sticks, 28, 45, 92, 139, 227–228, 246
Crayons, 22–24, 30–31, 33, 35, 39, 92, 94, 99, 100,
    103, 105, 136, 138, 141, 145, 182, 204–206, 222,
    235, 245, 270

Cream of tartar, 46–47
Creamy paint, 46
Creative movement, 180–184
Creativity, 21–47
Crepe paper, 180, 187, 207, 221
Critical thinking, 279–288
    overview, 279–280
Cross-lateral movements, 273
Cubbies, 256
Cultural diversity, 50, 73, 90, 107, 143–144, 172, 261,
    264–266
Cups, 54, 138, 147, 148, 157, 206, 218, 246–247, 283
    lids, 42
    measuring, 43–47, 51–62, 64, 84, 102, 151–152,
        167
    paper, 218
    plastic, 247
    teacups, 265
Curtains, 71

D

Daily schedules, 168
Dancer materials, 64
Dancing, 133, 179, 187–190
Dashikis, 73
Day/night, 168
Deodorant bottles, 26
Designs, 29–33
Detergent
    bottles, 186
    laundry, 47
    liquid, 33–34, 43–44, 84, 202, 213
Diffusion, 217, 219–220
    defined, 210
Dish tubs, 36, 142, 151, 167, 202, 219–220, 237
Dishes, 35, 64–65, 69, 270
Disk magnets, 227–228

Diving masks, 65

Dolls, 89, 100

    clothes, 219

    paper, 227

Donut recipe, 61–62

Double boilers, 46

Dramatic play, 63–75, 119–120, 161

    creative play, 72–75

    imaginative play, 66–72

    overview, 63–64

    prop boxes, 64–66

Drawing, 22–24, 235, 260–261, 263

    tools, 22

Dress-up clothes, 72–73

Drinking glasses, 51, 89, 134, 167, 172, 214, 219, 228, 239, 285

Drinking straws, 30, 67, 74, 84, 134, 140, 166, 185, 191, 212–213, 229, 259

Drive-throughs, 69

Drums, 186, 190

    homemade, 186

Dustpans, 229

Dyes, 248

E

Easel paper, 32

Easels, 64, 219

Egg cartons, 130, 150, 162, 269, 296

    Styrofoam, 246

Eggbeaters, 230

Eggs, 60, 102

    plastic, 151, 200

    shells, 38, 239

Electric skillets, 60–61

Embroidery hoops, 214

Emery boards, 287

Envelopes, 64, 106, 113, 151, 269

Environmental awareness, 269–272

Epsom salt, 43

    paint, 28

    solution recipe, 43

Erosion, 222

Evaporation, 219

Evergreens, 238

Expanding stories, 93

Extracts, 47, 136, 241

Eye charts, 64

Eye doctor prop box, 64

Eyedroppers, 30, 202, 205–206, 218, 229, 242, 246

Eyeglasses, 64, 72, 235

    frames, 232

F

Fabric scraps, 39, 41, 132, 135, 186–187, 214, 217, 219, 221, 239, 248

Face paint recipe, 44

Families, 261–262

    as partners, 295–297

Fans

    electric, 212, 214

    hand, 268

    paper, 212, 265

Father's Day, 23

Feather dusters, 27

Feathers, 22, 28, 39, 135, 211, 213, 226

Felt, 161

Fences, 207, 219, 264

Field trips

    home viewings, 264

    nature walk, 31, 38, 207, 237, 240–241, 252

    neighborhood walk, 80, 144, 224

    treasure hunt, 246

File folders, 269

Film canisters, 80

Fine motor skills, 21–47, 50, 92, 102–104, 110, 116, 126–127, 132, 139, 141, 162, 168, 189, 193, 202–208, 226, 235, 260–261, 263

Finger puppets, 207

Fingerpaint, 25, 29, 47, 218, 220
    paper, 28
    recipe, 44

Fingerplays
    "Dance, Thumbkin, Dance," 189
    "Five Little Monkeys," 162
    "Teasing Mr. Alligator," 162
    "Where Is Thumbkin?" 107

Fire safety, 278

Firefighter's hats, 67

Fishing line, 150

Fishing poles, 64

Flannel boards, 161
    characters, 100, 220
    stories, 93

Flash cards, 65

Flashlights, 64, 146, 207, 232–233, 234, 237

Florist Styrofoam, 72

Florist wire, 64, 72

Flour, 43, 46–47, 102
    whole wheat, 60

Flower/gift shop prop box, 64

Flowers, 38, 73, 239, 288
    artificial, 64, 72, 238
    seeds, 244

Fluids defined, 210

Foil, 22, 64, 224

Folders, 158, 296

Food allergies, 50, 53, 157, 170, 172, 249

Food cans, 71

Food coloring, 30, 43, 45–47, 51, 55, 73, 205, 220–231, 271

Food containers, 64, 71, 111

Food pyramids, 275

Force, 214, 221–222
    defined, 210

Forks, 34
    plastic, 22, 29, 138
    tuning, 217

Forms
    story map, 118
    word web, 119

Fractions, 172, 281
    defined, 123

Free exploration, 121, 123–125
    defined, 122

Friction, 222–224
    defined, 210

Friendship mix, 114
    recipe, 54

Fruit cocktail, 57, 59

Fruit juice, 169
    grape, 51
    lemon, 56, 236
    orange, 59

Fruit kebobs, 139
    recipe, 56

Fruits, 131, 171
    apples, 53, 56, 172
    bananas, 54, 57, 59, 152, 230, 239
    blackberries, 248
    dried, 54, 56–57, 60, 135, 157, 214
    grapes, 56, 139
    oranges, 56
    peaches, 52
    pineapple, 56–57, 59, 139
    strawberries, 56, 139

Funnels, 64, 167, 221, 229–230, 283, 286
    homemade, 270

G

Gak, 40

   recipe, 45

Games

   Beanbag Throw, 155

   Bingo, 106

   Bowling, 222

   Can Race, 222

   Can You Find It? 124

   Card Match, 158

   Circle 'Round the Zero, 159

   Cooperative Musical Chairs, 191, 338

   Did You Ever See a Lassie? 175

   Drop the Handkerchief, 338

   Duck, Duck, Goose, 338

   Ears Up, 82

   Farmer in the Dell, 339

   Follow the Leader, 195

   Follow the Sound, 81

   Freeze, 190

   Freeze Tag, 339

   Gossip, 82

   Hand Match-Up, 125

   Hopscotch, 192

   Hot and Cold, 339

   Hot Potato, 340

   I Spy, 84, 124, 340

   I've Got Rhythm, 83

   In and Out the Windows, 340

   Inchworm Race, 192

   Leap Frog, 341

   Letter Tic Tac Toe, 104

   London Bridge Is Falling Down, 341

   Lucky Letters, 105

   More or Less, 148

   Musical Beanbags, 190

   Musical Chairs, 148

   Musical Hot and Cold, 81

   Musical Numbers, 158

   Musical Shapes, 164

   Number Bingo, 159

   One Elephant, 342

   Opposites Hunt, 90

   Pair, Think, and Share, 104

   Paper Chase, 192

   Partner Match, 145

   Pass the Beanbag, 190

   Pass the Purse, 287

   Pick a Pair, 97

   Ping-Pong Races, 283

   Rebus Treasure Hunt, 113

   Rhyme or Reason, 97

   Rhyming, 97

   Ring Around the Rosie, 342

   Shoo Fly, 342

   Shopping Fun, 88

   Simon Says, 84, 343

   Singing, 175

   Snack Pass, 191

   Statues, 343

   String a Story, 91

   Tablecloth Lotto, 105

   Telephone, 343

   Tree Tag, 124–125

   Twister, 129

   Wallpaper Lotto, 101

   What's Missing? 99

   Where's the Button? 127

   Where's the Sound? 81

   Who Has the Button? 344

   Who's That Traipsing on My Bridge? 191

Garbage can lids, 249

Garden hoses, 42, 68

Gardening, 244, 246–248, 272

Garlic presses, 208

Gas station, 68

Gas, 217, 219, 242

    defined, 210

Gears, 64

Gelatin, 44, 47, 54, 59, 243

    jigglers, 243

    recipe, 59

Gerbils, 93

Gifts, 23

Gloves, 72, 133

    work, 64

Glue, 30–31, 33, 37–38, 41, 43, 45, 47, 69, 71–72, 74, 80, 92, 102–105, 130, 139, 146, 150, 158, 206–207, 212, 217, 220, 227, 246, 251, 258, 265, 271, 275, 287

    bottles, 99

    colored, 43

Glycerin, 34, 43–44, 46

Goldfish, 93

Golf balls, 29

Golf tees, 160

Goop, 40

    recipe, 45

Grade books, 65

Grapes, 56, 139

    juice, 51

Graphing, 131, 169–171

    defined, 123

Grass, 206, 222

    seed, 247

    skirts, 188

Graters, 56

Gravel, 80, 104, 186–187, 230

Gravitation, 213

    defined, 210

Gravity, 225–226

    defined, 210

Greeting cards, 42, 205, 269, 287, 296

Gritty paint, 46

Grocery bags, 39, 64, 75, 111, 212, 245

Grocery store

    items, 88

    prop box, 64

Gross motor skills, 50, 91, 129, 133–134, 142, 164, 174, 176–177, 179–185, 187–201, 291–292

H

Habitats, 251–252

Hair gel, 33, 102, 104

Hair spray bottles, 65, 67

Hairdryers, 65, 67

Hammers, 64

Hand lotion, 217

Hand-eye, 126, 140, 150, 153, 155, 160, 162, 197, 200, 222

    defined, 79

Hanger hooks, 258

Hats, 67, 72–73, 96

    baker's, 64

    baseball caps, 67, 267

    berets, 67

    caps, 69, 73

    conductor's, 67

    cowboy, 67

    fezzes, 67

    firefighter's, 67

    homemade, 72–73

    military, 67

Health/safety issues, 272–278

Height, 149

Hole punches, 103, 110, 203, 212, 221, 23, 31, 38, 64, 72, 234, 263

Holidays, 23, 35, 73

Hooks, 281

Hot plates, 44–47

    recipes, 60–62

Hourglasses, 262

House play, 70–71

Hula hoops, 195

I

Ice cream, 51

    recipes, 52

    salt, 104

Ice, 218, 240

    cubes, 51, 218, 242

    trays, 59

Icing paint, 28

    recipe, 45

Index cards, 102–106, 110, 147, 155–158, 162, 258

Ink pads. See Stamp pads

Insects, 251, 253

Insolubles, 217, 220

Instant pudding, 54

International Feast Day, 264

Ivory Flakes, 44

Ivory Snow, 44

J

Jars, 30, 32, 152, 240, 248, 296

    baby food, 23, 32, 51–52, 247

    lids, 138

    plastic, 38, 54, 229

Jelly, 57–58

Jewelry boxes, 41, 126

Jewelry, 73, 296

    homemade, 74, 243

Jingle bells, 80, 151

Job fairs, 267

Journals, 247

Juice cans, 259

Juice squeezers, 268

Jumper cables, 64

Junk boxes, 123

K

Kazoos, 216

Kerchiefs, 67

Keys, 64, 123, 267

Kimonos, 73

Kinetic energy, defined, 210

Kitchen tools, 230

Kits, 212

Knives, 56

    plastic, 54, 242

    X-acto, 240

Knox gelatin, 44

L

Lab coats, 65

Labels, 111, 256, 259, 296

Lace, 127, 207

Laces, 110

Laminate, 110, 153, 207

Lamps, 74, 146, 188, 207

Language/literacy development, 49, 77–120

    comprehension, 117–120

    dramatic play, 63–75

    letter knowledge, 99–107

    listening, 80–86

    oral language, 86–94

overview, 77–79

phonological awareness, 94–99

print awareness, 107–116

Lanterns, 64, 268

Laundry baskets, 207

Laundry detergent, 47

Laundry starch, 44

Learning domains, 17

Leaves, 38, 42, 136, 219, 230, 238–239, 245–246

Left-to-right progression, 108–109

defined, 79

Lemon extract, 47

Lemon juice, 56, 236

Length, 150

Leotards, 64

Letter cards, 104

Letter recognition, 78, 99–107

Light, 231–236, 271

scattered, 235

Liquid detergent, 33–34, 43–44, 84, 202, 213

Liquid soap, 46

Liquid starch, 26, 37, 44–46

Liquids, 217–218

defined, 210

Listening skills, 77, 80–86, 143

Listening stories, 84

Lists, 115

Locks, 98

Lumpy paint, 46

Lunch bags, 162, 211

M

Magazines, 38, 42, 64, 67, 69, 87, 104, 159, 203, 208, 261, 264, 276, 287

Magnetic letters, 103

Magnetic strips, 227

Magnetic tape, 228

Magnetic vinyl, 228

Magnetism, 227–229

defined, 210

Magnets, 150, 227–229

Magnifying glasses, 24, 65, 223, 235, 250

Magnolia leaves, 245

Mail carrier

materials, 64

Mail sacks, 64

Mail sorters, 64

Manicure supplies, 65

Manila folders, 252, 265

Maracas, 186, 240

Marbles, 29, 145, 225–226, 235

Margarine, 55, 57, 60

Margarine tubs, 269

with lids, 160, 206

Markers, 22, 24, 30, 35–36, 38–39, 74, 160, 162, 232, 244, 270

permanent, 271

scented, 23

Marzipan recipe, 59

Masking tape, 33, 67, 74, 87, 115, 119, 126, 130, 132, 155, 167, 185, 189, 191–192, 197–200, 211, 222, 229, 235, 243, 283

Masks, 72

diving, 65

Massage oils. See Scented oils

Matching activities, 71, 103, 111, 125, 130, 132, 145–147, 158, 165, 252, 260, 282, 288

Materials, 64–65

Math, 121–172, 296

classification, 130–137

cooking, 49–62

fractions, 172

free exploration, 123–125

graphs, 169–171

measurement, 165–169

numeration, 154–162

one-to-one correspondence, 145–149

ordering, 149–154

overview, 121–123

patterning, 138–145

shapes, 163–164

spatial relationships, 126–129

Measurement, 50–62, 149–154, 165–169

capacity, 167

defined, 123

height, 149

length, 150

linear, 165–166

liquid, 151–152

size, 152–153

temperature, 167–168

time, 168–169

weight, 151, 166

Measuring cups, 43–47, 51–62, 64, 84, 102, 151–152, 167

Measuring spoons, 34, 43–47, 51–62, 64, 84, 102, 167, 229, 242

Meatball presses, 205

Megaphones, 215

Memory skills, 100–102

auditory, 79

visual, 79

Menus, 64–65

Metal, 217, 227–228

mirrors, 235

Microscopes, 65

Microwave ovens, 60, 270

Milk, 51–52, 54

buttermilk, 23

cartons, 40, 129, 162, 246, 272

evaporated, 55

powdered, 53

sweetened condensed, 59

whipping cream, 52

Mirrors, 65, 73, 91, 235

metal, 235

Mittens, 146

Mixers, 47, 234

Mixing bowls, 64

Mobiles, 31

Modeling clay, 42, 202, 204

Mondrian, Piet, 32

Money, 64–65, 67, 262, 267

Months, 144

Mother's Day, 23

Motion, 214

defined, 211

resistance to, 222–224

Moving freely, 185

Muffin tins, 203, 205, 270

Music. See Recorded music; Songs

Music/movement, 173–191

chants, 178–180

creative movement, 180–184

dances, 187–190

games, 190–191

moving freely, 185

music makers, 185–187

overview, 173

songs, 174–178

Music boxes, 81

Music makers, 185–187

Mylar, 235

The Instant Curriculum

N

Nails, 228

Name cards, 293

Nametags, 111

Napkins, 64–65, 147–148, 208

Nature items, 38

Nesting bowls, 286

Newsletters, 297

Newspaper, 22, 26, 30, 33, 40, 75, 96, 103–104, 108, 112, 116, 180, 182, 185–186, 188, 192, 221

No-cook recipes, 51–57

Non-soluble, defined, 211

Numbers

cards, 155–156

charts, 157

plastic, 156

wooden, 156

Numeration, 154–162

defined, 123

Nursery rhymes, 91, 94, 98, 114

Nutrition, 49–62

Nuts, 203, 248

acorns, 239, 272

almonds, 203

hazelnuts, 248

metal, 123

peanuts, 53, 157, 170, 248

pecans, 203, 248

walnuts, 203, 248

O

Oak leaves, 245

Oatmeal boxes, 200, 232

Office prop box, 66

One-cup salad

recipe, 59

One-to-one correspondence, 131, 145–149, 154, 282, 296

defined, 122

equal sets, 145–147

unequal sets, 147–149

Onomatopoeia, 77

defined, 79

songs, 96

Open-ended questions, 93

Opposites, 89–90

Oral language

defined, 79

development, 77, 86–94

Order forms, 64–65

Ordering, 83, 100, 149–154

by comparing sets, 153–154

by height, 149

by length, 150

by liquid measurement, 151–152

by position and size, 152–153

by weight, 151

defined, 123

Outdoor activities, 23–24, 31, 38, 42, 68, 69, 136, 144–145, 161, 166, 192, 195, 212, 219, 221, 229, 231, 234, 236–237, 240–241, 244, 249–250, 264, 271, 290

Ovens, 102

microwave, 60, 270

recipes, 57–58, 102

Overhead projectors, 74, 146, 188, 207, 232–233

P

Pails. See Buckets

Paint rollers, 27

Paint, 22, 27, 64, 71, 166, 228, 232, 263, 277

acrylic, 40

creamy, 46

Epsom salt, 28

face, 44

fingerpaint, 25, 29, 44, 47, 218, 220

icing, 28, 45

lumpy, 46

poster, 40

powdered, 30–32, 44, 84, 245

puff, 28, 47

recipes, 44–47

rough, 46

salt, 28, 47

scratch-and-sniff, 25, 47

shiny, 46

slimy, 46

slippery, 46

soap, 47

sparkly, 46

tempera, 26–30, 32, 34–36, 43, 46–47, 142

thick, 46

Paintbrushes, 26, 28, 30, 32, 37, 38, 44, 64, 94, 219, 245, 277

Painting, 25–28

Pallets, 64

Pans, 42, 47, 56, 64, 73

cake, 64, 104, 142

double boilers, 46

lids, 187

muffin tins, 203, 205, 270

pie, 36, 228

plastic, 249

shallow, 30, 206, 214

Pantyhose, 74, 197, 251, 269, 271

Paper bags, 69

grocery, 39, 64, 75, 111, 212, 245

lunch, 162, 211

Paper baking cups, 153

Paper cups, 218

Paper pads, 66

Paper plates, 31–32, 72, 92, 141, 157, 181, 187, 217, 234, 260, 276, 287

Paper towels, 29–30, 34, 36, 43, 247, 283

tubes, 140, 149, 187, 212, 225, 276

Paper, 22, 24, 26, 28–31, 33–35, 37–38, 44, 64–65, 84, 92, 105, 116, 126, 129, 138–139, 141, 145, 150, 154, 157, 159, 163, 168, 172, 181–182, 195, 197–198, 206, 211, 223, 228, 232–233, 235, 240–241, 259–261, 269, 271, 282, 288

art, 23, 26–27, 30, 36–37, 263

butcher, 26, 36, 39, 60, 105, 136, 142, 182, 191, 220, 238

chart, 83, 86, 103, 112, 114, 119

construction, 35–36, 39, 87, 103, 110, 116, 130–131, 141, 146, 153, 156, 169, 198, 203, 206, 214, 233, 236, 238, 245–246, 257, 259, 264, 277, 284, 28

contact, 129, 156, 164

craft, 218

crepe, 180, 187, 207, 221

easel, 32

fingerpaint, 28

heavy, 25, 215

newspaper, 22, 26, 30, 33, 40, 75, 96, 103–104, 108, 112, 116, 180, 182, 185–186, 188, 192, 221

slick, 218

stiff, 33

tissue, 37, 39, 72, 91, 192, 213, 238

tracing, 103, 204

wax, 22, 216, 218, 249

wrapping, 35, 39, 64

Paperclips, 80, 103, 136, 141, 150–151, 156, 157, 165, 204, 214, 227–229

Papier-mâché paste, 40

recipe, 46

Parents, 295–297

Party pops

recipe, 59

The Instant Curriculum

Paste, 157, 159, 164, 217

    papier-mâché, 40

    recipe, 46

    wheat, 46

Pastry brushes, 58, 208

Pattern blocks, 235

Patterning, 52, 83, 108, 121–122, 138–145

    circular, 141

    cultural, 143–144

    defined, 122

    environmental, 144–145

    movement, 142

    musical/sound, 142–143

    vertical, 140

    wrap-around, 141–142

Patterns

    butterflies, 35

    counting, 156

    helicopters, 214

    ice cream cones, 146

    megaphones, 215

Peanut butter, 53, 57, 249

    recipe, 53

Peanut butter balls recipe, 53

Peanuts, 53, 157, 170, 248

Pebbles, 92, 145, 151, 218, 282, 285

Pegboards, 142

Pencils, 22, 36, 64–65, 67, 94, 103, 134, 149, 185–186, 204, 234, 288

    colored, 22

Pennies, 136, 147, 158–159, 162

Pens, 22, 64–65, 241, 270, 296

Peppermint extract, 47, 55, 274

Periscopes, 235

Permanent markers, 271

Pets, 170

Phonics, 78

Phonological sensitivity, 77–78, 94–99

    defined, 79

Photo albums, 87

Photocopiers, 104, 207, 215

Photos

    of children, 87, 207, 268

    of families, 87, 281

Physical development, 193–208

    fine motor, 202–208

    gross motor, 195–201

    overview, 193–194

Picasso, Pablo, 24

Pictures, 159, 198

    animals, 252

    cultural diversity, 265

    food, 69, 275–276

    happy faces, 38

    insects, 253

    meadows, 251

    morning activities, 269

    nature items, 243

    trees, 251

    water, 251

Pie pans, 36, 228

Pine needles, 245

Pine seedlings, 272

Pineapple

    chunks, 56, 139

    crushed, 57, 59

Pinecones, 249

Ping-pong balls, 200, 212, 283

Pipe cleaners, 42, 127, 136, 202, 208

Pitchers, 64

Pizza boxes, 64

Pizza cardboards, 234

Pizza face recipe, 58

Pizza place prop box, 64

Pizza sauce, 58

Plants, 134, 237–238, 243–248

    Bonsai, 265

Plastic, 27, 217, 228, 235

    animals, 170

    bags, 41

        zippered, 29, 45–46, 52, 54–55, 87, 102, 115, 136, 154, 159, 242, 282

    bottles, 229, 251

        ½-liter, 186, 222, 239, 242, 271

        1-liter, 167, 220

        2-liter, 65

        soda, 220, 251, 269

    containers, 158, 218

    eggs, 151, 200

    forks, 22, 29, 138

    jars, 38, 54, 229

    knives, 54, 242

    lids, 33, 186–187, 204, 206, 221

    tubing, 231

    tubs, 67, 142, 151, 167, 202, 219, 237, 271

Plates, 36, 148

    paper, 31–32, 72, 92, 141, 157, 181, 187, 217, 234, 260, 276, 287

    plastic, 187

Play money, 64–65, 67

Playdough, 41–42, 64, 73, 102, 133, 140, 163, 202, 208, 231, 234

    cloud dough, 40, 43

    recipes, 46–47

    scented, 47

Playing cards, 158

Pliers, 64

Pocket charts, 258

Pointillism, 24

Poker chips, 139

Pompoms, 147, 182, 185

Popcorn poppers, 60

Popcorn, 60, 203, 240

Popsicle sticks, 59

Positional words, 84, 89, 92–93, 107, 126–129, 152–153

Post office prop box, 64

Poster

    board, 106, 110, 158–159, 164, 227, 258, 260

    paint, 40

Potato chip canisters, 80, 83, 187

Potato mashers, 24, 34, 208, 230

Pots, 64, 248

    clay, 246

Potter's clay, 72

Potting soil, 244, 246–247

Powder puffs, 241

Predictions, 165, 225

Prepositions, 84

Pretzels, 54, 135, 191

    recipe, 102

Price tags, 64

Print awareness, 78, 107–120

    defined, 79

Print-making, 34–36

Prisms, 233

Problem solving, 210, 256, 279–288

    overview, 279–280

Projector screens, 74, 188

Prop boxes, 64–67, 266

Pudding, 54, 114, 152

    recipes, 54

Puff paint, 28

    recipe, 47

Pulleys, 229

Puppets

    finger, 207

    magnetic, 227

shadow, 207, 232

stick, 92

Purple cow shakes, 114

recipe, 51

Purses, 73, 89, 287

Puzzles, 286

cereal box, 110

greeting card, 205, 287

letter, 110

me, 207

name, 110

Q

Questioning strategies, 93, 117

R

Raisins, 56–57, 60, 135, 157, 214

Rebus activities, 113–114

Recipes, 93

apple–carrot salad, 56

arts and crafts, 43–47

baggie ice cream, 52

banana pudding, 54

banana wheels, 54

bear claws, 58

body paints, 44

bubble liquid, 84

bubble soap, 43

butter, 52

can ice cream, 52

candy mints, 55

chili popcorn, 60

cloud dough, 43

colored glue, 43

colored rock salt, 43

donuts, 61–62

Epsom salt solution, 43

face paint, 44

fingerpaint, 44

friendship mix, 54, 114

fruit kebobs, 56, 139

gak, 45

gelatin jigglers, 59

glittery sugar mallows, 55

goop, 45

grilled cheese delights, 62

hotplate/popper, 60–62

icing paint, 45

marzipan, 59

milkanilla, 51

mix it myself snacks, 157

no-cook, 51–57

one-cup salad, 59

paints, 46

papier-mâché paste, 46

party pops, 59

paste, 46

peanut butter, 53

peanut butter balls, 53

pigs in a blanket, 58

pizza faces, 58

playdough, 46–47

pretzel dough, 102

puff paint, 47

purple cow shakes, 51, 114

rebus, 114

refrigerator/freezer, 59

salt paint, 47

sandwich animals, 56

sandwich fillings, 57

scented playdough, 47

scratch-and-sniff paint, 47

shake-a-puddin', 54, 114

shooting stars, 60

skillet cookies, 60–61

soap paint, 47

soapsuds clay, 47

sun salad, 52

toast tidbits, 57

toaster oven/oven, 57–58

toothpaste, 274

tooty fruity, 56

Recorded music, 92, 105, 133, 148, 158, 164, 180–182, 185, 187–188, 190, 192, 196–197, 224, 260, 276, 287, 290–291

Recycling, 244, 269–272, 296

Refrigerator/freezer recipes, 59, 242

Reinforcement stickers, 157

Responsibility, 258–259, 263–264

Restaurant materials, 65

Rhymes, 113–114

   "Autumn Leaves," 320

   "Baby Bumblebee," 321

   "Big and Small," 134

   "Five Little Monkeys Jumping on the Bed," 122, 323

   "Five Little Pumpkins," 122

   "Gelatin Jigglers" by Pam Schiller, 243

   "Good Morning to You," 325

   "Gray Squirrel," 325

   "Hey, Diddle Diddle," 325

   "Hickory, Dickory, Dock," 325

   "Hicky Picky Bumblebee," 94, 257

   "Humpty Dumpty," 326

   "Jack and Jill," 94, 98, 327

   "Jack Be Nimble," 91, 98, 327

   "Johnny Works With One Hammer," 327

   "Little Bo Peep," 91, 328

   "Little Boy Blue," 328

   "Little Jack Horner," 91

   "Mary Had a Little Lamb," 94, 98, 328

   "Old Mother Hubbard," 94

   "One Potato, Two Potato," 94

   "Open, Shut Them," 331

   "Pat-a-Mint" by Pam Schiler, 55

   "The Purple Cow," by Gelett Burgess, 51

   "Say and Touch," 99

   silly sentences, 95

   "Teddy Bear, Teddy Bear," 334

   "Wee Willie Winkie," 336

   "Who Has Seen the Wind?" by Christina Georgina Rossetti, 213

Rhyming, 77, 94, 96–97, 293

   defined, 79

Rhythm instruments, 81–82, 185–187, 290

   homemade, 186–186

Rhythm sticks, 186

Ribbons, 39, 41, 64, 72–73, 127, 207, 208, 221, 270, 282

Rickrack, 207

Riding toys, 69, 166, 219, 230

Rock salt, 33, 43, 52

   colored, 43

Rocks, 96, 98, 219, 222–224, 226

Rollers, 65, 67

Rolling pins, 56, 64, 73

Ropes, 229–230, 263

Rough paint, 46

Rubber bands, 64, 140, 187, 216

Rubber bath mats, 147, 202

Rulers, 235, 237

S

Sacks, 38, 246

   mail, 64

Safety notes, 22, 43–44, 50, 53, 56, 60–62, 67, 71–72, 136, 140, 148, 157, 170, 172, 212, 214–215, 225, 229, 231, 234, 249, 263, 270

Safety rituals, 272

Salon/spa prop box, 65, 67

Salt 28, 45–47, 53, 60, 102, 218–219, 240, 285

    coarse, 102

    paint, 28

        recipe, 47

    rock, 33, 43, 52

Saltshakers, 30–31, 57, 61

Sand, 35, 46, 104, 186, 212, 218, 221–222, 238–239, 285, 286

    colored, 31–21

    making, 223

    play, 24, 42

Sandboxes, 24, 42, 161

Sandpaper, 22, 105, 223–224, 235

Sandwich animals recipe, 56

Sandwich fillings recipe, 57

Scales

    balance, 166

Scarves, 73, 92, 187, 267

Scented markers, 23

Scented oils, 47, 136, 241

Scented playdough recipe, 47

Science, 209–253

    air, 211–217

    animals, 249–253

    change of state, 242–243

    cooking, 49–62

    force and motion, 221–229

    light and color, 231–236

    materials, 65

    overview, 209–211

    plants, 243–248

    senses, 239–241

    simple tools, 229–230

    water, 217–220

    weather and seasons, 236–239

Scissors, 31, 36, 38, 64, 99–100, 110, 146, 203, 208, 214–215, 264, 265

Scoops, 208, 247

    homemade, 270

Scrabble tiles, 106

Scratch-and-sniff paint, 25

    recipe, 47

Scuba diver prop box, 65

Sculpting/molding, 40–42

Seashells, 65, 223, 239, 250

Seasons, 144, 236–239, 245

Seeds, 96, 203, 246, 249

    apple, 203, 239

    birdseed, 259, 285

    carrot, 244

    flower, 244

    grass, 247

    grass, 247

    lima bean, 247

    pine, 249, 272

    pumpkin, 203, 239

    radish, 247

    rye grass, 244

    sunflower, 147

Self-esteem, 256–259, 280

Sensory experiences, 135–136, 239–241

    cooking, 49–62

    smell, 239–241

    taste, 49–62, 240

    touch, 22, 25–26, 28, 39–40, 42, 46–47, 49–62, 104–105, 224, 240, 242, 265

Sentences, 94–95

Sequencing, 88, 101–102, 115, 268

    defined, 123

Service bells, 81, 200

Seurat, Georges, 24

Shadows, 74, 146, 188, 207, 231–234, 237

Shake-a-puddin', 114
  recipe, 54
Shampoo bottles, 65, 67, 186
Shapes, 31–33, 39, 49, 132–133, 138, 153, 156, 163–164, 204, 228, 277
Sharing, 262
Shaving cream, 47, 104, 204
Sheets, 68, 74, 119, 188, 197, 233, 236
Shelves, 111, 149
Shiny paint, 46
Shirts, 64–65
Shoeboxes, 41, 156, 222
Shoelaces, 134
Shoes, 72–73, 131, 146, 288
  ballet, 64, 67
  boots, 64
  tap, 64
Shooting stars recipe, 60
Shopping baskets, 64
Shovels, 200
Shower curtain liners, 60, 96, 129, 221
Sign language, 90, 107
Signs, 64
Silverware, 65, 69
Size, 49, 133–134
Skewers, 56, 139
Skillet cookies recipe, 60–61
Sleeping bags, 64
Slick paper, 218
Slides, 65
Slimy paint, 46
Slippery paint, 46
Smell, 239–241
Smocks, 64–65, 67
Snacks, 131, 152, 157, 191, 239–240, 243 (*See also* Cooking)
Snowflakes, 239

Soap paint recipe, 47
Soap, 36, 68, 142, 202, 213, 218–219, 230, 288
  bits, 269, 271
  bubble, 26, 34, 43, 84, 202, 213, 241, 287
  flakes, 44, 47
  liquid, 46
  powder, 47
  recycled, 271
Soapsuds clay, 42
  recipe, 47
Social studies, 255–278
  alike and different, 264–266
  community workers, 266–267
  emotions, 259–260
  environmental awareness, 269–272
  families, 261–262
  health/safety, 272–278
  overview, 255–256
  participating/contributing, 263–264
  self-esteem, 256–259
  sharing/cooperating, 262
  time, 268–269
Social/emotional development, 49, 90, 92, 104, 113, 116, 182, 199, 206, 215–216, 225, 237, 256, 259–260
  dramatic play, 63–75
Socks, 96, 98, 146, 198, 288
Soda bottles, 220, 251, 269
  ½-liter, 186, 222, 239, 242, 271
  1-liter, 167, 220
  2-liter, 65
Soft blocks, 75
Solids, 218
  defined, 211
Songs, 113, 174–178
  "ABC Song," 85, 319
  alliterative, 95

"The Alphabet Song," 101, 319

"The Ants Go Marching," 319

"Apples and Bananas," 320

"Are You Sleeping?" 320

"The Bagel Song," 62

"Bingo," 321

"Come and Listen," 85

"Dance of the Sugar Plum Fairies" by Pytor Ilvich Tchaikovsky, 290

"Dance, Thumbkin, Dance, 189

"Days of the Week," 143–144

"Did You Ever See a Lassie?" 175

"Did You Ever See My Tiffany?" 257

"Do Your Ears Hang Low?" 322

"The Donut Song," 61

"Doodle-li-do," 95

"Five in the Bed," 322

"Five Little Ducks," 96, 122

"Five Little Speckled Frogs," 162, 323

"Five Speckled Frogs," 95

"Flight of the Bumblebee," 187

"Go In and Out the Windows," 142, 176

"Happy Birthday," 174

"Head, Shoulders, Knees, and Toes," 107, 142

"Here We Go 'Round the Mulberry Bush," 142, 330

"If You're Happy and You Know It," 177, 273, 326

"The Insect Song," 253

"It's Raining, It's Pouring," 326

"The Itsy Bitsy Spider," 86, 95, 177, 326

"The Little Ants," 201, 250

"Miss Mary Mack," 95, 329

"Months of the Year," 144

"The More We Get Together," 329

"Old MacDonald's Farm," 96, 106, 331

onomatopoeia, 96

"The Peanut Butter Song" by Pam Schiller, 53

"The Reader Wiggle," 109

"Rime Time," 97

"Row, Row, Row Your Boat," 332

"She'll Be Comin' Round the Mountain," 332

"Sing a Song of Opposites" by Pam Schiller, 89

"Skip to My Lou," 196, 333

"This Is Quinn," 256

"This Is the Way," 85

"This Is the Way We Brush Our Teeth," 274

"This Is the Way We Wash Our Face," 275

"This Old Man," 142, 334

"Time to Pick Up the Toys," 290

"Tiny Tim," 95

"Touch and Stretch," 174

"Twinkle, Twinkle, Little Star," 85, 177, 335

"Two Little Ducks," 335

"We'll Be Coming to the Table Very Soon," 273

"The Weather Song," 236

"The Wheels on the Bus," 96, 336

"Where Is Thumbkin?" 336

Sound canisters, 80

Sound vibrations, 215–217

Soup, 242

cans, 71

Spark plugs, 64

Sparkly paint, 46

Spatial relationships, 121, 126–129

defined, 122

Spices, 136

chili powder, 60

cinnamon, 57, 60, 239

cumin, 60

pepper, 219

Splatter painting, 25

Sponges, 23, 27, 29, 35, 206, 226, 277

Spools, 123, 151, 226

Spoons, 54, 64, 217, 283

    measuring, 34, 43–47, 51–62, 64, 84, 102, 167, 229, 242

    plastic, 29

    wooden, 186

Spray bottles, 26, 96

Spray paint, 160

Square dancing, 189

Squeeze bottles, 43, 211

Squirt bottles, 27, 212, 236

Stamp pads, 64, 103, 155

Stamps, 64, 159

Staplers, 87, 115, 130, 153, 159, 215

Starch

    laundry, 44

    liquid, 26, 37, 44–46

Stick puppets, 232

Stickers, 106, 159, 269, 296

    reinforcement, 157

Stick-on dots, 154, 168

Stick-on notes, 115, 171

Sticks, 24, 64, 134, 152, 161, 186, 204

Stocking balls, 195

Stockings. See Pantyhose

Stories

    action, 120, 127–128, 161

    expanding, 93

    feelings, 260

    flannel board, 93

    "The Gingerbread Man," 161

    "Going on a Bear Hunt," 120, 127–128, 324

    "Goldilocks and the Three Bears," 119

    "The Great Big Turnip," 161

    listening, 84

    "The Little Red Hen," 117, 143

    "Little Red Riding Hood," 117

    magnetic, 228

    "The Old Gray Cat," 120

    pantomime, 120

    reenacting, 119

    starters, 114

    telling, 91, 98, 112, 115

    "The Three Bears," 88, 143

    "The Three Billy Goats Gruff," 119

    "The Three Little Pigs," 88, 143

Story maps, 118

Stoves, 44–47

Strainers, 25, 285

Straws. See Drinking straws

Streamers, 125, 181, 187, 207, 212

String, 74, 110, 132, 141, 150, 212, 221, 226, 250, 263

Stuffed animals, 67, 93

Styrofoam

    chips, 74, 200, 205, 211–212, 226–230, 244

    egg cartons, 246

    florist, 72

    meat trays, 23, 33, 35–36, 127, 269, 296

Subtraction, 162

Sugar, 23, 46, 51–52, 55, 57, 59–60, 219, 240

    powdered, 55, 61

Suitcases, 72

Sun salad recipe, 52

Sundials, 234

Surface tension, 218

Syllables, 85

Symmetry, 235

T

Tablecloths, 64–65, 69, 156, 197

Tables, 25, 66, 69, 111, 119, 156, 166, 195–196, 204, 225, 228

Tagboard, 87, 159, 215, 260

Talcum, 44

Tap shoes, 64

Tape, 64, 71, 75, 105, 166, 180, 182, 188, 195, 215, 221–222, 225, 247, 265

    colored, 87, 115

    masking, 33, 67, 74, 87, 115, 119, 126, 130, 132, 155, 167, 185, 189, 191–192, 197–200, 211, 222, 229, 235, 243, 283

    magnetic, 228

    vinyl, 149

Tape dispensers, 66

Tape recorders, 83–84, 143, 175, 177, 240

Tatami mats, 265

Tea strainers, 230

Teachable moments, 19

Teacher/school prop box, 65

Telephones, 64–67

Tempera paint, 26–30, 32, 34–36, 43, 46–47, 142

    powdered, 30–32, 44, 84, 245

Templates, 26, 33

Tennis balls, 162, 222, 225

    canisters, 140

Tents, 64, 68

Terrariums, 247

Textures, 22, 25–26, 28, 39–40, 42, 46–47, 49–62, 104–105, 224, 240, 242, 265

Thick paint, 46

Ties, 72–73

Tiles, 224

    color, 140

    Scrabble, 106

Time, 268–269

Timers, 83, 262

Tire pumps, 64

Tires, 42, 68

Tissue paper, 37, 39, 72, 91, 192, 213, 238

Toaster oven/oven recipes, 57–58, 102

Toilet paper tubes, 91, 149, 216, 276

Tomorrow boxes, 268

Tongs, 203, 205

Tongue depressors. See Craft sticks

Tongue twisters, 113

    "Peter Piper," 95

    "Six Sneezing Sneetches," 95

    "Twenty Twirling Twigs," 95

Toolboxes, 68

Tools, 27, 53, 64, 158

    filters, 230

    kitchen, 56, 64, 73, 203, 205, 230

    movers, 230

    pulleys, 229

    simple, 229–230

Toothbrushes, 25, 274

Toothpicks, 30, 54, 248

Towels, 36, 67–68, 214, 236

    paper, 29–30, 34, 36, 43, 247, 283

Toys, 97

Tracing paper, 103, 204

Transitions, 65, 289–293

    overview, 289

Trays, 25, 59, 104, 136, 212, 221, 239–240, 238, 246

    pizza, 64

    shallow, 27–28, 34–36

    warming, 22, 270

Trees, 272

True/not true, 117

Tubes, 166

Tuning forks, 217

Tweezers, 203, 206

Twigs, 22, 38, 42, 238

Typewriters, 66

U

Umbrellas, 67

V

Vanilla extract, 47, 51–52, 60

Vases, 64, 288

Vegetables, 238, 242

    beets, 248

    broccoli, 248

    cans, 140

    carrots, 56

    onions, 244

    red peppers, 58

    sweet potatoes, 248

Vinyl tape, 159

Viscosity, 217

Visual assessment/discrimination, 148–149, 239

    defined, 79

Visual memory, defined, 79

Vocabulary development, 86–94, 124–125

    defined, 79

    reading, 86

    singing, 86

W

Wallpaper, 39, 100, 153, 224, 260, 264

    paste, 45

    textured, 22, 105

Warming trays, 22, 270

Washboards, 219, 268

Washcloths, 283, 288

Washers, 135, 154, 160, 213, 227

Water, 23–24, 26, 30, 34, 36, 42–47, 55, 59, 60, 68, 84, 96, 102, 142, 151–152, 161, 167, 172, 202, 205–206, 213–214, 217–218, 222, 228–230, 239–240, 245–249, 271–272, 274

    learning about, 217–220

    play, 42, 151, 283

    soda, 214

Watering cans, 24

Wax paper, 22, 216, 218, 249

Weather, 236–239

Weight, 151

Wheat paste, 46

Wheels, 230, 287

Whisks, 34

Whole/part relationships defined, 79

Wiggle eyes, 131

Willow leaves, 245

Wind wheels, 221

Wind, 221

Wiring, 64

    florist, 64, 72

Wisp brooms, 27

Wood, 41, 217, 223

    dowels, 150, 186, 230, 234

    numbers, 156

    spoons, 186

Word cards, 104

Word webs, 119

Work gloves, 64

Workbooks, 65

Wrapping paper, 39, 64

    homemade, 35

    tubes, 149, 226

Writing, 87, 103, 113, 116

X

X-acto knives, 204

Xylophones, 183

Y

Yardsticks, 221, 227, 235

Yarn, 23, 31, 67, 74, 91, 127, 163, 166, 207, 226, 232, 102

    balls, 162

Z

Zippered plastic bags, 29, 45–46, 52, 54–55, 87, 102,

The Instant Curriculum

The Complete Book of Rhymes, Songs, Poems, Fingerplays, and Chants

Over 700 Selections

By Jackie Silberg and Pam Schiller

Build a strong foundation in skills such as listening, imagination, coordination, and spatial and body awareness with over 700 favorite rhymes, songs, poems, fingerplays, and chants. 512 pages. 2002.

★ Parent's Choice Award
★ Parent's Guide to Children's Media Award
★ National Parenting Publications Award

Gryphon House / 18264

The Complete Book of Activities, Games, Stories, Props, Recipes, and Dances

For Young Children

By Pam Schiller and Jackie Silberg

Are you searching for just the right story to reinforce your theme? Trying to play a game but can't remember the rules? Looking for your favorite no-bake cookie recipe? It's all right here! This book is chock full of over 600 ways to enhance any curriculum. The companion to *The Complete Book of Rhymes, Songs, Poems, Fingerplays, and Chants,* it's a teacher's best friend! 640 pages. 2003.

Gryphon House / 16284

The Complete Resource Book

An Early Childhood Curriculum

By Pam Schiller and Kay Hastings

The Complete Resource Book is an absolute must-have book for every teacher. Offering a complete plan for every day of the year, this is an excellent reference book for responding to children's specific interests. Each daily plan contains:

- circle time activities
- music and movement activities
- suggested books
- six learning-center ideas

The appendix, jam-packed with songs, recipes, and games, is almost a book in itself. *The Complete Resource Book* is like having a master teacher working at your side, offering you guidance and inspiration all year long. 464 pages. 1998.

Gryphon House / 15327

The Complete Daily Curriculum for Early Childhood

Over 1200 Easy Activities to Support Multiple Intelligences and Learning Styles

By Pam Schiller and Pat Phipps

Because there's more than one way to be smart! This innovative book for three-to six-year-olds offers a complete plan for every learning style. Organized by theme, *The Complete Daily Curriculum* includes a morning circle and end-of-day reflection, and different activities for each learning center. With over 1200 activities to engage multiple intelligences, plus assessment tools and a comprehensive appendix of songs, stories, games, dances, props, recipes, patterns, chants, rhymes, and arts and crafts, you'll find everything you need to captivate and challenge every child in your classroom. 608 pages. 2002.

★ *Early Childhood News* Director's Choice Award

Gryphon House / 16279